THE LAW OF REINSURANCE

SECOND EDITION

THE LAW OF REINSURANCE

SECOND EDITION

COLIN EDELMAN QC
ANDREW BURNS

OXFORD
UNIVERSITY PRESS

Great Clarendon Street, Oxford, OX2 6DP,
United Kingdom

Oxford University Press is a department of the University of Oxford.
It furthers the University's objective of excellence in research, scholarship,
and education by publishing worldwide. Oxford is a registered trade mark of
Oxford University Press in the UK and in certain other countries

First edition published 2005
Second edition published 2013

Impression: 1

British Library Cataloguing in Publication Data

Data available

ISBN 978–0–19–966504–4

Printed in Great Britain by
CPI Group (UK) Ltd, Croydon, CR0 4YY

FOREWORD TO THE FIRST EDITION

The general contract lawyer who strays into reinsurance could well feel that he (or, of course, she) has entered a different world, one where the conversational currency of the natives is to do with fronting and retrocession, treaties and quota shares, fac/oblig arrangements, and scratching of slips. All very baffling.

In reinsurance, as in other fields of law, it is of course essential to understand the terms in which business is transacted in the marketplace. But when that has been done (a task which the authors of this new and welcome book make easy) the familiar landscape of contract becomes quickly recognizable: there must be an offer and an acceptance, the terms of the contract must be interpreted, and so on. Not baffling at all.

But a contract of reinsurance has its own special characteristics, addressed by the courts in an unending series of cases coming before them. So it is necessary for the newcomer to know what has been decided and, in particular, what has been decided recently.

This book provides an excellent guide. The authors lucidly explain the underlying principles and offer expert (not always uncritical) summaries of the relevant case law, all in short, easily assimilable paragraphs. London is rightly proud of its dominant role in the world reinsurance market, and a book such as this can only serve to entrench that position.

Lord Bingham
London
December 2004

FOREWORD TO THE SECOND EDITION

This is a small book on a big subject, but what it foregoes in size it compensates with its clarity and elegance.

Those virtues can be seen from the very start. Chapter 1 is a model exposition of the nature, purposes, and types of reinsurance. The ensuing chapters deal concisely, but with a proper regard for recent jurisprudence, with formation, interpretation, the reinsurer's obligations and rights, defences, applicable law, and jurisdiction. The reader is quickly led to the heart of the subject.

The authors have not attempted to cover the whole of insurance law, but to show how that law operates in the context of reinsurance. For instance, the problems caused by follow the settlements and claims co-operation clauses are systematic-ally explained. Particular problems of the operation of the doctrine of good faith as they arise between reinsurer and reinsured are discussed. The analysis is shrewd and helpful.

In their Preface to this Second Edition, the authors regret the fact that so much of modern reinsurance law is hidden from outside gaze by the confidentiality by which arbitration awards are protected. In the absence of sufficient publication of even anonymized awards, the development of the law in this important financial service is stultified, and the wheel has to be constantly reinvented. The authors, who, as practitioners, are familiar with many such recent arbitrations, have drawn as far as they properly can on that knowledge for the purposes of their analysis, but cannot cite explicitly from the awards. As they remark, 'the learning must remain hidden'. For those concerned with ensuring that reinsurance law remains fit for its purpose, which means not only for writers on the subject and practitioners, but also brokers and ultimately reinsurers and reinsureds themselves, this is an ill which needs a solution, and all the more so since London and English law are significant elements in a worldwide industry.

In the meantime, this excellent book will continue to do much to fill the gap.

Bernard Rix
July 2012

PREFACE

In the Preface to the First Edition we noted that the London market is one of the world's largest reinsurance markets, a focal point for reinsurance capacity and underwriting expertise. The position has not changed substantially over the last six years and London still takes a key role in difficult and complex risks. It has grown from modest beginnings at the end of the nineteenth century to one of the dominant reinsurance marketplaces in the world. The London Companies' market together with the members of Lloyd's provide reinsurance cover to insurers throughout the world. The industry has developed flexibly, adopting new products and methods of reinsurance to suit an insurer's every need. Brokers in the London market now offer innovative ways of reinsuring larger and larger risks in complex and sometimes impenetrable reinsurance programmes.

Despite the growth of the international reinsurance market, it is still the case that a large proportion of reinsurance business is placed and led in London and is subject to English law, making the law of reinsurance in England and Wales of real importance to the world's reinsurance industry. As reinsurance has become more complex and the amounts of money at stake have grown, so, inevitably, has the complexity of litigation. Over the past decades the insurance industry worldwide has suffered a number of extraordinary financial setbacks arising from long-tail liabilities for pollution and asbestos related claims, financial collapses, and natural and man-made catastrophes. The old-fashioned notion of insurers and reinsurers paying claims on the basis of a 'gentleman's agreement' without contesting whether the claims fall within the strict terms of the reinsurance is long gone. Now reinsurance contracts are carefully examined for conditions, warranties or exclusions that might relieve a reinsurer of a very expensive liability. Both reinsurers and reinsureds have turned to the lawyers and to litigation to help apportion some of the substantial losses suffered by the market in recent years. As the sums at stake are often very large, parties have often been willing to contest every possible point in the case, raising numerous and convoluted claims and defences.

An additional complicating factor is that sometimes vast reinsurance risks can be agreed using the briefest of formality and paperwork although the use of standard forms in the London market, particularly the MRG documentation has improved certainty in recent years. However, a reinsurance contract may still range from the shortest slip to the longest and most complicated bespoke wording. As a result of these factors, coupled with the many layers and towers of a typical reinsurance programme, the law of reinsurance can often appear to be an unfathomable maze of intricate and opaque concepts.

This and the considerable overlap with the law of insurance means that it can be hard to find a simple and straightforward path through the complexity of the issues involved in reinsurance. It is too easy to meet a difficult subject with a difficult book, which is as long and convoluted as the concepts that it is attempting to unravel. Our aim in the First Edition was to do the opposite: to set out the law of reinsurance with brevity and clarity. Although this Second Edition is necessarily enlarged by new case law and arguments which have been raised over the last few years, we have tried again to cut through the complexity and the detail and refine the case law into a concise and accessible structure. We have added a glossary of common reinsurance terms which we hope will be of assistance to those new to the area. We hope that this Edition will continue to provide a practical guide to difficult topics and make the essential answers quickly and readily available. Except where essential to explain the reinsurance issue, we have avoided setting out principles of insurance law. Like the First Edition, this Edition does not purport to provide a comprehensive explanation of insurance principles and case law. It assumes a basic knowledge of insurance law and focuses on how insurance principles translate to the reinsurance context and on exclusively reinsurance concepts. We wholeheartedly recommend readers to refer to the very well-known leading texts on insurance law if they need to know more about insurance principles and case law.

The law of reinsurance has blossomed from its foundations in the law of contract and has developed out of and, occasionally, even away from the law of insurance. Reinsurance lawyers now have to deal not only with particular market jargon and peculiar practices, but also particular legal points that arise only or mainly in the reinsurance field, such as those relating to follow the settlements or claims co-operation clauses. It is upon these peculiarities and niceties of reinsurance law that this book focuses its attention.

A further aim of this book is to achieve a review of reinsurance law without lengthy quotations from case law or recitation of factual details in each case. We have included classic or particularly helpful quotations and discussed the facts where they are necessary to understand the principles, but have tried to avoid verbose discussion. We hope that this book, and in particular its footnotes, will indicate the way to all the relevant case law on a particular topic, so that the reader can then go straight to the cases to research further factual detail or judicial discussion.

One frustration that we know has been felt by readers of the First Edition and which is shared by us is the fact that some of the most illuminating recent decisions in this field must remain confidential. We have been prevailed upon to discuss the legal analysis in arbitration awards which address some of the most controversial subjects in reinsurance law. However the market requires and even desires that these awards remain secret and we are unable to disclose the content of arbitrations, whether we have had personal involvement or not. Some of the finest judges and lawyers in the reinsurance field have produced detailed arbitration awards in difficult areas of reinsurance litigation, but the learning must remain hidden. Due to the confidential nature of arbitrations, it normally requires both parties to consent to publication of the existence, never mind the content, of arbitration decisions. As a result the majority of contested decisions are not available to the researcher and the reinsurance wheel has to be reinvented time and again. For this reason there are numerous decisions of which we are aware, but unfortunately cannot be referred to in this book. It is an omission that we regret, but can do little to rectify.

The structure of this book tries to accommodate both the interested cover-to-cover reader as well as being an immediately accessible reference guide. The opening chapters address and define reinsurance in its many different guises, looking at the many varied types of contract that are commonly offered and then go on to look at the legal principles involved in the formation of each type of contract. We have sought to explain and categorize slips, slip policies, and formal policy wordings, going on to explain how terms in a reinsurance contract should be discovered and interpreted. The special principles relating to the different types of follow the settlements clauses are examined in detail, together with the reinsurance aspects of aggregation and limitation. The rights of the reinsured and reinsurer are compared and contrasted, and the conflict of follow the settlements and claims control are discussed. Many aspects of insurance law such as the duty of utmost good faith and the particular effects of breaches of conditions and warranties have been developed in the reinsurance context. Indeed, in an interesting reversal of the norm, some of the leading reinsurance cases that we discuss are also used and referred to in the insurance field. Finally, we deal with aspects of conflicts of laws and jurisdiction that appear in reinsurance litigation due to their frequently international nature: involving parties and risks in different parts of the world.

We must once again thank Oxford University Press for their good-natured patience and encouragement. Also thanks go to our colleagues at Devereux for their suggestions and comments (sometimes conscious and sometimes not), to Akash Nawbatt and David Craig who contributed so much to the First Edition and to our families for their support and tolerance of the long hours associated with writing and practising in this area of the law. We are also indebted to Sir Bernard Rix for agreeing to write the foreword. The law is as stated at July 2012.

Colin Edelman QC
Andrew Burns
Devereux Chambers, August 2012

CONTENTS–SUMMARY

CONTENTS–DETAILED

TABLE OF CASES

TABLE OF LEGISLATION

1

FUNCTIONS, DEFINITIONS, AND TYPES OF REINSURANCE

A. Historical Background

The earliest recorded reinsurance arrangement[1] appears to have been effected in the **1.01** fourteenth century when an underwriter reinsured the hazardous part of a marine voyage from Genoa to Sluys. Professional reinsurers, however, did not emerge until the nineteenth century, some two centuries after the first professional insurers were founded. The first of these was the Cologne Reinsurance Company, which was formed in 1846 after a catastrophic fire in Hamburg had led to losses well beyond the reserves of the insurers—the Hamburg Fire Fund.[2]

By the middle of the nineteenth century London had become firmly established as **1.02** the central market for marine insurance. This was in part because the conducting

---

[1] According to CE Golding, *The Law and Practice of Reinsurance* (5th edn, London: Witherby & Co Ltd, 1987).

[2] Cologne Reinsurance Company was followed relatively swiftly by the formation of Swiss Re in 1863 and Munich Re in 1880.

of reinsurance business was prohibited by statute[3] in England until as late as 1864,[4] and this had forced direct insurers to join together into syndicates in order to cover risks beyond their individual financial means, which in turn had led to the availability of considerable insurance capacity in the London market. It is not entirely clear why reinsurance was rendered illegal in the middle of the eighteenth century. Lord Mansfield speculated that the reason for the prohibition was that reinsurance was viewed as gambling at a time when gambling was clearly a widespread social problem in England.[5] Park J[6] ascribed the prohibition to the fact that reinsurance was being abused by insurers to relieve themselves of risks which they had 'incautiously undertaken', stating:

> [T]he law of England...permitted the underwriters upon policies to insure themselves against those risks for which they had inadvertently engaged to indemnify the insured; or where perhaps they had involved themselves to a greater amount than their ability would enable them to discharge. Although such a contract seems perfectly fair and reasonable in itself, and might be productive of very beneficial consequences to those concerned in this important branch of trade; yet, like many other useful institutions, it was so much abused, and turned to purposes so pernicious to a commercial nation, and so destructive of those very benefits it was originally intended to promote and encourage, that the Legislature was at last obliged to interpose, and by a positive law to cut off all opportunity of practising those frauds in future, which were become thus glaring and enormous.[7]

1.03 Lord Hoffmann explained in *Charter Reinsurance Co Ltd v Fagan*:[8]

> Contracts of reinsurance were unlawful until 1864. Such a contract [of reinsurance] is not an insurance of the primary insurer's potential liability or disbursement. It is an independent contract between reinsured and reinsurer in which the subject matter of the insurance is the same as that of the primary insurance, that is to say, the risk to the ship or goods or whatever might be insured. The difference lies in the nature of the insurable interest, which in the case of the primary insurer, arises from his liability under the original policy.

---

[3] Reinsurance was rendered illegal by the Marine Insurance Act 1745 (19 Geo 2, c 37). Note that s 4 of the Act provided that 'reinsurance' was prohibited 'unless the insurer should be insolvent, become a bankrupt, or die; in either of which cases the insurer, his executors, administrators, or assigns were permitted to provide reinsurance to the amount of the sum insured, provided it was expressed in the policy to be reinsurance'. It should be recognized that this was not a limited exception to the provision of 'reinsurance' as understood by that word today; rather it referred to the provision of a new policy of insurance being effected with a new insurer.

[4] In 1864 the Revenue No 2 Act (27 & 28 Vict, c 56) effectively rendered reinsurance lawful.

[5] 1745 also saw the enactment of legislation to outlaw the playing of roulette (also known as 'roly-poly' at that time), and the first half of the eighteenth century saw a flurry of legislative activity to prevent gambling.

[6] In his book *A System of the Law of Marine Insurances* (8th edn, 1842, reprinted 1987: Professional Books) 596–597.

[7] Hobhouse J cited this passage with apparent approval in *Phoenix General Insurance Co of Greece SA v Halvanon Insurance Co Ltd* [1985] 2 Lloyd's Rep 599, 611.

[8] [1997] AC 313, 392.

When the prohibition was lifted, the discriminating and capable reinsurer flour- **1.04**
ished. In 1911 Scrutton J, in *Glasgow Assurance Corp v Symondson*,[9] stated:

> When one finds, as one frequently does at Lloyd's, A agreeing to reinsure B against
> every risk insured by B at a premium based on a percentage of the premiums received
> by B, and always therefore smaller, one is naturally inclined to think that B has a temp-
> tation to accept every risk, however bad, and pass it on to A at a smaller premium, and
> therefore at a certain profit such system is absurd and cannot work. But as Bowen LJ
> said in *Sanders v McLean*, anyone who attempts to follow and understand the law of
> merchants will soon find himself lost if he begins by assuming that merchants conduct
> their business on the basis of attempting to insure themselves against fraudulent deal-
> ing. Credit, not mistrust, is the basis of commercial dealings, and mercantile genius
> consists principally in knowing whom to trust and with whom to deal.

The turmoil created by two world wars saw England and the United States com- **1.05**
ing to the forefront of international reinsurance business, usurping the dominant
position that had previously been held by German reinsurers. The City of London
became the leading reinsurance market in the world, using both companies and
Lloyd's 'names' to provide unparalleled technical expertise and market capacity. It
remains a major reinsurance centre today, working in partnership particularly with
companies based in the United States, Bermuda, and Germany.[10]

As Lord Collins commented in *Wasa International Insurance Co v Lexington* **1.06**
Insurance Co:[11]

> [A]fter banking, insurance is the United Kingdom's largest invisible export, of
> which reinsurance forms a large part, and amounted to at least £1.2bn in 2007.

B. The Functions of Reinsurance

Lord Mance has neatly encapsulated the basic function of reinsurance on a number **1.07**
of occasions; first as follows:

> In insurance, the matching of exposure and protection to assure both solvency and
> profitability is absolutely fundamental. Reinsurance—of whatever type—is a prin-
> cipal means to this end.[12]

Summarizing the way in which reinsurance works in *Wasa International Insurance* **1.08**
Co v Lexington Insurance Co he said:[13]

> Reinsurance is a settled business conducted worldwide by experts, often (even
> if past experience indicates not invariably) possessing very considerable legal

---

[9] (1911) 16 Com Cas 109, 110–111.
[10] For a more detailed history of reinsurance see Golding, n 1.
[11] [2010] 1 AC 180; [2009] 2 Lloyd's Rep 508, para 55 citing the Office for National Statistics,
United Kingdom Balance of Payments: The Pink Book 2008, 52.
[12] Per Mance J as he then was in *Charter Reinsurance Co Ltd v Fagan* [1997] AC 313, 343.
[13] [2010] 1 AC 180; [2009] 2 Lloyd's Rep 508, para 33.

knowledge and expertise. The well-recognised analysis which neither side gainsaid before your Lordships is that a reinsurance such as the present is an independent contract, under which the subject matter reinsured is the original subject matter. The insurable interest which entitles the insurer to reinsure in respect of that subject matter is the insurer's exposure under the original insurance. The principle of indemnity limits any recovery from reinsurers to the amount paid in respect of that insurable interest . . . Reinsurance business is classified in accordance with this well-settled analysis for regulatory purposes: Financial Services and Markets Act 2000 (Regulated Activities) Order 2001 (SI 2001/544). Reinsurance slips are underwritten identifying the subject matter insured (here, against the headings 'Interest' and 'Situated') as the original insured's property, rather than the insurer's exposure or liability under the original insurance . . . There is no basis or justification for courts to throw unnecessarily into doubt an accepted analysis with business significance.

1.09 The broad purpose of reinsurance is for the direct insurer to be covered in respect of his liability under an original insurance policy, pursuant to which the original insured is entitled to recover from him.[14] The direct insurer gives protection to individuals and businesses against the uncertain risks associated with life and commerce. The reinsurer takes a share of those risks (and a share of the premium), thus spreading the consequences of the losses should a risk event take place.[15] Furthermore, an insurer cannot predict with certainty which part of the business that it writes will result in profits and which part in losses each year, and reinsurance enables the insurer to smooth the peaks and troughs of his business results.

1.10 The functions of reinsurance, however, are not only protective—there are significant business advantages to be gained by an insurer that can obtain reinsurance. Primarily reinsurance provides capacity to an insurer, thereby enabling the insurer to insure a volume, type or size of risk that it would not be able to cover in the absence of reinsurance. In effect, the reinsurer enlarges the direct insurer's underwriting capacity by accepting a share of the risks and by providing part of the necessary reserves for losses.

1.11 Reinsurance also increases the capital available to the direct insurer which would otherwise be earmarked to cover potential losses. This is of some significance to the conducting of reinsurance business both in England and elsewhere. A yardstick commonly used by regulatory bodies[16] in controlling insurance companies is the margin of their solvency—defined under the Insurance Companies

---

[14] Per Potter LJ *in Skandia International Corp v NRG Victory Reinsurance Ltd* [1998] Lloyd's Rep IR 439, 459.

[15] One consequence of the drive to spread risks as widely as possible is that reinsurance often involves international transactions so that parts of each large risk are taken by the major reinsurance markets across the globe. This not only permits risks to be spread more effectively, but also provides international experience.

[16] The insurance industry in England is now regulated by the Financial Services Authority (pursuant to the Financial Services and Markets Act 2000). The FSA has four objectives under the Act: maintaining market confidence; promoting public understanding of the financial system; appropriate protection for consumers; and fighting financial crime.

Act 1982[17] as the excess of the value of its assets over the amount of its liabilities. Regulatory authorities will frequently have minimum margins or ratios below which they will not allow insurers to operate.[18] Reinsurance, therefore, can strengthen the solvency ratio of the direct insurer.

C. Parties to a Reinsurance Contract

The parties to a reinsurance contract can be referred to by different titles depending **1.12** on the context. Essentially a reinsurer agrees to provide cover to a reinsured by entering into a contract of reinsurance. However the reinsured will itself be an insurer and the reinsurer will often itself be reinsured under a further contract of retrocession. The terms insured and reinsured are often used interchangeably in the market with assured and reassured.[19] Where the reinsurer is reinsured under a contract of retrocession it is referred to as a 'retrocedant', whilst its reinsurer is a 'retrocessionaire'.

The parties to the insurance and reinsurance contracts are necessarily different and **1.13** the insurance and reinsurance are separate contracts. This was explored when a reinsurer, Meadows, claimed not only a declaration as to the validity of its contract of reinsurance but also a declaration as to the validity of the underlying contract of insurance, entered into between its reinsured, I.C.I. and the underlying insured, I.C.B.[20] Neill LJ dismissed the second claim for a declaration pointing out that:

> These two parties have no rights or obligations against or to each other; they are not in a contractual relationship. Although there is of course a connection between the contract of insurance on the one hand and of re-insurance on the other, Meadows' rights are in no way involved in the existing dispute between I.C.I. and I.C.B. Whether I.C.I. has to pay I.C.B. depends upon the terms and circumstances of the insurance contract between them and, if relevant, any non-disclosure or misrepresentation that occurred between them. In so far as Meadows is concerned, any liability on their part will depend upon the contract of re-insurance and the factual situation which existed between them when this was entered into.

In *Markel Capital Ltd v Gothaer Allgemeine Versicherung*[21] the Court considered **1.14** the definition of 'Reinsured' in the slip of a reinsurance of a Directors' and Officers' cover. The defendant's agent was listed as the reinsured, but the Court noted that

---

[17] s 32.

[18] This approach was put on a statutory footing in England in 1946. Previously regulation under the Assurance Companies Act 1909 required insurers (and reinsurers after the decision of the House of Lords in *Forsikringsaktieselskapet National of Copenhagen v Attorney General* [1925] AC 639) to lodge deposits with the High Court in order to conduct business.

[19] The term 'reassured' is particularly used in relation to life insurance and marine reinsurance. When someone is a party to a reinsurance treaty, they are commonly referred to as a 'cedant' as there is a cession of part of the risk (and premium) to a reinsurer. However for the purposes of simplicity the word reinsured is preferred in this book.

[20] *The Meadows Insurance Co Ltd and The Insurance Corporation of Ireland plc v International Commercial Bank plc* [1989] 2 Lloyd's Rep 298.

[21] [2009] Lloyd's Rep IR 433.

it was not unnatural for a slip contract to specify that the reinsureds were entering into it through an agent. The Court took into account all the uses of the word 'reinsured' in the slip contract, including the fact that the agreement was to reinsure the 'reinsured's' interest, and the interest was to indemnify 'the Reinsured'. It was the reinsureds and not their agents who were to be indemnified.

D. Fronting

1.15 The availability of reinsurance can enable smaller insurers notionally to accept risks that are considerably beyond their capacity, and perhaps expertise, by 'fronting' the insurance, whilst reinsuring the entirety, or the vast majority, of the risk to a reinsurer that specializes in that type of business. The use of fronting is also common in circumstances where the reinsurer is not permitted to conduct direct insurance business in a certain country (or state) and therefore has to find a local insurer notionally to insure the risk. The local insurer can issue a direct policy and pass all the risk (and premium)[22] to the reinsurer which, in effect underwrites the risk. The use of 'fronting' can result in a reversal of the traditional course of business, with reinsurers agreeing to reinsure the entirety of a risk with an individual or business and then having to find an insurance company prepared to act as the fronting insurer.[23] Alternatively the local insurer may retain some of the risk and the reinsurer will take account of the amount of risk retained by the reinsured in considering whether to accept the cession and on what terms.

1.16 The availability of reinsurance has facilitated the development of 'captive' insurance companies in places such as Bermuda and the Isle of Man. The reinsurance of 'captive' insurance companies is often in substance a form of fronting arrangement. Rather than placing its insurance cover in the insurance market, a group of companies may set up an offshore 'captive' insurance company, the only purpose of which is to provide insurance cover to the group. All or a substantial part of the risk will then be reinsured by those who would otherwise have been the insurers under a comprehensive programme of reinsurance protection which controls and limits the net exposure of the captive.

1.17 Where a reinsurer accepts the risk with the reinsured acting as the front, there ought to be a claims control clause in the reinsurance so that the reinsurer can control the investigation and adjustment of the underlying claim.[24] This can lead to tension when a local insurer fronting a local risk is commercially inclined to pay

---

[22] Retaining a commission for the cession of the risk.
[23] See *Commonwealth Insurance Co of Vancouver v Groupe Sprinks SA* [1983] 1 Lloyd's Rep 67 for an early reported example of such an arrangement.
[24] See paras 5.07 et seq.

out on the claim in circumstances where the reinsurer takes a very different view about the agreement or adjustment of the claim.

E. Retrocession

For the same reasons that insurers need reinsurance, prudent reinsurers will also use the reinsurance market in order to cede part of their potential exposure to other reinsurers. This is known as 'retrocession', with the reinsurer of the reinsurer known as the 'retrocessionaire'. Where an insurer insures part of his liability, that is reinsurance. However, where a reinsurer insures part of his liability, that is a retrocession.[25] In simple terms, then, a retrocession agreement is a form of insurance contract under which a reinsurer insures the liability of another reinsurer in respect of reinsurances that the latter has entered into.[26]   **1.18**

Retrocession arrangements may also involve the use of fronting. Fronting may be used where the insurer or reinsurer is not confident in the solvency or security of the proposed reinsurer or retrocessionaire and a fronting company, in whom the insurer or reinsurer has confidence, is interposed to front the cover, with the fronting company then retroceding the cover to the proposed ultimate reinsurer. The insurer/reinsurer can then rely on the solvency and security of the fronting reinsurer, rather than that of the ultimate reinsurer, see *Wace v Pan Atlantic Group Inc.*[27]   **1.19**

F. A Legal Definition of Reinsurance

Reinsurance eludes a simple concrete legal definition. This is due in large measure to the fact that reinsurance is primarily a product that exists in, and has been responsive to, a marketplace and which has therefore spawned numerous and varied types; it is not a monolithic whole.   **1.20**

An early definition of reinsurance was furnished by Lord Mansfield in *Delver v Barnes.*[28] He said this: **1.21**

> This contract...does not fully amount to a reassurance, which consists of [1] a new assurance, effected by a new policy, [2] on the same risk which was before insured,

---

[25] Lloyd J in *Commonwealth Insurance Co of Vancouver v Groupe Sprinks* [1983] 1 Lloyd's Rep 67, 87 said: 'It may well be that a retrocession agreement is sometimes described as reinsurance; in so far as it is a reinsurance of a reinsurer, the use of the word is accurate. But I have never heard a reinsurance of the original insurer described as a retrocession. I had thought the meaning of the word was well understood.'

[26] Per Hirst J in *Transcontinental Underwriting Agency SRL v Grand Union Insurance Co Ltd* [1987] 2 Lloyd's Rep 409.

[27] [1981] 2 Lloyd's Rep 339, 344. See also *Sirius International Insurance Corp v FAI General Insurance Co Ltd* [2004] Lloyd's Rep IR 47 in which Sirius fronted reinsurance for FAI because the reinsured was not happy with the security of FAI as reinsurer.

[28] (1807) 1 Taunt 48.

[3] in order to indemnify the underwriters from their previous subscription' and [4] both policies are in existence at the same time [numbers added].

1.22 The definition provides a useful heuristic. However, it is not all-encompassing. For example, it does not grapple with the modern practice of reinsurance being arranged before the insurance policy is entered into, either through fronting or where, for example,[29] a risk is so great or of such a type that underwriters will only subscribe if they are also offered reinsurance. In such circumstances, brokers will often first find reinsurers who are prepared to reinsure the risk (and offer to do so) before they obtain subscriptions from direct insurers.[30] It also fails to address certain types of non-facultative reinsurance (for example general or whole account excess of loss reinsurance) where what is reinsured is the risk that all or a defined part of the reinsured's account will suffer an aggregate loss in excess of a specific amount or a catastrophic loss in excess of a specific amount.

1.23 In *Toomey v Eagle Star Insurance Co Ltd*[31] Hobhouse LJ stated that the word 'reinsurance' had been used very loosely and often simply to describe a contract of insurance which had been placed by or for the benefit of the insurer. He suggested that reinsurance is not 'a mere liability insurance'; rather, reinsurance properly defined 'is the insurance of an insurable interest in the subject matter of an original insurance and that the principles of subrogation apply'.[32] Hobhouse LJ approved the definition enunciated by Buckley LJ in *British Dominion General Insurance Co v Duder*[33] that:

> A contract of insurance and a contract of re-insurance are independent of each other. But a contract of re-insurance is a contract which insures the thing originally insured, namely, [in this case] the ship. The re-insurer has an insurable interest in the ship by virtue of his original contract of insurance. The thing insured, however, is the ship and not the interest of the re-insurer in the ship by reason of his contract of insurance upon the ship.

---

[29] See, eg, *General Accident Fire and Life Assurance Corp v Tanter* (The Zephyr) [1984] 1 Lloyd's Rep 58; [1985] 2 Lloyd's Rep 529, CA; *Commonwealth Insurance Co of Vancouver v Groupe Sprinks SA* [1983] 1 Lloyd's Rep 67; *CNA International Reinsurance Co Ltd v Companhia de Seguros Tranquilidade SA* [1999] Lloyd's Rep IR 289.

[30] Insofar as a contract is concluded at this stage it is not a bilateral contract of insurance; rather it is akin to a unilateral contract by which the reinsurer offers to provide reinsurance in the future if required; the reinsurer effectively offers to reinsure any underwriter falling within the class or category described in the slip, whether or not the broker has at that time obtained any subscription to the original line or an order for reinsurance. The reinsurance contract, properly understood, is only made when the broker conveys the reinsurer's offer to the underwriter and the underwriter accepts both the risk and the reinsurance. The insurance and the reinsurance are, therefore, effected simultaneously.

[31] [1994] 1 Lloyd's Rep 516.

[32] [1994] 1 Lloyd's Rep 516, 523.

[33] [1915] 2 KB 394, 400. This case effectively settled the issue as to whether a contract of reinsurance was a contract of indemnity that had troubled the courts for some time in the late nineteenth and early twentieth centuries, see *Uzielli & Co v Boston Marine Insurance Co* [1884] 25 KB 11; *Nelson v Empress Assurance Corp Ltd* [1905] 2 KB 281.

Hobhouse LJ also cited with approval the statement of Viscount Cave LC in **1.24** *Forsikringsaktieselskapet National of Copenhagen v Attorney General*[34] that:

> The reinsuring party insures the original insuring party against the original loss, the insurance interest of the original insuring party being constituted by its policy given to the original assured.

In *Toomey* a syndicate at Lloyd's had reinsured to close the totality of certain **1.25** accounts to Eagle Star. Hobhouse J took the view, on the basis of his rather narrow definition, that this was not reinsurance; rather it was a 100% stop-loss policy,[35] covering the 'run-off' of liabilities on the relevant accounts, and was effectively in the nature of an original insurance rather than reinsurance, properly so called.

The reinsurance market would doubtless view stop-loss insurance as a species of **1.26** reinsurance and it is difficult to understand why such an arrangement should be excluded from a definition of reinsurance, particularly against a background in which Hobhouse J had previously stated that, as a matter of reinsurance law, there was no inconsistency between the idea of reinsurance and a nil retention by the reinsured.[36] The courts should strive to ensure that their approach to a definition of reinsurance is consonant with the market's understanding and practice. In numerous cases, they have done so, notwithstanding the approach taken by Hobhouse J.[37]

The approach of Hobhouse J to a definition of reinsurance was largely echoed by **1.27** Lord Hoffmann in *Charter Reinsurance Co Ltd v Fagan*[38] who suggested that a contract of reinsurance is:

> ...not an insurance of the primary insurer's potential liability or disbursement. It is an independent contract between reinsured and reinsurer in which the subject matter of the insurance is the same as that of the primary insurance, that is to say, the risk, the ship, the goods or whatever might be insured. The difference lies in the nature of the insurable interest, which in the case of the primary insurer arises from his liability under the original policy: see Buckley LJ in *British Dominion General Insurance Company v Duder*.[39]

However, Lord Mustill was rather less keen to narrow the definition. He said **1.28** that:[40]

> This is not the place to discuss the question, perhaps not yet finally resolved, whether there can be cases where a contract of reinsurance is an insurance of the reinsurer's liability under the inward policy or whether it is always an insurance on

---

[34] [1925] AC 639, 642.
[35] See para 1.66.
[36] *Phoenix General Insurance Co of Greece SA v Halvanon Insurance Co Ltd* [1985] 2 Lloyd's Rep 599, 611.
[37] See, eg, *Baker v Black Sea & Baltic General Insurance Co Ltd* [1990] Lloyd's Rep IR 327, 334.
[38] [1997] AC 313, 392.
[39] [1915] 2 KB 394, 400.
[40] [1997] AC 313, 385.

the original subject matter, the liability of the reinsured serving merely to give him an insurable interest.

Thus he left open the possibility, without deciding the point, that in some cases a contract of insurance may more properly be regarded as being in the nature of liability insurance rather than a reinsurance of the original subject matter.[41] Potter LJ in *Skandia International Corp v NRG Victory Reinsurance Ltd*[42] was equally reluctant to resolve the general question as to whether, or where, the line should be drawn between reinsurance 'properly' or 'narrowly' so called and 'mere' liability insurance effected by a reinsurer.

1.29 It is suggested that for a contract properly to be understood as reinsurance there must be a contract between insurer and reinsurer whereby the insurer lays off some or all of its risk to the reinsurer for the payment of a premium in circumstances where the reinsurer has no contractual relationship directly with the ultimate insured.[43] Furthermore, the fact that the insurance is a reinsurance means that the extent of the reinsured's insurable interest has to be identified by reference to the terms of the original policy and that the reinsured must therefore give to the reinsurer the benefit of any protection which the reinsured is entitled to enjoy, or may have obtained under the original policy.[44] The indemnity afforded by reinsurance is therefore against the discharge of liability by the reinsured—the reinsured cannot make a profit out of the reinsurance.

1.30 However the possibility left open by Lord Mustill gives rise to the problem identified by Lord Mance in *Wasa International Insurance Co v Lexington Insurance Co*:[45]

> A conclusion that 'what is insured is the insurer's own liability' would not entitle the insurer to indemnity against whatever liability it might be found to have in any court in which it was sued, under whatever law was there applied. Insurance against liability may, like any other insurance, be subject to specific terms which have to be satisfied before any indemnity can be sought.

1.31 Lord Philips regarded it as a well-established principle when he commented in *Wasa*:[46]

> Essentially the result of this appeal is dictated by the agreed fact that the reinsurance contract that is the subject of the appeal is governed by English law and by the

---

[41] Certainly he did not think that was the case in the policy before him when he observed: '...the policy covers...the occurrence of a casualty suffered by the subject matter insured through the operation of an insured peril. The Inward policies and the reinsurance are wholly distinct.'

[42] [1998] Lloyd's Rep IR 439, 457.

[43] In *Forsikringsaktieselskapet Vesta v JNE Butcher* [1989] 1 AC 852, 908 Lord Lowry stated that 'reinsurance is prima facie a contract of indemnity...under which the reinsurer indemnifies the original insurer against the whole or against a specified amount or proportion...of the risk which the latter has himself insured'. See also *The Zephyr* [1985] 2 Lloyd's Rep 529, 531–532.

[44] Hobhouse LJ in *Toomey* at 522–523. See also, eg, *British Dominion General Insurance Co v Duder* [1915] 2 KB 394, 401–402.

[45] [2010] 1 AC 180; [2009] 2 Lloyd's Rep 508, para 34.

[46] At para 2, citing *British Dominions General Insurance Co Ltd v Duder* [1915] 2 KB 394, 400.

well established principle, not challenged in this case, that under English law a contract of reinsurance in relation to property is a contract under which the reinsurers insure the property that is the subject of the primary insurance; it is not simply a contract under which the reinsurers agree to indemnify the insurers in relation to any liability that they may incur under the primary insurance.

The concept of reinsurance was held to exist where the reinsurance contract was an **1.32** insurance of surety bonds rather than of an underlying insurance risk. Contracts of reinsurance are excluded from the charge to insurance premium tax and in *Travellers Casualty v Commissioners of Customs and Excise*[47] the question for a VAT Tribunal was whether an insurance of surety bonds were contracts of reinsurance. Surety contracts are not themselves insurance,[48] but they are part of the business of an insurer and so when that insurer took out insurance with a reinsurer in respect of those bonds, that was held to be a reinsurance contract.

G. Types and Methods of Reinsurance

Reinsurance is essentially a contract under which an insurer agrees to pass a **1.33** defined part of an insurance risk to a reinsurer. The distinction between the two main types of reinsurance is in the way that this part is defined—proportional or non-proportional.

(1) Proportional Reinsurance

In the first main type of reinsurance, proportional reinsurance, the reinsurer agrees **1.34** to take a proportional part or share of the liability of the insurer on a single risk or a number of risks and also takes an equivalent proportion of the premium (less commission). The reinsurer has an interest in all the insurer's losses as it will pay the proportion of such losses that he has agreed to reinsure, leaving the remainder to be paid by the insurer. For example, an insurer enters into a contract of insurance providing for £1 million of cover in the event of fire damage to a factory. The insurer then enters into a contract of reinsurance with a reinsurer who agrees to reinsure 75% of the risk. The reinsurer receives 75% of the premium (less commission). If a fire takes place at the factory and damage of £1 million results then the reinsurer will be liable for the payment of £750,000 (ie his proportion of the total liability), and the net cost to the insurer will be £250,000 (ie that part which he has retained).

---

[47] [2006] Lloyd's Rep IR 63.
[48] The VAT Tribunal noted that the fact that s 95(a) of the Insurance Companies Act 1982 includes the effecting and carrying out of suretyship contracts did not make them contracts of insurance.

(2) Non-Proportional Reinsurance

1.35 In the second main type of reinsurance, non-proportional excess of loss reinsurance, the reinsurer reinsures a layer (or part of a layer) of the liability of the insurer on a single risk or a number of risks. Non-proportional reinsurance enables a reinsured to assume a risk or size of risk which it might not otherwise write, but for the protection afforded by the reinsurance.

1.36 The non-proportional reinsurer has little interest in any loss until it reaches a certain amount: the excess point. For a loss which is greater than the excess point, the insurer pays everything below the excess and the reinsurer pays that part which he has insured above the excess point.[49] Take the same example of an insurer entering into a contract of insurance providing for £1 million of cover in the event of fire damage to a factory. The insurer enters into a contract of reinsurance with reinsurer A for 100% of its liability in excess of £250,000 but up to a liability of the insurer of £500,000 (ie £250,000 in excess of £250,000) and a contract of reinsurance with reinsurer B for 100% of the liability in excess of £500,000 up to £1 million (ie £500,000 in excess of £500,000). Both reinsurers have reinsured a layer of the risk. If a fire takes place causing £200,000 of damage to the factory, neither reinsurer will be called upon to pay any part of the loss. If the loss caused by the fire is £450,000, the insurer will be liable for the first £250,000 but reinsurer A's layer of cover will also be caught and reinsurer A will therefore be liable for £200,000 (ie that part of the damage in excess of £250,000). If the loss caused by the fire is £1 million (or more), reinsurer A will be liable for £250,000 and reinsurer B for £500,000.

1.37 The difference between proportional and non-proportional reinsurance is fundamental. As Waller LJ said in *Bonner v Cox*:[50]

> Reinsurance is very much the life blood of the market. It may be proportional, such as a quota share which is in the nature of a joint venture between the reinsured and his reinsurer. Or it may be non-proportional, such as an excess of loss, which is written to protect an exposure to a particular risk (facultative), a particular class of risk or a whole account; it is a way in which an underwriter manages an underwriting account. The fundamental difference between these two types of reinsurance is that the former involves a sharing of risks (premium and losses) between reinsured and reinsurer. The latter, (with which we are concerned) does not.

1.38 A non-proportional reinsurer does not usually exercise any underwriting judgement as to the particular risks which he reinsures.[51] The assessment a reinsurer makes at the outset relates to the skill which it believes the reinsured has as the reinsurer will expect to follow the fortunes of that reinsured.

---

[49] See, eg, *Balfour v Beaumont* [1982] 2 Lloyd's Rep 493, 496.
[50] [2006] Lloyd's Rep IR 385, paras 87–88.
[51] Indeed other than in facultative reinsurance, a reinsurer rarely exercises independent underwriting judgement: see Waller LJ said in *Bonner v Cox* [2006] Lloyd's Rep IR 385, para 89.

Excess of loss reinsurance is comparatively modern, probably dating from transac-   **1.39**
tions arranged by CE Heath (an underwriter at Lloyd's) in the United States in
the last two decades of the nineteenth century.[52] Under such non-proportional
reinsurance, the premium may be fixed but where the reinsurance is not simply
protecting a single risk, it is commonly a minimum and deposit premium adjust-
able by reference to a percentage of the reinsured's net premium income. Claims
on the risk(s) within the scope of the reinsurance are payable in excess of a specified
figure, whether the cover relates to individual losses or to an accumulation of losses
or on the whole or a particular part of the reinsured's account.[53] The more likely
it is that a layer of reinsurance is going to be breached, the more the reinsurer will
expect to be paid by way of premium.

H. Facultative and Treaty Reinsurance

A reinsurance programme will often be comprised of a combination of propor-   **1.40**
tional and excess of loss or non-proportional reinsurances. These can be provided
on a 'one-off' basis, with specific contracts of reinsurance designed to cover a particular risk ('facultative' reinsurance), or the insurer and reinsurer can enter into
a continuing relationship under a 'treaty' whereby a class of risks or an insurer's
entire account can be reinsured. The different forms of reinsurance, ie facultative
and treaty, represent different tools which an insurer may deploy, frequently in
conjunction with one another, to pass on or protect exposure either on particular
risks or on the whole or part of its insurance account. The purpose is self-evidently
to protect the insurer from exposures of the type reinsured which could otherwise
either individually or cumulatively imperil the insurer's solvency or profitability.[54]

I. Facultative Reinsurance

Facultative reinsurance is reinsurance for individual risks and each risk is con-   **1.41**
sidered individually. The central distinguishing feature of facultative reinsurance is that both insurer and reinsurer have a choice as to whether to enter into a
reinsurance contract in respect of each risk. There is no obligation on the insurer
to reinsure the risk. If the insurer does seek reinsurance, there is no obligation on
the reinsurer to provide it.

Facultative reinsurance can be proportional or non-proportional. It was the predom-   **1.42**
inant form of reinsurance probably until the early part of the twentieth century. It

---

[52] Per Lord Mustill in *Charter Reinsurance Co Ltd v Fagan* [1997] AC 313, 390.
[53] Per Mance J in *Charter Reinsurance Co Ltd v Fagan* [1997] AC 313, 341.
[54] Per Mance J in *Charter Reinsurance Co Ltd v Fagan* [1997] AC 313, 342.

has a number of obvious drawbacks. The administrative costs of having to consider risks on an individual basis are relatively high, and the time taken to do so may also be somewhat lengthy. Unsurprisingly, therefore, one most often sees facultative reinsurance being used to reinsure unusual or large risks.[55] Furthermore, an insurer will generally want a degree of certainty that if he insures a risk he will be able to obtain appropriate reinsurance for it. The facultative method, in its most traditional form (ie where insurance is effected first and reinsurance is then sought), is intrinsically uncertain—an insurer can take on a risk and then discover that he cannot obtain any reinsurance (or any reinsurance for a price that he wishes to pay).

(1) Proportional Facultative Reinsurance

1.43 The basic concept of facultative proportional reinsurance was summarized by Lord Griffiths in *Forsikringsaktieselskapet Vesta v JNE Butcher*:[56]

> An insurer who has accepted a risk by issuing a policy of insurance goes to reinsurers to lay off part of that risk. Before the reinsurer accepts part of the reinsurer's risk, he will wish to assess the risk for himself. The reinsurer can only assess the risk if he is shown the terms on which the insurer has accepted the risk; in other words if the reinsurer is shown the policy that has been or is to be issued by the insurer. When the reinsurer has assessed the risk covered by the policy he can then decide whether or not he will reinsure the risk. In the ordinary course of business reinsurance is referred to as 'back-to-back' with the insurance, which means that the reinsurer agrees that if the insurer is liable under the policy the reinsurer will accept liability to pay whatever percentage of the claim he has agreed to reinsure.

1.44 This is not, however, a complete description of facultative proportional reinsurance.[57] In many cases reinsurance is arranged, at least in principle, before insurance is effected. Furthermore, the description does not address the common and accepted practice of 'signing down' facultative proportional reinsurance[58]—whereby a broker will over-subscribe reinsurance (ie obtaining reinsurance cover for more than 100% of the risk, or for more than the amount which the reinsured has asked him to obtain, and then 'signing down' the over-subscription proportionately to 100%).[59]

---

[55] In the insurance market, the problems posed by the placement of small facultative risks can be addressed by the broker arranging a line slip, which is an arrangement whereby the leading underwriter on the line slip has the authority to accept risks falling within its ambit on behalf of all the following underwriters subscribing to the line slip. Such an arrangement can also be set up for facultative reinsurance business that a broker anticipates receiving—see, eg, *Brotherton v Aseguradora Colseguros SA* [2002] 1 Lloyd's Rep IR 848.

[56] [1989] 1 AC 852, 893.

[57] As recognized by Tuckey LJ in *Groupama Navigation et Transports v Catatumbo CA Seguros* [2000] 2 Lloyd's Rep 350.

[58] Signing down lines can apply to any form of reinsurance which is over-subscribed.

[59] The percentage of a liability that the reinsurer will actually bear in practice will therefore depend on the extent to which the broker goes on recruiting subscribers after 100% of the risk has been written.

The classic description of market practice was described by Mustill LJ in *The* **1.45**
Zephyr:[60]

> ...a practice has developed whereby a broker instructed to obtain a primary cover
> will on his own initiative approach potential reinsurers to obtain from them in
> advance a binding promise to provide reinsurance for whatever person may subse-
> quently write a line on the primary cover and desire to reinsure the whole or part
> of that line. The reinsurer conveys this promise by initialling a percentage line on
> a slip, which identifies the subject-matter, the nature of the risk and the value. The
> slip does not, however, identify the reassured and could not do so: for at the stage
> when the potential reinsurer is approached, it is not known whether the primary
> insurance will ever be written at all, and if so by whom; or whether any of the pri-
> mary insurers will desire to effect reinsurance; or whether any insurer who does
> desire to reinsure will be willing to do so with the reinsurer whom the broker has
> approached, and on the terms which he has offered. With this promise 'at large'
> in his pocket, the broker can offer to an underwriter a package consisting of the
> opportunity to take a line on the primary cover, and at the same time to place an
> order for reinsurance.

The commercial intention of proportional facultative reinsurance is for the original **1.46**
insurer to reinsure part of its own risk and for the reinsurer to accept that part of the
risk. Therefore the relevant terms in the reinsurance contract should be construed
so as to be consistent with the contract of insurance as a matter of commercial common sense. Consequently the starting point for the construction of the reinsurance
policy is that the scope and nature of the cover in the reinsurance is co-extensive
with the cover in the insurance. As Staughton LJ said:[61]

> One can...readily assume that a reinsurance contract was intended to cover the
> same risks on the same conditions as the original contract of insurance, in the
> absence of some indication to the contrary.

An early example of this principle is found in a reinsurance of cargo in *Joyce v Realm* **1.47**
Marine Insurance Co.[62] The reinsurance was 'to commence from the loading of the
goods' at West African ports. Goods were lost a day after the ship's arrival from
Liverpool into an African port. Under the wording of the reinsurance it might
seem as if the Liverpool cargo was not covered. However the terms of the insurance indicated that the outward cargo was to be considered as covered homeward
cargo 24 hours after the ship's arrival at her first port of discharge. The Court held

---

[60] [1985] 2 Lloyd's Rep 529, 532. The Court of Appeal approved Hobhouse J's approach that the
above, as a matter of market practice, produced a binding promise, but also that on a strict contractual analysis there was a binding contract once the reinsurance had been accepted, and even without
communication of that acceptance to the reinsurers. Once a reinsurer had scratched the slip offering the reinsurance that was an open offer capable of acceptance simply by the offeree accepting or
renewing the cover on the basis of that offer of reinsurance. See also *Bonner v Cox* [2006] Lloyd's
Rep IR 385.
[61] In *Youell v Bland Welch & Co Ltd* [1992] 2 Lloyd's Rep 127, 132.
[62] (1872) LR 7 QB 580.

that 'loading' in the reinsurance applied to outward cargo from Liverpool which was left on board and considered as homeward cargo under the insurance. The reinsurance was read in the light of the insurance and showed that what was meant between the parties was not the actual loading, but a constructive loading. What was important was what the original underwriters had agreed to treat as a loading on board for the purpose of the homeward voyage.

1.48　The existence of back-to-back reinsurance is a matter of construction of the wording used by the parties in the context of the type of reinsurance and not any rule of law, as was emphasized in *Wasa International Insurance Co v Lexington Insurance Co*.[63] The fact that a reinsurer could offer non back-to-back cover if it selected the correct wording was explained by Lord Griffiths in *Vesta*[64] when he said:

> A reinsurer could, of course, make a special contract with an insurer and agree only to reinsure some of the risks covered by the policy of insurance, leaving the insurer to bear the full cost of the other risks. Such a contract would I believe be wholly exceptional, a departure from the normal understanding of the back-to-back nature of reinsurance and would require to be spelt out in clear terms. I doubt if there is any market for such a reinsurance.

(2) Non-Proportional Facultative Reinsurance

1.49　Non-proportional, excess of loss, facultative reinsurance is a somewhat rarer feature on the reinsurance landscape, although it is commonly found on the reinsurance of captives above a 'working' layer. The reinsurer will offer to reinsure only on a sum in excess of a particular figure on the risk. The insurer and reinsurer are free not to offer and not to accept. If accepted, the insurer will then retain liability for the entire loss below that excess; and the reinsurer for that part of the loss that he has agreed to pay above the excess. Reinsurers may favour this method as a mechanism for limiting their exposure and also for negotiating premium rates (ie not simply taking a share of the premium proportionate to the percentage of the risk that they have reinsured).

J. Treaty Reinsurance

1.50　Treaty reinsurance is an agreement ('treaty') for reinsurance, at least in principle,[65] for a number of risks. By this method, insurer and reinsurer agree that all risks of the insurer of a certain type or types, and potentially the entirety of the insurer's book of business, will be reinsured by the reinsurer. Individual risks are not assessed

---

[63] [2010] 1 AC 180; [2009] 2 Lloyd's Rep 508.
[64] *Forsikringsaktieselskapet Vesta v Butcher* [1989] AC 852.
[65] The reason for the use of the words 'in principle' is that it may transpire that the insurer will not in fact have any business of a particular type during the currency of the agreement, and therefore will not cede any business of that type to the reinsurer.

by the reinsurer and premiums are decided in advance, reducing administrative costs and ensuring certainty of reinsurance cover simultaneously with the direct insurance being placed. The central distinguishing feature of the treaty method of reinsurance is that the insurer is obliged to cede to the reinsurer such risks as he has agreed to cede under the treaty and the reinsurer is obliged to accept those risks. It is the predominant method of reinsurance.

In *Hanwha Non-Life Insurance Co Ltd v Alba Pte Ltd*[66] the High Court of Singapore **1.51** had to construe a reinsurance contract to decide whether it was facultative or obligatory. Both on a traditional construction of its brief terms (including a fixed premium, a limit of cover and monthly declarations) and when adopting the contextual approach outlined in *Investors Compensation Scheme Ltd v West Bromwich Building Society*,[67] the reinsurance was held to be open obligatory in nature. This meant that the reinsurance risk run by the reinsurer commenced immediately whenever the reinsured accepted a risk on the underlying insurance policy. Such obligatory or treaty reinsurance can be effected proportionally and non-proportionally, and there are various mechanisms of doing so within each category.

K. Proportional Treaty Reinsurance

Under a proportional treaty the insurer agrees to cede a proportional share of all its **1.52** business within the limits of the treaty, and the reinsurer agrees to accept that share. The limits of the treaty can be in relation to the type of risk, the amount of risk, the area for which the risk is provided (eg, only certain countries). However, once agreed the reinsurance is automatic—the insurer is obliged to cede and the reinsurer is obliged to accept all risks that are within the compass of the treaty. As with other proportional arrangements, the reinsurer will take a share of the premium equivalent to the proportion of the risk that he has reinsured (less commission).

There are two main types of proportional reinsurance treaty: quota share and sur- **1.53** plus. These are considered in turn.

(1) Quota Share

By a quota share treaty, insurer and reinsurer are obliged to cede and accept a fixed **1.54** share of each and every risk within the scope of the treaty. This is a simple form of treaty. In practice, it is common for reinsurers to limit the amounts that they will be required to pay in respect of each risk ceded. To give an example, the reinsurer

---

[66] [2012] Lloyd's Rep IR 505. The Court held that the reinsurer had no right to reject a later endorsement as the attachment of risk under the reinsurance contract was independent of the submission of declaration of the risk, applying *Glencore International AG v Ryan (The Beursgracht)* [2002] 1 Lloyd's Rep 574 and [2002] Lloyd's Rep IR 335.
[67] [1998] 1 WLR 896 at 912.

agrees by a quota share treaty to provide reinsurance to the insurer on all of its fire business in Scotland for the year 1 January to 31 December 2005 to the extent of 75% on each risk, and not to exceed £1 million on each risk. The insurer issues 1,000 policies for fire insurance in Scotland that year for a premium of £1,000 each. The reinsurer will take £750,000 of the premium (subject to any commission payments). There are five fires upon which the insurance cover is called. Four fires cause losses of £100,000, and the fifth causes a loss of £1,500,000. The reinsured is liable to pay his 75% share of £75,000 for the first four fires, but only £750,000 for the fifth fire (having limited his liability to £1 million for each risk).[68]

1.55   By this arrangement the reinsurer is dependent upon the insurer to write his business prudently, but has the comfort of knowing that both bad and good business will be ceded automatically. The reinsured cannot simply pick out the duff and keep the plums for himself.

(2) Surplus

1.56   By a surplus treaty, the reinsurer agrees to accept the liability above that which the insurer wishes to retain for itself. The insurer decides what sum it wishes to cede to the reinsurer depending on the size and the type of risk. The insurer's retention is called a line and rather than being expressed as a percentage total of the risk (as with quota share treaties) it is referred to as a specific monetary sum. The treaty will usually provide for a monetary limit to the retention. Any risk that falls within the retention is not passed to the reinsurer(s). However, where a risk is larger than the insurer's retention, that part over the retention is ceded to the surplus share treaty reinsurer(s) as a multiple of the sum retained by the insurer. At first blush this treaty appears to be somewhat complex, but in fact it is relatively simple—although it is perhaps best understood by way of example. An insurer wishes to obtain reinsurance for its fire business in circumstances where it wants to retain a maximum exposure of, say, £100,000 for each risk. It enters into a treaty with reinsurers to provide nine lines (ie nine times the retention of the insurer up to £100,000 each line, in this example a maximum available reinsurance of £900,000). Thereafter the insurer issues a policy of insurance to company A for fire damage insurance in the sum of £100,000 and decides to retain the entire risk itself. There is no surplus to cede to reinsurers under the treaty and the entire risk falls on the insurer. However, the insurer then issues a policy to company B for fire damage insurance of £100,000 but decides that it wants to retain only £10,000 of that risk. There is a surplus of £90,000 over the reinsured's retention. Under the treaty nine lines of £10,000 each (the sum retained by the reinsured) are automatically ceded to the reinsurers.

---

[68] See *Forsikringsaktieselskabet National (of Copenhagen) v Attorney General* [1925] AC 639 for an early example of a quota share treaty coming before the courts.

A difficulty for the reinsured will of course arise if he wishes to reinsure a risk **1.57** of, say, £2,000,000. Under the treaty, the maximum amount that the reinsured can retain for itself is £100,000 and the maximum amount that can be ceded to the reinsurers under the treaty is £900,000 (nine lines of £100,000 each). That leaves a reinsurance shortfall of £1 million and the reinsured will accordingly have to make alternative arrangements, perhaps facultatively, for the reinsurance of that part.

In practice, a reinsured will enter into a number of treaties with a number of rein- **1.58** surers to cover the surplus; the treaties should generally be in identical form, and reinsurers will often reinsure part of a line rather than a whole line.

The insurer, through deciding what part of any risk that it wishes to retain, has the **1.59** advantage of deciding what business it wishes to cede (although some surplus treaties may oblige the insurer to cede all business of a certain type). From the reinsurer's perspective this may be somewhat unattractive—the insurer may retain most of the lines on low risks but cede most of the lines on high risks.

There can be more than one surplus treaty, one effectively sitting on top of **1.60** another.

L. Non-Proportional Treaties

Non-proportional reinsurance is based more on claims than risks. The liability of **1.61** the insurer is capped at a certain level (the deductible). Within that retained layer the insurer will remain liable for all losses. The reinsurer will be liable for sums that exceed the deductible (usually subject to a maximum limit), and it is not uncommon to have different layers of excess of loss reinsurance. Different types of non-proportional treaty are geared to the type of business being underwritten. There are two main types: excess of loss and stop loss.

(1) Excess of Loss

In a proportional treaty the reinsurer will be involved in every loss that is ceded **1.62** under the treaty according to the predetermined amount for which it has agreed to be liable. In excess of loss treaties, the reinsurer only becomes involved in a loss when it exceeds the insured's deductible. Where the loss on any risk exceeds the deductible, the reinsurer becomes liable for that layer of the loss that it has agreed to reinsure. Clearly, the more likely it is that a layer of reinsurance is going to be caught, the more the reinsurer will expect to be paid by way of premium. Unlike quota share treaties, the premium paid does not have a proportional relationship to the premium paid by the insured to the insurer. The 'loss' covered can be referable just to losses on individual risks or can extend, for example, to all losses arising from one event.

1.63   An issue as to the order of presentation of losses arose in *Teal Assurance Co Ltd v WR Berkley Insurance (Europe) Ltd*,[69] in which the Court of Appeal found that a tower of insurance contracts was to be regarded as exhausted by reference to the order in which the insured's liability was established and ascertained or the insured incurred covered costs and expenses rather than by reference to the order in which the reinsured paid the losses, as the reinsured contended for the purposes of recovery from its reinsurers. An engineering company had a tower of insurance contracts providing it with worldwide cover for US$60 million any one claim, and in the aggregate annually in excess of the deductible and self-insured retention. Above the initial layer in the tower, there were three layers of excess of loss insurance written by the insured's captive insurer which were reinsured. Above the tower was a 'top and drop' insurance of £10 million per claim which operated once the tower was exhausted. This layer was also insured by the captive and was separately reinsured. However in the 'top and drop' insurance there was an exclusion of North American claims. The insurances issued by the captive each provided that liability should not attach until the underlying insurance had paid its limit. The question was whether the insurer could choose to pay the American claims first within the lower layers, thus leaving the reinsurer exposed to non-American claims at the top.

1.64   The top and drop insurance contract provided that once the indemnity provided by the underlying policies was exhausted then 'this policy shall continue in force as Underlying policy'. That provided for the 'drop'. Each excess insurance had an equivalent drop down clause and therefore as losses arose, each dropped down and became the underlying policy until it in turn was exhausted. The reinsured contended that the clause which provided that liability should not attach until the underlying insurance had paid its limit meant that a layer was not exhausted until payment was made under the policy and that this meant that the order of losses for the purposes of the programme was the order of payment by the reinsured. The Court of Appeal rejected this contention and held that the reinsured could not rely on the clause so as to re-arrange the order of losses by applying the limits of the tower to the payment of American claims leaving reinsurers of the 'top and drop' insurance to face non-American claims where those claims, according to the order in which the insured's liability was established and ascertained or the insured incurred covered costs and expenses, should have been paid by the tower. Such ability to manipulate liabilities was unlikely to have been the intention of the parties. As Longmore LJ said:[70]

> The fact is that the construction of the policies of insurance…does not lead to a sensible commercial result, while the reinsurers' construction (that the policies are exhausted in an orderly manner depending on the time when liability is established against Black and Veatch) does produce a commercially sensible outcome. In these circumstances, however much one may feel that [the insurers'] construction is one

---

[69] [2012] Lloyd's Rep. IR 315 (at the time of writing there is an appeal to the Supreme Court pending).
[70] At para 16.

possible construction, there is no doubt that the policies can bear the construction for which Mr Edelman QC contends on behalf of reinsurers. In these circumstances it is the more sensible commercial construction which is to be preferred, see *Rainy Sky S.A. v Kookmin* [2011] 1 WLR 2900 paras 21–30 per Lord Clarke of Stone-cum-Ebony.

The nature of excess of loss reinsurance was explored by Lord Mance in *Wasa* **1.65** *International Insurance Co v Lexington Insurance Co* when he said:[71]

> Excess of loss reinsurance is underwritten on either a losses occurring or risks attaching basis. In other words, it is fundamental that such a reinsurance will respond in the one case to losses occurring during the reinsurance period, in the other to losses occurring during the period of policies attaching during the reinsurance period. To treat excess of loss policies as covering losses through contamination occurring during any period, so long as some of the contamination occurred or existed during the reinsurance period, would be to change completely their nature and effect.

(2) Stop Loss

Stop loss reinsurance comes in two principal forms (although sometimes also an **1.66** amalgamation of the two)—namely excess of loss ratio and aggregate excess of loss, which are considered individually at paras 1.67 et seq. The difference lies in the way in which the stop loss excess is expressed to operate—in the former it is expressed as a percentage of loss to premium income; in the latter it is expressed as a particular sum. Stop loss reinsurance is a product commonly used to cover against an attritional level of losses on an account or part of an account and may or may not relate to losses of a particular type. They are usually written annually, but this is not invariably so, for example reinsurance for seasonal damage to, say, crops.

(3) Excess of Loss Ratio

By this method of reinsurance the reinsurer agrees to provide insurance to the rein- **1.67** sured in excess of an agreed annual loss ratio—based on the ratio of losses suffered by the insurer to the premiums received by it in a given year. For example, the reinsurer may agree to reinsure an amount of 20% in excess of 110% of the insurer's loss ratio. If in any given year the insurer's losses exceed 110% of its premium income, the reinsurer will be liable for all losses until the total amount paid out by the insurer amounts to 130% of the ratio. Thereafter the loss will fall back onto the reinsured. Because these treaties will generally run annually, it is common to see payments being made by reinsurers at the end of the year. However, such treaties frequently provide for payments to be made earlier when it is clear that the ratio excess will be breached, with any necessary reconciliation taking place at the year end.

In the light of the fact that it may become clear early in the year that the excess ratio **1.68** will be breached, reinsurers will often want to ensure that the reinsured has some

---

[71] [2010] 1 AC 180; [2009] 2 Lloyd's Rep 508, para 41, citing *Balfour v Beaumont* [1984] 1 Lloyd's Rep 272.

incentive to deal with further claims prudently. This is usually done by providing that the reinsurer will only be liable for, say, 85% of the aggregate of the losses that are represented by the losses that it has reinsured, thus furnishing the insurer with an incentive to keep losses to a minimum.

(4) Aggregate Excess of Loss

1.69 This form of reinsurance, sometimes called cumulative excess of loss or catastrophe excess of loss, performs essentially the same function as excess of loss ratio reinsurance—providing protection in respect of the general result of the reinsured—the difference being that a specific monetary amount is defined in the treaty.

1.70 An obvious danger for the reinsurer in underwriting this sort of reinsurance is that the reinsured may write much more business than the reinsurer anticipated when the reinsurance was effected. As such the losses incurred may reach an excess point rather more readily than at first had been anticipated. It is perhaps not unsurprising, therefore, that one often finds hybrid stop loss policies being effected in which the ratio and specified sums are both included, with the reinsurance cover provided expressed to be a maximum of one or the other.

M. A Hybrid Method of Reinsurance— Facultative Obligatory

1.71 A facultative obligatory ('fac/oblig') arrangement (sometimes referred to as 'open cover') works in much the same fashion as a quota share treaty (ie a set proportion of a risk is ceded to the reinsurer), save for the very important difference that the insurer has a choice whether to cede any given risk to the treaty. The insurer cannot cede a risk unless it falls within the limits of the treaty; but he is not obliged to cede if it does. The reinsurer, however, has no choice; he cannot insist on a risk being ceded, and is obliged to take his share of the cessions. Thus the arrangements are facultative so far as the reinsured is concerned because he retains the choice as to whether or not to cede. So far as the reinsurer is concerned, the arrangement is obligatory, like a treaty.

1.72 Fac/oblig treaties are, unsurprisingly, less attractive to reinsurers than quota share treaties. They are subject to the obvious risk that the insurer will retain good business for its own account and cede poor business to the treaty. The main constraint upon the insurer in this regard appears to be a commercial one—it will have to exercise some restraint if it wishes to maintain a good reputation in the market and to conduct future business with existing and prospective reinsurers.[72] As Lord

---

[72] Per Lord Millett in *Aneco Reinsurance Underwriting Ltd v Johnson & Higgins Ltd* [2002] 1 Lloyd's Rep 157, 192.

Steyn said in *Aneco Reinsurance Underwriting Ltd v Johnson & Higgins Ltd*,[73] the difference between quota share and fac/oblig treaties is that:

> …a quota share treaty is not facultative so far as the reassured is concerned: he must cede a set proportion of every risk which falls within the limits of the contract, so that everything which meets those criteria is automatically ceded. By contrast fac/oblig treaties are plainly open to abuse. The reassured is able to put on to his reinsurer the least attractive pieces of qualifying business in his book, while keeping that he considers to be the best business for himself. A reinsurer will tend only to reinsure another underwriter on fac/oblig terms if he has considerable trust in the way that the reassured will use it.

However, it has been argued that there are also legal restrictions on the conduct of business by the insurer under a facultative obligatory reinsurance treaty. In *Phoenix General Insurance Co of Greece SA v Halvanon Insurance Co Ltd*[74] Hobhouse J held that facultative obligatory reinsurance, which imposes no restriction on the reinsured's right to choose whether to cede or not, without giving the reinsurer any equivalent right, necessitated the implication of a term, or terms, that the reinsured should conduct the business involved in the cession prudently, reasonably carefully, and in accordance with the ordinary practice of the market.[75]   **1.73**

In *Phoenix v Halvanon*[76] Hobhouse J said: **1.74**

> The implication of these terms was not controversial before me. Both [expert] witnesses thought them appropriate. Even though the opinion of the witnesses as to what is appropriate and reasonable does not itself suffice to show that such terms should be implied, I am satisfied that such terms are necessary in the present transactions. The fac. oblig. nature of the transaction which imposes no restriction on the reassured's right to chose whether to cede or not to cede, without giving the reinsurer any equivalent right, does necessitate that the reinsured should accept the obligation to conduct the business involved in the cession prudently, reasonably carefully and in accordance with the ordinary practice of the market. In the general formulation the word 'reasonable' is to be preferred to 'due' and the duty to act prudently as if not reinsured is not an alternative but it is really a restatement of the same obligation, provided it is realised that the obligation does not preclude the plaintiffs from taking into account the added capacity to write business that the availability of the reinsurances give them. Such is, after all, one of the important purposes of any reinsurance. In general terms, it must also be pointed out that the overrider commission being paid to the plaintiffs in part specifically covers the cost of carrying out these obligations.

---

[73] [2002] 1 Lloyd's Rep 157, 183.

[74] [1985] 2 Lloyd's Rep 599.

[75] See also section on implied terms in Chapter 3.

[76] [1985] 2 Lloyd's Rep 599, 613. Note that this was a case in which the contractual material was sparse and where the true contractual intention of the parties had to be inferred or implied. In many cases, therefore, matters will be dealt with expressly and there will be no need to imply such a term or terms. Hobhouse J stated that this term (or terms) was innominate and therefore the consequences of any breach for any particular cession or any individual claim or for the contract as a whole must depend on the nature and gravity of the relevant breach—at 614. Note further that the decision of Hobhouse J was overturned by the Court of Appeal, but not in respect of the matters set out above, in *Phoenix General Insurance Co of Greece SA v Administratia Asigurarilor de Stat* [1986] 2 Lloyd's Rep 552.

1.75   Although Hobhouse LJ seemed to endorse, in passing, his own earlier judgment as a general statement of the implied terms appropriate to reinsurance in *Toomey v Eagle Star Insurance Co Ltd*[77] this has received qualified judicial support since. In *Toomey* Hobhouse LJ suggested that *Phoenix v Halvanon* dealt with the terms to be implied into reinsurance contracts 'in order to ensure that the interests of the reinsurers or those to whom risks are ceded, are sufficiently protected'. However the Court of Appeal in *Bonner v Cox*[78] held that non-proportional reinsurance was not subject to such implied terms and was a different type of contract from the proportional facultative obligatory treaty.

---

[77] [1994] 1 Lloyd's Rep 516, 523. It was also followed by Tuckey J in *Economic v Le Assicurazioni d'Italia* (unreported, 27 November 1996).
[78] [2006] Lloyd's Rep IR 385.

2

THE FORMATION OF THE REINSURANCE CONTRACT

A. Elements of a Contract

A reinsurance contract is formed according to normal contractual principles. There **2.01** needs to be an offer and an acceptance of that offer to form an agreement, with consideration for the bargain and an intention by the parties to create legal relations between them. The relationship between reinsurer and reinsured may be one of utmost good faith when concluding the contract, but the essential requirements for the formation of a contract are the same.

(1) Offer

An offer to enter into a contract must disclose an apparent intention to be bound **2.02** on an objective analysis.[1] An offer of reinsurance is generally in the form of a slip, wording or proposal proffered by the reinsured's broker to a reinsurer or reinsurers in the market, but it is not confined to these conventional categories and, in theory, could be in any form setting out the terms of the offer. This would conventionally

---

[1] *Ignazio Messina & Co v Polskie Linie Oceaniczne* [1995] 2 Lloyd's Rep 566, 571.

be carried around the market by the broker until the slip was fully subscribed by a number of reinsurers each accepting a proportion of the risk. Offer documents are now often sent around the marketplace by electronic means. An oral offer will in theory suffice, but is uncommon and uncommercial as it is important to be able to evidence the terms of the reinsurance when the offer is accepted. The broker may already have a good knowledge of the categories of business that are written by the prospective reinsurers or he might have already contacted them to discuss potential terms.[2] The reinsured or its agent either offers the opportunity to reinsure on express terms as set out in the offer, proposal or slip, or, unusually, could apply for reinsurance cover on the basis of the reinsurer's standard terms.[3] In normal circumstances an offer may be withdrawn at any time before it is accepted, by communication with the offeree. An unaccepted offer will lapse after a reasonable time.[4]

2.03 The circumstances of a reinsurance agreement may need to be analysed in some detail to avoid jumping to an erroneous conclusion as to even such a basic contractual notion as offer and acceptance. A slip stamped and signed by a reinsurer may not be the acceptance that it first appears, but an offer or even an invitation to treat. If a reinsured instructs a broker to see if reinsurance is available before the underlying insurance is agreed, the terms obtained from the lead reinsurer and signed lines subscribed on a slip may only amount to an offer or even an invitation to treat.

(2) Acceptance

2.04 Once all the relevant terms of the reinsurance are in place, a binding contract will arise when the reinsurer signifies its acceptance of the offer or counter-offer. The reinsurer should accept by a final and unqualified assent to the terms of the offer. This will usually be signified by a scratch, stamp and/or signature on the proposal, slip or policy.[5] An oral acceptance or acceptance by conduct will technically suffice, but may be difficult to prove, particularly if it falls within the course of negotiations between the parties over the terms[6] and would be highly unusual in practice.

2.05 In cases where the broker has been instructed by the reinsured to see if reinsurance is available before the underlying insurance is placed and secures the reinsurers' agreement to write the reinsurance, the reinsurance contract is only concluded

---

   [2] Such pre-contractual contact which may include a quotation slip is not an offer, but merely an invitation to treat: *Assicurazioni Generali SpA v Arab Insurance Group* [2003] Lloyd's Rep IR 131; *Brotherton v Aseguradora Colseguros SA* [2002] Lloyd's Rep IR 848. A broker may make an invitation to treat to enquire about whether a potential reinsured wishes to make an offer to a reinsurer for a particular reinsurance product.
   [3] *Nsubuga v Commercial Union Assurance* [1998] 2 Lloyd's Rep 682.
   [4] *Canning v Farquar* (1886) 16 QBD 727.
   [5] *Denby v English and Scottish Maritime Insurance Co* [1998] Lloyd's Rep IR 343.
   [6] *Sphere Drake Insurance v Denby* [1995] LRLR 1.

when the reinsured actually places the order for the reinsurance, having decided to take the underlying risk.[7]

An acceptance can be made by the reinsurer itself or an agent with actual or osten- **2.06** sible authority.[8] An acceptance which includes new or different terms for the reinsurance cover is actually a counter-offer, which itself needs to be accepted in order for a contract to be concluded. Silence cannot generally be an acceptance unless coupled with some conduct or course of dealing indicative of an intention to be bound, or unless an estoppel arises which prevents the offeree from resiling from the bargain.[9]

Once the reinsurance contract has been accepted and becomes binding, the rein- **2.07** sured's general duty of utmost good faith[10] comes to an end. A reinsured therefore does not have to disclose material facts that come to its knowledge after acceptance, but before the cover commences.[11] However, the duty continues in force up to the moment of acceptance.[12]

(3) Consideration

A reinsurance agreement must be supported by sufficient consideration.[13] This is **2.08** invariably supplied by the premium.[14] A reinsurance premium is paid by the reinsured to the reinsurer and is calculated to reflect the element or proportion of the underlying risk that is passed to the reinsurer. Other sums payable in relation to the reinsurance contract may include ceding commission (payable to the reinsured as a reward for finding business for the reinsurer) and brokerage (paid to the broker under the separate agency contract between reinsured and broker).[15] A binding reinsurance contract will exist before the premium is actually paid unless, unusually, payment is expressly made a condition precedent of the policy. If a premium warranty clause is a term of the reinsurance a failure to pay the premium will (in the absence of waiver) discharge the reinsurer from liability under the policy.[16]

---

[7] *General Accident Fire & Life Assurance v Tanter* [1985] 2 Lloyd's Rep 529. See also *Mander v Commercial Union Assurance Co* [1998] Lloyd's Rep IR 93 in which reinsurers had signed up to a retrocession facility which did not lead to a binding contract until valid declarations were made by the broker under the facility.

[8] *Eagle Star v Spratt* [1971] 2 Lloyd's Rep 116. For an outline of some of the principles of agency in reinsurance see para 2.50.

[9] *Spiro v Lintern* [1973] 1 WLR 1002, but see *Rust v Abbey Life Insurance Co* [1979] 2 Lloyd's Rep 355 where silence coupled with keeping an insurance policy for a number of months was an acceptance. See also *New Hampshire Insurance v MGN* [1997] LRLR 24 in which a policy tendered was different from the slip and so was a counter-offer which needed to be accepted. It was unsuccessfully contended that the failure to object to the differences was an acceptance.

[10] See paras 6.02 et seq.

[11] For discussion about any continuing duty of utmost good faith see paras 6.08 et seq.

[12] *Looker v Law Union & Rock Insurance* [1928] 1 KB 554 (a case involving life assurance).

[13] See the insurance case of *Clark v Tull* [2002] Lloyd's Rep IR 524.

[14] See para 5.01.

[15] See para 2.50.

[16] See para 5.02.

The amount of the premium may be a rate to be agreed, and if no agreement is reached then the premium is taken to be a reasonable premium.[17]

(4) Complete and Certain Terms

2.09 The terms on which the parties are contracting must be complete and reasonably certain in order for a contract to exist.[18] It is possible to find the terms of a reinsurance contract wholly within one document signed by all the parties.[19] More common is a reinsurance contract contained within a slip followed by a formal policy with terms and conditions incorporated by reference to another document or documents, such as the standard market LMP or other London market form.[20] Where such standard terms and conditions are being incorporated it is usually necessary for them to be drawn to the attention of the reinsured[21] unless the reinsured knows about them from a course of dealing or market notoriety. Proportional reinsurance may often be referred to as 'back-to-back' with the insurance: if the reinsured is liable under the underlying policy, the reinsurer will accept liability to pay whatever percentage of the claim it has agreed to reinsure. The reinsurance contract is found by taking the slip or reinsurance policy together with the underlying insurance policy.[22] In a proportional reinsurance of this kind there is a presumption that, in the absence of clear words to the contrary, the scope and nature of the cover afforded is the same as the cover afforded by the insurance.[23]

2.10 Words of incorporation should be interpreted so as to give effect to the context from which they had been drawn and into which they have been inserted.[24] This process involves an intelligent and not a mechanical approach to interpretation. The principles applicable to the incorporation of terms into a reinsurance contract

---

[17] See the insurance case of *Banque Sabbag v Hope* [1973] 1 Lloyd's Rep 233.

[18] *Frota Oceania Brasileira v Steamship Mutual Underwriting Association* [1996] 2 Lloyd's Rep 461.

[19] All the terms will usually be in one document in the case of treaty reinsurance. In reinsurance initially written by slip, it is increasingly common for the formal policy to replace the slip: *HIH Casualty & General Insurance v New Hampshire Insurance* [2001] Lloyd's Rep IR 596.

[20] See para 2.12; *Cigna Life Insurance v Intercaser SA de Seguros y Reaseguros* [2001] Lloyd's Rep IR 821; *Wyndham Rather Limited v Eagle Star & British Dominions Insurance Co Ltd* (1925) 21 Ll LR 214.

[21] *Circle Freight International Ltd T/A Mogul Air v Medeast Gulf Exports Ltd T/A Gulf Export* [1988] 2 Lloyd's Rep 427, 430 and 433 and *Nsubuga v Commercial Union Assurance Co Plc* [1998] 2 Lloyd's Rep 683, 685. See *Trygg Hansa v Equitas* [1998] 2 Lloyd's Rep 439 in relation to incorporation of arbitration clauses.

[22] *Forsikringsaktieselskapet Vesta v Butcher* [1989] 1 AC 852, 894–898 per Lord Griffiths at 895. See also Lord Mustill in *Axa Reinsurance (UK) plc v Field* [1996] 1 WLR 1026, 1033–1034; *Groupama Navigation et Transports v Catatumbo CA Seguros* [2001] Lloyd's Rep IR 141. For further discussion, see paras 3.15–3.29.

[23] However, the same does not necessarily apply to provisions relating to ancillary or procedural matters such as claims control, law and jurisdiction, and arbitration: *Forsikringsaktieselskapet Vesta v Butcher* [1989] 1 AC 852.

[24] *Union Camp Chemicals v ACE Insurance* [2003] Lloyd's Rep IR 487.

by the words 'as original' or similar were set out by David Steel J in *HIH Casualty & General Insurance Ltd v New Hampshire Insurance Co*:[25]

> I have been referred to a number of cases that have considered the effect of such general words in the fields of insurance and carriage of goods. I would summarise their effect as follows. Incorporation of a specific term (or condition) is only achieved if:
>   i. The term is germane to the reinsurance.
>   ii. The term makes sense, subject to permissible 'manipulation', in the context of the reinsurance.
>   iii. The term is consistent with the express terms of the reinsurance.
>   iv. The term is apposite for inclusion in the reinsurance.

An incomplete contract, which is missing vital terms such as the amount of the price or premium, is not a binding contract.[26] Similarly, if a necessary term or condition is uncertain and is not reasonably ascertainable from the documents or the surrounding circumstances,[27] then the contract will be void for uncertainty.[28] **2.11**

(5) Formality

There is no common law requirement that a reinsurance contract must be contained in a written policy document,[29] but this is compulsory in the marine insurance field.[30] However, it is unusual to find reinsurance effected any other way except by a written reinsurance policy, treaty or slip as it is common market practice to assess the risk by reference to a slip or schedule and then scratch that document to demonstrate agreement to providing cover by a stamp and signature. In practice this means that it will be straightforward in most cases to show that the parties intended to enter into legal relations when the offer was accepted.[31] It is possible to enter into reinsurance by an oral agreement which perhaps refers to a standard wording: such an agreement would be binding in theory, but difficult to rely upon in practice. **2.12**

---

[25] [2001] Lloyd's Rep IR 224, 234, approved by Rix LJ on appeal: [2001] Lloyd's Rep IR 596. This subject is dealt with more fully in Chapter 3.

[26] A contract to negotiate is too uncertain to be enforced: *Walford v Miles* [1992] 2 AC 128, but if there is some agreed mechanism for agreeing a premium a contract should be valid: *Gliksten & Son v State Insurance* (1922) 10 Ll LR 604.

[27] Courts will never construe words in a vacuum. To a greater or lesser degree, depending on the subject matter, they will wish to be informed of what may variously be described as the context, the background, the factual matrix or the mischief: *Arbuthnott v Fagan* [1996] LRLR 135, see also *Investors Compensation Scheme Ltd v West Bromwich Building Society* [1998] 1 WLR 896.

[28] *Walford v Miles* [1992] 2 AC 128 and see s 26(1) of the Marine Insurance Act 1906.

[29] *Sphere Drake Insurance v Denby* [1995] LRLR 1.

[30] Marine Insurance Act 1906, ss 22 and 23: which arguably does not apply even to a purely marine reinsurance policy since the formalities of reinsurance would not have been in the mind of the legislators as reinsurance was still rare and, in part, illegal at the turn of the twentieth century.

[31] But see *Orion Insurance v Sphere Drake Insurance* [1990] 1 Lloyd's Rep 465 and *Clark v Tull* [2002] Lloyd's Rep IR 524 in relation to insurance contracts.

B. Slips and Policies

(1) The Slip

2.13   Reinsurance is often placed on the London market by way of a slip.[32] This document contains the bare essentials of the risk and the cover and is passed around
the market, being shown to prospective insurers. The slip was traditionally passed
around in card or paper form by a broker or sent to insurers by post or fax. The trend
towards electronic slips and endorsements has been gathering momentum since
the Lloyd's and companies markets[33] contracted out policy processing and back
office facilities to XIS.[34] This trend was assisted by the adoption for the London
market of the Market Reform Group's standard MRC slip.[35]

2.14   The system of placing a risk by the use of a slip has been judicially described:

> Contracts of insurance are placed at Lloyd's by a broker acting exclusively as agent
> for the assured. It is he who prepares the slip in which he indicates in the custom-
> ary 'shorthand' the cover that the assured requires. He takes the slip in the first
> instance to an underwriter whom he has selected to deal with as leading under-
> writer, i.e. one who has a reputation in the market as an expert in the kind of
> cover required and whose lead is likely to be followed by other insurers in the
> market…The broker and the leading underwriter go through the slip together.
> They agree on any amendments to the broker's draft and fix the premium. When
> agreement has been reached the leading underwriter initials the slip for his propor-
> tion of the cover and the broker then takes the initialled slip around the market to
> other insurers who initial it for such proportion of the cover as each is willing to
> accept. For practical purposes all the negotiations about the terms of the insurance
> and the rate of premium are carried on between the broker and the leading under-
> writer alone. Where, as is often the case, the slip gives to the assured options to
> cover additional aircraft or additional risks during the period of the cover it does so
> on terms to be agreed with the leading underwriter. This is indicated by the abbre-
> viation 'tba L/U'.[36]

---

[32]   Although sometimes parties will contract without even a slip: *Sun Life Assurance Co of Canada
v CX Reinsurance Co Ltd* [2004] Lloyd's Rep IR 58 in which the basis of the contract was a 'management and administration agreement'.

[33]   Comprising the London Insurance and Reinsurance Market Association (LIRMA) and the
Institute of London Underwriters (ILU), which merged to form the International Underwriting
Association of London (IUA), which is based at the London Underwriting Centre.

[34]   Xchanging Ins-Sure Services (providing services formerly offered by the Lloyd's Policy Signing
Office (LPSO)).

[35]   Market Reform Contract, for all risks incepting on or after 1 November 2007. Its predecessor
was the London Market Principles (LMP) slip. These standard slips were introduced to offer a clear
structure so that every broker presents reinsurance contracts in a consistent manner. They must be
used for all risks (except certain contracts relating to motor business, personal lines business or term
life insurance business which are not processed by XIS).

[36]   Lord Diplock in *American Airlines Inc v Hope* [1973] 1 Lloyd's Rep 233, 243.

A slip typically contains the following sorts of information: **2.15**

(a) the broker's reference;
(b) the type or category of risk or cover;
(c) the form—whether a Lloyd's Underwriters Non-Marine Association (NMA) or other London market standard form is to be used or whether the terms are as original;
(d) the identities of the underlying insured and reinsured;
(e) the period of reinsurance;
(f) the sums reinsured and limits, deductibles, and the reinsured's retention;
(g) the premium, commission, and brokerage;
(h) any reinsurance clause or special reinsurance terms and conditions such as a follow settlements clause or terms relating to costs;
(i) information about the underlying insured or losses, noting as attached any survey, report, accounts or other presentation documents.

The standard open market MRC form contains six sections: Risk Details (contain- **2.16** ing details of the terms of the contract); Information; Security Details, including each reinsurer's share of the risk and their references; Subscription Agreement (detailing processing and administration of post-placement amendments and transactions); Fiscal and Regulatory information, and Broker Remuneration and Deductions (brokerage, fees and premium deductions).

The MRC slip will, if correctly completed, add considerable clarity to the slip. If **2.17** an MRC slip is incorrectly completed it may give rise to some novel arguments (for example if a condition precedent is listed under the conditions heading, without qualification). Separate headings are provided for different terms, including:

(a) conditions (mandatory);
(b) express warranties (where applicable);
(c) conditions precedent (where applicable);
(d) choice of law and jurisdiction (mandatory);
(e) original conditions (specifically for reinsurance).

When using the MRC, the options are to present the full wording in the contract **2.18** during the placing process or to use specific references to a particular wording (whether standard or bespoke). A model or registered wording is often incorporated by reference within the Conditions section of the MRC slip but sometimes the parties use a bespoke wording which ought to be attached to the back of the MRC for certainty as to what terms are incorporated. If the wording is not attached or incorporated by reference at the time of placing, the broker may be exposed to an argument that the wording was not incorporated.

(2) Information on the Slip

A slip fulfils a number of functions in the procurement of reinsurance. Not only is **2.19** it the document which constitutes the offer and acceptance, and which sometimes is the whole contract itself, but it will normally also adopt the role taken by the proposal form in insurance. The proposal form is only a pre-contractual document (except insofar as warranties are incorporated by virtue of a basis clause) but will contain information about the risk and other material representations from the insured. In a similar way a reinsurance slip will often have an information section. This is information that is volunteered by the reinsured or its broker in discharge of its duty of good faith. Such information will not be, without some special term or condition, a warranty of the reinsurance contract, but is part of the performance of the duty of disclosure. All information disclosed on the slip is information which the reinsurer is entitled to assume is correct, but is not warranted as correct.[37]

2.20 The provision of information on the slip reflects the inequality in knowledge between the reinsured and reinsurer which is the *raison d'être* of the duty of utmost good faith.[38] The reinsured should be in a position to provide accurate information about the nature of the risk, previous losses or protective measures taken in respect of the subject of the underlying insurance. The reinsurers use the information as part of the material on which to decide whether or not to write the risk. Therefore information on a slip will usually be regarded as a statement of fact by the reinsured, not merely a statement of its belief.[39]

2.21 Information on a slip is therefore of great importance, but as a representation of the facts upon which the reinsurance is offered and not as a warranty.[40] Since basis clauses rarely appear in reinsurance slips, such information can only become a warranty (or indeed any part of the contract) by very clear words that indicate an intention to this effect. Information on a slip may well give rise to an evidential presumption that the information on the slip is material to the risk, since its inclusion tends to suggest it was considered relevant to the reinsurer's decision whether to write the risk and at what premium. However, at best this will only be a presumption of materiality that can be negated by appropriate evidence that information which was in fact irrelevant was included by the broker in its presentation.

(3) Scratching the Slip

2.22 Each reinsurer can consider the outline terms on the slip and decide whether they want to reinsure the risk. What is most curious about the mechanism of reinsurance placement is how many reinsurers will enter into very substantial contracts based on a single summary document and sometimes without immediate sight of the full terms and conditions of the contract. If a reinsurer wants to cover the

---

[37] *Wise Underwriting Ltd v Grupo Nacional Provincial* [2004] Lloyd's Rep IR 764, per Longmore LJ at para 114 in which he points out that a careful underwriter may still ask for further information.
[38] See para 6.04.
[39] *Highlands v Continental* [1987] 1 Lloyd's Rep 108 in which Steyn J held that 'information' on the slip constituted a representation.
[40] *Sirius International Insurance Corp v Oriental Assurance Corp* [1999] Lloyd's Rep IR 343. On warranties see paras 6.54 et seq.

risk it will write a line on the slip or scratch the slip. This is most often done by the reinsurer or its authorized agent stamping the slip with the official stamp of the reinsurer including its reference code. Then the authorized person writes the percentage placement that the reinsurer wishes to take and either initials or signs the slip against the stamp and proportion (known as 'scratching' the slip).[41]

It should be noted that the placing of a reinsurer's stamp on the slip is generally a **2.23** preparatory step to the writing of a line and does not normally complete a contract in itself without a signature or initials. The purpose of the stamp is to assist to clearly identify the syndicate or company and to provide a box in which the reference number can be written. If the reinsurer does not sign the slip over the stamp, this can be evidence of an absence of an intention to bind.[42] Further, it is an essential part of the underwriting process that the underwriter should state on the slip the amount or proportion of risk ('the line') which he is accepting for that syndicate.

(4) Contractual Nature of the Slip

The object of the reinsured is to secure the full desired cover on acceptable terms **2.24** and this is commonly achieved by the slip method of participation. The total cover results from the conclusion of the individual contracts of reinsurance made with the various syndicates or companies on whose behalf the participating lines are written. The broker will often try to approach an influential reinsurer to be the leading underwriter whose scratch will impress and induce the following market also to sign up to the risk.[43] If and when a claim arises, the reinsured can only claim against the individual reinsurers to the extent of the proportion which they have underwritten. Although there is only one slip it should not be forgotten that this method results in the conclusion of separate contracts with the various subscribers of the slip.[44] Therefore it is very common for a reinsurance contract actually to be a bundle of reinsurance contracts, each reinsurer who subscribes entering into a separate contract of reinsurance with the reinsured.

This slip procedure leads to the formation of the reinsurance contract. Market **2.25** practice is that the slip is an offer presented by the broker, which each reinsurer accepts when writing its line and which becomes binding on the scratching of

---

[41] The slip must be scratched by a person with authority or apparent authority to do so: *Eagle Star Insurance v Spratt* [1971] 2 Lloyd's Rep 116. The underwriter may also scratch accompanying documents to prove that they have been seen. The scratch normally binds the reinsurer: *ERC Frankona Reinsurance v American National Insurance Co* [2006] Lloyd's Rep IR 157.

[42] *Denby v English & Scottish Maritime Insurance Co* [1998] Lloyd's Rep IR 343, in which it was said that it was the practice of the market that it is the signature or initials which bind.

[43] The leading underwriter does not need to subscribe to the greatest proportion on the slip, but will usually be the first to subscribe: *Roar Marine v Bimeh Iran* [1998] 1 Lloyd's Rep 423. For an overview of leading underwriters see para 2.41.

[44] *General Re v Forsakringsaktiebolaget Fennia Patria* [1983] 2 Lloyd's Rep 287, 289.

the slip, subject only to the contingency that it may fall to be written down[45] on closing to some extent if the slip turns out to have been over-subscribed.[46] The slip will either be returned to the reinsured fully subscribed, with all the proportions on offer accepted and scratched by the reinsurers, or potentially there may only be partial acceptance or indeed over-subscription of the risk. In any event the contract is concluded between the parties insofar as the slip is subscribed and the reinsured has no right to cancel the contract resulting from the writing of each line.[47] If the reinsured no longer wants the cover then he has to negotiate a cancellation of the cover with the reinsurers, which they may agree to on payment of a 'time on risk' premium.

2.26   In *Mopani Copper Mines v Millennium Underwriting*[48] the parties started with a slip which was limited to Construction/Erection All Risks, but they then moved to discussing, but not agreeing, the inclusion of operational cover. It was argued that the words of the reinsurance slip included operational risks within the cover. Christopher Clarke J noted that negotiations which had not matured into an agreement were inadmissible, but prior agreements were admissible.[49] The judge found that the finalized contract comprised an amended slip together with emails, which showed that the parties decided against additional operational cover. He therefore read words that were in the slip as non-contractual as they had been introduced in anticipation of cover that was never agreed. The judge found that part of the slip—normally the written contract between the parties—had not been agreed when the wider evidence was considered. He also found that it was legitimate to take account of deleted words in the slip as they helped to show what the parties were (and were not) agreeing by way of additional reinsurance cover.

(5) The Slip Policy

2.27   The reinsurance slip will often indicate that the parties intend that it should be followed up by the creation of a full and formal policy containing all the express

---

[45]   On writing down see para 2.31.

[46]   *General Re v Fennia* [1983] 2 Lloyd's Rep 287, disapproving the contrary obiter view in *Jaglom v Excess Insurance Co Ltd* [1972] 2 QB 250 that the writing of each line constituted an offer by the underwriter and that there was no concluded contract until the slip had been fully subscribed. See also *Morrison v Universal Marine Insurance Co* (1873) LR 8 Ex 40 and 197 where the loss occurred before the slip had been fully subscribed. Also note that offers or 'agreements' prior to the scratching of the slip (including 'quotation slips' or earlier drafts of wordings) are unlikely to be contractual: *Assicurazioni Generali SpA v Arab Insurance Group* [2003] Lloyd's Rep IR 131; *Brotherton v Aseguradora Colseguros SA* [2002] Lloyd's Rep IR 848.

[47]   *General Re v Fennia* [1983] 2 Lloyd's Rep 287, 295. It rejected the argument that the reinsured has a right, until the time when the slip is fully subscribed to the extent of 100%, to rescind any or all of the contracts resulting from the lines on the partially subscribed slip. See also Marine Insurance Act 1906, s 21. The assured owes a duty of utmost good faith when offering a slip to a reinsurer: *Abrahams v Mediterranean Insurance and Reins Co* [1991] 1 Lloyd's Rep 216, which comes to an end when the slip is fully subscribed: *Morrison v Universal Marine Insurance Co* (1873) LR 8 Ex 197.

[48]   [2009] Lloyd's Rep IR 158.

[49]   *HIH Casualty and General Insurance Ltd v New Hampshire Insurance Co* [2001] 2 Lloyd's Rep 161.

terms and conditions of the reinsurance. The broker will need to get this wording approved by the parties (sometimes the lead underwriter will have authority from the following reinsurers to do this or a number of reinsurers nominated pursuant to a general underwriters agreement or GUA). A policy is then officially issued.[50] Still common in facultative reinsurance is the 'Slip Policy', which may be headed as such. The slip policy often specifies that the terms and conditions of the reinsurance are those in a standard London market or other form or are those of the underlying insurance by use of words such as 'terms and conditions as original' or 'as underlying'. The slip document that was prepared for circulation around the market becomes the actual policy or contract document. In the words of Hobhouse J in *The Zephyr*:[51]

> Another point which emerged clearly from the evidence was that the slip is a record of the contract between the assured and the underwriter. It is the contract; it is not merely evidence of an oral contract; it is not open to either party to contend that part of the contract between the assured and the underwriter is to be found elsewhere.[52]

Where there is no subsequent policy, the slip policy should be construed to ascertain the terms of the reinsurance, together with any standard wording incorporated by reference.[53] However, that is not to say that the slip policy should be construed in a vacuum; there is always a setting in which they have to be placed. Normal rules of contractual construction require the context and factual matrix to be considered when looking at the words of the written document.[54] The context in relation to a slip policy may consist of: **2.28**

(a) documents already in existence incorporated in the slip policy by reference, or otherwise referred to in it;
(b) documents which were relevant to the risk and were read by the underwriters when they initialled the slip policy (such as financial accounts, business records or details of previous losses); and
(c) other background documents or other background facts.

One of the features of slip placements is that the completion of the slip may well take days and sometimes weeks. In most cases, the first line, which has been written by the leading underwriter, will be followed by the remainder writing different proportions **2.29**

---

[50] By XIS, which replaced the old Lloyd's Policy Signing Office.

[51] *General Accident Fire & Life Assurance v Tanter (The Zephyr)* [1984] 1 Lloyd's Rep 58, 69.

[52] Hobhouse J went on to observe that the evidence correctly reflected the legal position as stated in *Thompson v Adams* (1889) 23 QBD 361, 365 and *American Airlines Inc v Hope* [1973] 1 Lloyd's Rep 233, 243.

[53] *Quinta Communications v Warrington* [2000] 1 Lloyd's Rep IR 81; but see *HIH Casualty & General Insurance v New Hampshire Insurance* [2001] Lloyd's Rep IR 596, and paras 3.19 et seq.

[54] *Balfour v Beaumont* [1982] 2 Lloyd's Rep 493, 499 (aff'd [1984] 1 Lloyd's Rep 272); see Lord Hoffmann in *Investors Compensation Scheme Ltd v West Bromwich Building Society* [1998] 1 WLR 896 and Lord Wilberforce in *Reardon Smith Line Ltd v Yngvar Hansen-Tangen* [1976] 1 WLR 989.

(whether by way of percentage or amount) on identical terms and at the same rate of premium until the required level of subscription has been achieved. If a policy is over-subscribed it will be signed down proportionally in accordance with market practice, unless insurers/underwriters have scratched 'To stand' or equivalent on the slip.[55] The insurer's or reinsurer's ultimate line is referred to as the 'signed line' and the line initially scratched as the 'written line'. An under-subscribed slip remains binding on subscribers, unless they have scratched 'subject to 100 per cent signing' or equivalent.

2.30   The subscribed slip results in individual and several obligations to the reinsured. It is therefore possible that the subsequent reinsurers may insist on different terms to which the broker may agree, or there may be a change of circumstances or a change of mind by the reinsured which leads to different terms.[56] Indeed if the broker is unable to persuade reinsurers to sign up to the slip to achieve a 100% participation, he may need to offer different terms in order to complete the line. This leads to the unsatisfactory consequence that the cover is not afforded on identical terms. To overcome this problem the first or earlier reinsurers may contract on the basis of the most favourable terms, so that they get the benefit of any better bargain negotiated by any subsequent reinsurers.

(6) Writing Down

2.31   A different but related problem is when the broker obtains subscriptions for more than 100% of the risk. London market practice accepts a degree of over-subscription. The subscribers of a slip find on their ultimate closing notification (which they may not receive for weeks or even months after they have written their line) that their lines need to be written down proportionately so that the total subscription does not exceed 100%. This was described in *General Reinsurance Corporation v Forsakringsaktiebolaget Fennia Patria* by Kerr LJ:[57]

> Providing that this over-subscription does not occur to an unreasonable extent, it is accepted by the subscribers of a slip, albeit reluctantly that, upon 'ultimate closing'…this may fall to be written down proportionally to some extent so that the total subscription does not exceed 100%.

2.32   However, the reinsurers will have often been given an estimate by the brokers of the extent to which the risk is likely to be over-subscribed; known as a 'signing indication'.[58] This signing indication must be a reasonably accurate estimate else

---

[55]   Writing down is discussed at para 2.31.

[56]   The underwriters amended the clauses on the slip in *Pindos Shipping Corp v Raven (The Mata Hari)* [1983] 2 Lloyd's Rep 449.

[57]   [1983] QB 856, [1983] 2 Lloyd's Rep 287, 291.

[58]   *General Accident Fire & Life Assurance v Tanter (The Zephyr)* [1984] 1 Lloyd's Rep 58, [1985] 1 Lloyd's Rep 529. At the time of the loss of the Zephyr the broker had over-subscribed the slip by approximately 13% and had only signed it down to 88.48%, therefore, all three reinsurers were left with larger lines than they said they had anticipated. Hobhouse J rejected the reinsurers' argument that they were not bound to pay the original claim by the reassureds (and this was not contested on appeal).

the broker may be liable for breach of a collateral contract to the reinsurer to whom it was given.[59] There is offer and acceptance at the time of each scratch. The terms are fixed and the slip reinsurers are bound by their lines on the terms on which each were offered, subject only to the contingency that the line may have to be written down on closing if the slip turns out to have been over-subscribed.[60] A reinsurer may indicate an express refusal to agree to writing down on the slip by words such as 'to stand' alongside its proportion, or by signing up to a fixed amount rather than a proportion.

(7) Formal Policy Wording

Where a subsequent policy wording is produced, this may be an administrative for-   **2.33**
mality rather than a step which is intended to alter the terms of the contract specified in the slip. If merely administrative the wording must accord with the slip and
should not contradict it without there being separate agreement to a variation.[61]
Where the parties intend the slip to be the contract, unless expressly indicated by
the broker as containing matters inconsistent with the pre-existing slip, the tender
of a wording is not an offer to vary the contract. It has been said that it is essential
to the way in which the market operates that the slip should contain or identify all
the terms of any real significance that are intended to form part of the contract.[62]

There has been debate for some years over the effect of subsequently issued policy   **2.34**
wording. It has been held, for example, that a reinsurer's signature to the wording is not an acceptance of any variation, but only an acknowledgement that the
broker had accurately turned the slip contract into policy wording.[63] The alternative view is that once a policy is issued and agreed by the parties, this replaces
the slip which is then viewed as a merely provisional contract.[64] More recent
decisions[65] indicate that it is necessary to examine on a case by case basis what the

---

[59] *General Accident Fire & Life Assurance v Tanter (The Zephyr)* [1985] 1 Lloyd's Rep 529, 537.

[60] *General Reinsurance Corporation v Forsakringsaktiebolaget Fennia Patria* [1983] QB 856, [1983] 2 Lloyd's Rep 287, 291.

[61] It is essential to the way in which the market operates that the slip should contain or identify all the terms of any real significance that are intended to form part of the contract: *Burrows v Jamaica Private Power Co* [2002] Lloyd's Rep IR 466, 472 per Moore-Bick J.

[62] *Burrows v Jamaica Private Power Co* [2002] Lloyd's Rep IR 466.

[63] If the wording does not reflect the slip there would not be an amended contract, but only a wording inaccurately reflecting the true contract: *Assicurazioni Generali SpA v Ege Sigorta AS* [2002] Lloyd's Rep IR 480, 484. In *Eagle Star v Renier* [1927] 27 Ll LR 173 Salter J ordered rectification of the policy to accord with the terms of the slip.

[64] *Youell v Bland Welch & Co (Superhulls)* [1990] 2 Lloyd's Rep 423, although the same line was not taken on appeal by Staughton LJ and Beldam LJ [1992] 2 Lloyd's Rep 127. See also Potter J in *New Hampshire Insurance Co v MGN* [1997] LRLR 24 (not addressed by the CA). A slip policy may have continuing significance even where a formal wording is subsequently issued: *HIH Casualty & General Insurance v New Hampshire Insurance* [2001] Lloyd's Rep IR 596.

[65] *HIH Casualty & General Insurance v New Hampshire Insurance* [2001] Lloyd's Rep IR 596 (Steel J was affirmed by the Court of Appeal on this issue), see paras 3.31 et seq.

parties intended—there is no rule of law one way or the other. The terms of the slip will prevail unless and until the parties agree that a subsequent wording replaces it. Such agreement can be indicated, for example, by underwriters authorizing a leader to agree policy wording.[66] The extent to which a slip can be referred to as part of the factual matrix in which a subsequent policy is to be interpreted will depend on the circumstances and is discussed in Chapter 3, though in a proper case the slip could be referred to as a basis for seeking rectification of errors in a subsequent policy wording. Practical difficulties arise where the parties agree in the slip to later consign all the terms formally into a policy wording, but when the matter comes to be litigated, no such policy can be found. As Lord Mance commented in *Wasa International Insurance Co v Lexington Insurance Co*:[67]

> 'The reference in the slip to the use of form J.1 (designed for use with a full policy wording) or NMA 1779 (designed for use with the slip to constitute a slip policy) is itself not without interest, even though neither a formal nor a slip policy has been identified (one may question how premium was ever closed, unless at least the latter at some time existed). The understanding must have been that any formal policy would be on terms consistent with those of any slip policy. Form NMA 1779 provides for reinsurers '"to pay…all such loss as aforesaid as may happen to the subject matter of this reinsurance, or any part thereof during the continuance of this policy'"—confirmation of the basic nature of the reinsurance.'

(8) Binders and Line Slips

2.35 A slip can be in the form of a binding authority given by a number of underwriters to a broker[68] or underwriter. A binding authority is an authority to the cover holder to underwrite on behalf of the reinsurer. It may or may not circumscribe the extent of the authority to writing limited temporary cover and/or referring each risk to the underwriters or leading underwriter. It can also be or include an authority by the following underwriters to the leading underwriters to write risks on their behalf. The binder can also authorize the brokers to issue cover notes on behalf of the reinsurers and indeed to cancel the cover. This type of slip is accordingly referred to as a binder slip.[69]

2.36 The question in *American International Marine Agency of New York Inc v Dandridge*[70] was whether the words 'subject to the same clauses…as in the original policy or policies' were apt to refer to a binder (or at least to the terms of the claimants' participation in the reinsurance as recorded in a binder) which included a follow the leader

---

[66] As in *Youell v Bland Welch & Co (Superhulls)* [1990] 2 Lloyd's Rep 423.
[67] [2010] 1 AC 180, [2009] 2 Lloyd's Rep 508, para 38.
[68] For an overview of brokers see paras 2.43 et seq.
[69] For an example of a binder in practice see *Forsikringsaktieselskapet Vesta v Butcher* [1989] AC 852 where the issue was to identify whether the terms of the underlying insurance had been incorporated into the slip policy. See also *R+V Versicherung AG v Risk Insurance And Reinsurance Solutions SA* [2006] Lloyd's Rep IR 253 concering a conspiracy arising out of the use of binders.
[70] [2005] Lloyd's Rep IR 643.

clause under which the leader had agreed to a post-inception change of class for the insured vessel. The problem on the facts was that the binder postdated the reinsurers' subscriptions to the reinsurance slip by between two and four days. Therefore the reinsureds were not bound to the insurance until several days after the contract of reinsurance had been concluded. The references in the reinsurance to 'the original policy or policies' could not be references to the binder as that was not in existence at the time the reinsurance was agreed, but to the insurance as a whole.[71]

An insurer may be unwilling to write a particular risk offered by a broker because **2.37** of an uncertainty about the availability of reinsurance (or retrocession) cover. However, if he does not accept the risk, he has nothing to reinsure. The line slip and associated reinsurance policy provide an escape from this dilemma. The reinsurer agrees to reinsure original risks accepted by the insurer in accordance with the line slip. The underlying insurance is contained in a separate contract called an 'off slip', indicating that it is concluded under the auspices of the line slip and is reinsured under the reinsurance policy. Strictly any loss suffered by the insurer was suffered under the 'off slip' contract and not under the line slip, but in the London market such losses are referred to as occurring under the line slip.[72]

It should be noted that in insurance a 'line slip' is also an authority (known in the **2.38** London market as a 'facility') given in writing by a number of reinsurers which enables the leading reinsurer to agree to proposals for reinsurance of risks within a prescribed class on behalf of all subscribers to the line slip, provided that the proposed reinsurance is within the scope of the terms of the authority.[73] Such a facility can either be given to a particular broker or be made available to any broker operating in the market. The reinsurance only comes into being when there is a 'declaration' within the terms of the line slip, which is scratched as agreed by the lead reinsurer. The declaration can result in an 'off slip' which, when accepted and initialled, contains the terms of the contract of reinsurance between the reinsured and the group of reinsurers subscribing to the line slip.[74]

The line slip imposes no obligation whatsoever upon the broker to present any **2.39** risks to the lead reinsurer nor does it impose any liability whatsoever upon the lead reinsurer to accept any such risk. The line slip is not a binding legal contract

---

[71] Para 43. By signing the binder the claimants became bound to 15% participation in the insurance, but the original policy was held to refer to the insurance of the 100% which did not all contain follow the leader provisions.

[72] *Balfour v Beaumont* [1984] 1 Lloyd's Rep 272, 273, per Donaldson MR.

[73] Mandatory market line slips have been introduced in London, first the LMP line slip used from October 2005 which was replaced by the Market Reform line slip (MR line slip) with effect from 1 February 2007.

[74] For definitions of 'line slips' and 'off slips' see the judgment of Webster J in *Balfour v Beaumont* [1982] 2 Lloyd's Rep 493, 494, and 495, as approved in *Denby v English and Scottish Maritime Insurance Co* [1998] Lloyd's Rep IR 343. See also Lord Mustill in *Touche Ross v Baker* [1992] 2 Lloyd's Rep 207, 210 and 215.

in itself, it is simply a device whereby a number of insurers or reinsurers can give authority to a leader to enter into reinsurance on their behalf. Any participant can withdraw the authority except insofar as off slips have been agreed. No contract of reinsurance comes into existence unless and until the lead accepts the risk proposed in an 'off slip'.[75]

(9) Policy Amendments

2.40 It is not uncommon for the parties and most commonly the reinsured to want to vary the terms of the reinsurance contract during the course of the cover. Different or additional cover or limits of indemnity may be sought. The amendment, if agreed, commonly takes effect by a written document known as an 'endorsement' which is scratched by reinsurers in the same way as the original slip.[76] That is not to say that an endorsement is always a contractual variation as it may just record aspects of the contract or notify changes in the percentage participation in a reinsurance such as a long-term quota share treaty.[77] Where an endorsement is a variation, the normal contractual rules of offer and acceptance apply to reinsurance contracts and so an alternative and less formal method can be adopted if the parties agree[78] or variation may even be effected by estoppel.[79] The duty of utmost good faith applies to variations in a contract.[80] It is also common for the leading underwriter to be authorized to vary the contract on behalf of the following market under what is most likely to be an agency contract.[81] In order to standardize documentation in the London market, the Market Reform Group have introduced a standard form for contractual changes known as the Market Reform Contract Endorsement (MRCE) which should now be used in the London market to document variations.

(10) Leading Underwriters

2.41 In order to simplify the problems caused by a multiplicity of contracting parties to one insurance or reinsurance it is common for follow the leader clauses to appear.

---

[75] *Denby v English and Scottish Maritime Insurance Co* [1998] Lloyd's Rep IR 343, 355. See also *Limit No 2 Ltd v Axa Versicherung AG* [2008] Lloyd's Rep IR 330—no risks attached to a reinsurance treaty when the open cover itself was written. Risks only attached when they were declared under the open cover. This was not an issue on appeal ([2009] Lloyd's Rep IR 396).

[76] Or a formal written amendment that requires the signature of both parties: *Sun Life Assurance Co of Canada v CX Reinsurance Co Ltd* [2004] Lloyd's Rep IR 58.

[77] *Iron Trades Mutual Insurance Co Ltd v Companhia de Seguros Imperio* [1991] 1 Re LR 213 per Hobhouse J at 226.

[78] See, eg, the arguments in *Lark v Outhwaite* [1991] 2 Lloyd's Rep 132.

[79] *Lark v Outhwaite* [1991] 2 Lloyd's Rep 132; *Hiscox v Outhwaite* (No 3) [1991] 2 Lloyd's Rep 524.

[80] See para 6.08 et seq.

[81] *Roadworks (1952) v Charman* [1994] 2 Lloyd's Rep 99; see also *Unum Life Insurance Co of America v Israel Phoenix Assurance Co* [2002] Lloyd's Rep IR 374; *Barlee Marine Corp v Mountain* [1987] 1 Lloyd's Rep 471, but cf *Mander v Commercial Union Assurance Co* [1998] Lloyd's Rep IR 93 in which Rix J tried to avoid the multiplicity of claims that might arise from a breach of agency by suggesting that the leading underwriter was not the agent for the following market but just the trigger by which they became bound.

Such a clause may bind the insurers subscribing to a slip or treaty to follow the leading underwriters (or Agreement Parties) in regard to agreements, amendments, extensions, and cancellations of cover and may also commonly cover settlements.[82] So far as policy wording and endorsements are concerned the GUA is now the preferred basis for agreeing the leading underwriter's authority to bind the following market. The leading underwriter is by no means bound to take the larger share. Indeed, since he usually puts down his line first, he has no means of knowing whether other underwriters will or will not be more enthusiastic in their commitment.[83]

In relation to settlements the operation of a follow the leader clause on the London **2.42**
market is not necessarily conditional on the settlement being concluded in a proper and businesslike way. This is because there is mutuality of interest between leading and following reinsurers who, for better or worse, trust the leader and accept both the advantages and any risks of the leader's handling of settlements and of other matters affecting them.[84]

C. Formation of Treaties

The treaty wording will specify which type of reinsurance is provided in a reinsur- **2.43**
ing clause and will usually contain a number of exclusions of the types of business that the reinsurers do not want to cover. Such treaties are common enterprises and so it is common for both reinsurer and reinsured to share in each other's fortunes with a strong follow settlements clause. These clauses are express and normally contained in the treaty wording that is circulated by the reinsured or its brokers around the market. Each reinsurer scratches the signing sheet or schedule, stamping the sheet and indicating the proportion of the offered risk to which it wishes to subscribe.[85]

Many treaties will contain an 'as original' clause to equate their scope of cover with **2.44**
the underlying insurance. Some quota share treaties rely less on incorporation of terms from the underlying insurance, or from other standard wordings. Treaty

---

[82] Although often restricting the leading underwriter from having a completely free hand by excluding ex gratia or without prejudice settlements: see, eg, *Roar Marine v Bimeh Iran Insurance* [1998] 1 Lloyd's Rep 423. For an alternative form of the clause see *Barlee Marine Corp v Mountain (The Leegas)* [1987] 1 Lloyd's Rep 471. See also the obiter discussion by Richard Siberry QC sitting as a deputy High Court judge in *American International Marine Agency of New York Inc v Dandridge* [2005] Lloyd's Rep IR 643.

[83] *Roar Marine v Bimeh Iran Insurance* [1998] 1 Lloyd's Rep 423, 426.

[84] *Roar Marine v Bimeh Iran Insurance* [1998] 1 Lloyd's Rep 423, 430 rejecting an attempt to introduce concepts found in follow settlement clauses: see *Insurance Co of Africa v Scor (UK) Reinsurance Co Ltd* [1985] 1 Lloyd's Rep 312; *Baker v Black Sea and Baltic Insurance Co Ltd* [1995] LRLR 261, 283.

[85] On the importance of a treaty wording being signed see *Sun Life Assurance Co of Canada v CX Reinsurance Co Ltd* [2004] Lloyd's Rep IR 58.

terms typically provide a right to the reinsurer to inspect the reinsured's records[86] and a duty on the reinsured to provide to the reinsurer regular accounts or borderaux showing the paid claims, the outstanding claims, and the claims that the reinsured believes have been incurred but not yet notified to it. Amendments or extensions to the treaty cover can be made by addenda or endorsements and may particularly be used to renew the cover at the end of the year on the same or different terms.

D. Writing Reinsurance at Lloyd's

2.45 Lloyd's is not a reinsurer, but one of the largest markets in the world in which reinsurance is written. Every underwriting member of Lloyd's or 'Name' incurs liability on a basis which is several and not joint.[87] The Names participate in the insurance market through a complex series of agencies. Members' agents help them to band together in syndicates, some specialist and some composite, which are managed by managing agents. The Names give their authority to the active underwriter to enter into insurance and reinsurance contracts on their behalf. Therefore although the rights and liabilities are several, the individual Name never in practice acts on his own in insuring or reinsuring. They are obliged to underwrite contracts only through an underwriting agent and the standard form of underwriting agency agreement makes plain that business is conducted on a grouped basis, through the medium of syndicates. It is the active underwriter's duty to act in the interests of the Names in his syndicate: to make a gross profit and keep the risk of loss to an acceptable level.

2.46 When an underwriter takes a line on a reinsurance policy for his syndicate he calls into existence a bundle of individual contracts between each Name and the reinsured, identical save as to the respective proportions taken by each Name. This bundle of contracts is itself normally only part of the reinsurance programme with other syndicates or companies taking lines on the same reinsurance. Therefore as well as the reinsurance sharing the insurance load between reinsured and reinsurer, this mechanism shares the insurance risk even more widely: with numerous individuals and companies taking a small share in the risk. Where an insurer covers a very large risk, the reinsurance is often spread very widely in this way, with no one syndicate or company taking a disproportionate share. The business risks of reinsuring are thus reduced.

---

[86] See paras 5.45 et seq.

[87] Although the historical unlimited liability of individual Names which led to the ruin of many following the huge losses from 1988–1992 ('down to their last cuff-links') has now been abolished. An individual Name is limited and secured on specified and readily realizable assets. A corporate member's liability is limited by its nature as a limited liability company.

Within the Lloyd's market, there is a complete delegation by the Name to the **2.47** underwriting agent and active underwriter of all powers relating to the conduct of his underwriting business. Indeed the individual Name is expressly prohibited from interfering with the control and management of the business[88] and is more in the way of an investor than an insurer. If a corporate Name is the only member of a syndicate, it will be in a position to control the underwriting.

The accounts for each syndicate are supposed to be kept open only for a three-year **2.48** cycle. In year one the underwriting agent writes various insurance and reinsurance business on behalf of his members. After the end of year three, the first year's business is closed with each member receiving his share of the profit or loss made on the business written in that year. However, because Lloyd's syndicates often write long-tail business, there may be liabilities notified for many years to come. It is not possible to close the year without the syndicate assessing what outstanding liabilities exist and purchasing reinsurance to cover those outstandings. Therefore each Lloyd's year of account will have 'reinsurance to close'. As the practice has been for the members who make up the next year of account to reinsure year one, the syndicates would, in effect, reinsure themselves and thus were able to store up the massive losses that befell Lloyd's in the early 1990s. Once these huge long-tail losses (such as asbestos, pollution, and other US environmental claims) became known in the market it became impossible for all syndicates to obtain reinsurance to close and many years had to remain open and on the last open year the members remained liable for the historic losses,[89] hence the creation of Equitas to reinsure the run-off of open years.

At Lloyd's a reinsurance is effected by a Lloyd's broker presenting the slip for the **2.49** risk to the underwriters.[90] The broker will approach a market leader or specialist first, to see if it can secure him as the lead underwriter on the slip. The potential leader will study the slip and any attachments, look at the files of claims histories and other risk information, and discuss the risk with the broker. He will make a contract by scratching the slip and then the broker can use the leader's signed line to encourage the following market to subscribe. The broker can then visit other underwriters around the Lloyd's building showing them the slip, attachments, and the existing participation. Each additional scratch makes a new and separate contract. The subscribed slip is then sent to XIS[91] for checking and for the formal Lloyd's reinsurance policy to be issued.

---

[88] By the terms of the standard agency agreement.
[89] The downside of such huge losses, including catastrophe claims, being written in a relatively small and incestuous market was the LMX Spiral.
[90] Physically in his box at Lloyd's, which is how most Lloyd's brokers prefer to do business, but note the spread of electronic communications in Lloyd's as well as the companies market which are using systems such as XIS or eReinsurer. These are used for the processing of premiums and claims but are not so popular for the formation of the contracts.
[91] Formerly the Lloyd's Policy Signing Office (LPSO).

E. Brokers and Intermediaries

2.50 It has been said that 'the role of an insurance or reinsurance broker is notoriously anomalous for its inherent scope for engendering conflict of interest in the otherwise relatively tidy legal world of agency'.[92] At its simplest, the broker acts as agent for the reinsured, but normally receives his remuneration from the reinsurer in the form of commission. A broker may, in certain circumstances, act for both reinsured and reinsurer as the same broker may act on behalf of the underlying insured in placing the insurance and on behalf of the insurer (and reinsured) in placing the reinsurance. Where brokers wear the reinsured's hat and the reinsurers' hat side by side the concern must be that neither hat may fit properly.[93]

2.51 The initial oddity of the arrangement was explained by Mustill LJ in *The Zephyr*:[94]

> When a primary insurer is deciding whether or not to take a line on a particular risk, and if so in what amount, he may decide to participate only if he can obtain reinsurance. In such a case the broker will have a better prospect of persuading the underwriter to participate in the primary insurance if he is able to offer him reinsurance at the same time. Accordingly, a practice has developed whereby a broker instructed to obtain a primary cover will on his own initiative approach potential reinsurers to obtain from them in advance a binding promise to provide reinsurance for whatever person may subsequently write a line on the primary cover and desire to reinsure the whole or part of that line.

2.52 Generally a reinsurance broker is the agent of the reinsured and owes its principal duties to the reinsured rather than to reinsurers.[95] He is the agent of the reinsured to carry out the business of obtaining reinsurance cover from a reinsurer.[96] The broker may also be the agent of the reinsurer for specific purposes, such as proposing some retrocession in order to make the reinsurance more attractive.[97] However, this straightforward statement of first principles must be adapted in the light of modern practice. The complex chains of relationships within which reinsurance brokers often operate involve reinsured acting through producing brokers who instruct placing brokers or Lloyd's brokers, who in turn have relationships with reinsurers. The broker normally receives his payment ('commission' or 'brokerage')

---

[92] Auld LJ in *HIH Casualty and General Insurance Ltd v JLT Risk Solutions Ltd* [2007] Lloyd's Rep IR 717, para 61.

[93] *North and South Trust Co v Berkeley* [1971] 1 WLR 470, [1970] 2 Lloyd's Rep 467 per Donaldson J at 486; followed in *General Accident Fire and Life Assurance Corpn v Tanter (The Zephyr)* [1984] 1 Lloyd's Rep 58, 84 by Hobhouse J.

[94] *The Zephyr* [1985] 2 Lloyd's Rep 529.

[95] *General Accident Fire & Life Assurance v Tanter* [1985] 2 Lloyd's Rep 529; *Deny v Walker* [1996] LRLR 276, 282.

[96] Or paying the premium or receiving money in respect of claims.

[97] *Société Anonyme d'Intermédiaires Luxembourgeois (SAIL) v Farex* [1995] LRLR 116, see also *Group Josi Re v Walbrook Insurance Co* [1996] 1 Lloyd's Rep 345.

for his services not from his reinsured client, but from the reinsurer as a percentage of the full premium or deposit premium payable.[98]

In *Markel Capital Ltd v Gothaer Allgemeine Versicherung*[99] the Court rejected the   **2.53**
argument that the reinsured's pool manager had been held out as having ostensible authority to receive information on behalf of the reinsureds. The description of 'reinsured' in the reinsurance agreement, although including a reference to the pool manager, did not bear such a meaning and there was no evidence that the reinsurer relied upon the statement as having that meaning.

The knowledge of the broker can affect his reinsured principal, and is of particular   **2.54**
significance to the duty of utmost good faith.[100] This can arise in three ways. The first is where the agent is relied on by a reinsured for information concerning the subject matter of the proposed reinsurance.[101] The reinsured is deemed to know circumstances which such agents ought to have communicated to the reinsured in the ordinary course of business. The second situation is deemed knowledge where the agent has or appears to have full authority to act for the reinsured so that his knowledge can be regarded as the knowledge of the reinsured.[102] Thirdly where the agent has effected the relevant reinsurance the reinsurance will be affected by any non-disclosure by the agent of any circumstances that lie within the knowledge of the agent.[103] However, an exception to this is where the agent is acting in fraud of his principal and the knowledge that he possesses is relevant to that fraud. In those circumstances the knowledge will not be imputed to or affect the principal.[104]

Where the broker is just the reinsured's agent, it generally owes no contractual duties   **2.55**
to the reinsurer except where the broker holds the reinsurer's binding authority or is instructed to place retrocession or other cover on behalf of the reinsurer. Although he owes no tortious duty of care to advise or act for the reinsurer, he should avoid intentional or reckless falsity else he could be sued for the tort of deceit, and should also take care not to make a negligent misstatement to the reinsurer.

---

[98] Often the reinsured will not even know how much brokerage has been agreed and so the assumption is that the broker will be paid the ordinary amount; however, sometimes the amount of premium or its net equivalent will appear on the slip. If the amount of the commission is set or disclosed and the broker takes more, then he is guilty of dishonesty: *E Green & Son Ltd v G Tughan & Co* (1913) 30 TLR 64. This principle may apply to some undisclosed super commissions or volume discounts.

[99] [2009] Lloyd's Rep IR 433, para 36.

[100] *Blackburn Low v Vigors* (1887) 12 App Cas 531. See paras 6.25 et seq.

[101] *Proudfoot v Montefiore* (1867) LR 2 QB 511, 521.

[102] *Blackburn Low v Vigors* (1887) 12 App Cas 531. eg, where an agent has binding authority.

[103] s 19 of the Marine Insurance Act 1906 which provides that an agent to insure is deemed to know every circumstance which ought to be known by, or ought to have been communicated to, him. See also *Blackburn Low v Vigors* (1887) 12 App Cas 531, 539 per Lord Watson and *Blackburn v Haslam* (1888) 21 QBD 144.

[104] *Belmont Finance Corp Ltd v Williams Furniture Ltd* [1979] 1 Ch 250; *Group Josi Re v Walbrook Insurance Co* [1996] 1 Lloyd's Rep 345; *PCW Syndicates v PCW Reinsurers* [1996] 1 Lloyd's Rep 241.

2.56 In the simplest broking chain it can be demonstrated that separate contracts of agency are concluded first between the reinsured and its producing broker and secondly between the producing broker and the placing brokers who will approach the reinsurers. The producing broker owes direct contractual duties to its principal, the reinsured. The scope of the agency will depend on its express terms or what can be implied by necessity or the course of dealing between the parties. The broker has a duty to advise and place the reinsurance business with reasonable care and skill and will be liable to the reinsured for any default on the part of its own agent, the placing broker. Indeed the placing broker, as well as owing the producing broker contractual duties, can be directly liable to the reinsured.[105]

2.57 There are two routes by which a placing broker might find himself liable to an insured:

(a) by a claim under the Contracts (Rights of Third Parties) Act 1999; and/or
(b) breach of the duty of care in tort.

2.58 The Contracts (Rights of Third Parties) Act 1999[106] provides a right to a person who is not a party to a contract, but who is mentioned in the contract. The Act means that a third party may personally enforce a contractual term if the contract expressly provides that it may or the term purports to confer a benefit on it. The reinsured is a third party to the contract between the placing and the producing broker. Although such a contract may not expressly provide for enforcement by a reinsured, its terms do confer a benefit on the reinsured in the provision of suitable reinsurance cover for it. The Act requires that the third party be expressly identified in the contract by name, as a member of a class or answering a particular description and so a reinsured will probably be able to satisfy this requirement.

2.59 The reinsured's power to sue under the Act is excluded where the broker's contract includes a term that it will not be enforceable by the reinsured. If the broking contract is silent or neutral on the point, the reinsured will probably be able to rely on the Act. However, this just gives a right to sue and the reinsured will still need to show a cause of action: a breach of duty that caused loss. Therefore it is likely that most reinsureds who are looking to recover against a placing broker will continue to rely on a duty of care in tort either on its own or together with a contractual claim under the Act.

2.60 The placing broker can owe a duty of care to the reinsured,[107] although the cases from the insurance field should be relied on with caution as the duty may be limited

---

[105] Under the Contracts (Rights of Third Parties) Act 1999: see *Nisshin Shipping Co Ltd v Cleaves & Co Ltd* [2004] 1 Lloyd's Rep 38 where the third party enforced a term of the contract.

[106] Applying to all contracts made since May 2000.

[107] *European International Reinsurance Co Ltd v Curzon Insurance Ltd* [2003] Lloyd's Rep IR 793 in which the Court of Appeal held that a claim that three sub-brokers and their employers owed a duty of care to an insurer had realistic prospects of success.

in the particular circumstances of the reinsurance programme. What is important is to show an assumption of responsibility towards the reinsured by the placing broker. A placing broker may owe a duty to check that the policy wording and the exclusion clause contained within it accorded with an insured's instructions.[108] A broker might assume a responsibility by voluntarily undertaking to carry out a task for a reinsured. However, an instruction to obtain a quotation and subsequently to effect cover in accordance with the terms of that quotation was insufficient to amount to an assumption of direct responsibility to an insured.[109] Brokers involved in a transaction including a fronting arrangement can arguably owe duties to the fronting company.[110]

It is not uncommon for brokers to place both original cover and reinsurance cover. As Longmore LJ commented in *HIH Casualty and General Insurance Ltd v JLT Risk Solutions Ltd* [111] there may be excellent market reasons for that but the duty owed to each client should, in principle, be the same. If there is information which may potentially put cover at risk, both clients will want to know about it and, in normal circumstances, both clients should be informed.   **2.61**

Phillips J explored the situation where a broker has a dual role in the *Superhulls* case:[112]   **2.62**

> It is, however, possible to consider more generally the role that brokers customarily play where, as often happens, they have broked both original insurance and reinsurance. In such a case there are many activities which require to be performed in relation to both the original contract of insurance and the contract of reinsurance. Some are purely administrative such as accounting for premium. Others may be steps that are essential if cover is to bind, such as making declarations under a facultative/obligatory cover. The evidence of the insurers' witnesses on market practice in such circumstances was consistent and unchallenged. The brokers would be expected automatically to take such steps as were necessary to ensure that, if insurers came on risk under the original cover, the reinsurers came on risk under the reinsurance cover.

The fact that a broker places the insurance and reinsurance back-to-back suggests a duty of care on behalf of the broker to alert the reinsured to potential problems in relation to the reinsurance risk (at least once the underlying risk begins to go bad). A potential risk to the reinsurance cover would necessarily reflect a corresponding risk to the insurance cover. The fact that the broker might find itself in a conflict of interest between the underlying insured's concern to maintain the insurance cover   **2.63**

---

[108] *Tudor Jones & Marsh McLennan v Crowley Colosso* ([1997] EWCA Civ 2909, 4 December 1997, Lawtel Doc No AC0004108, but reported at first instance at [1996] 2 Lloyd's Rep 619).
[109] *Pangood v Barclay Brown & Bradstock* [1999] Lloyd's Rep IR 405 in which an insured claimed against the producing broker for failure to advise about a policy warranty and the producing broker joined in the placing broker claiming a contribution.
[110] *European International Reinsurance Co Ltd v Curzon Insurance Ltd* [2003] Lloyd's Rep IR 793.
[111] [2007] Lloyd's Rep IR 717, para 61.
[112] *Youell v Bland Welch & Co Ltd (The 'Superhulls Cover' Case) (No 2)* [1990] 2 Lloyd's Rep 431.

and the reinsured's possible wish to remove cover does not necessarily exclude such a duty.[113]

2.64   In the *Superhulls* case[114] the brokers broked both insurance for shipbuilders against construction risks and reinsurance for the insurers. The reinsurance differed from the insurance cover as it restricted the period of reinsurance cover to 48 months. The insured claimed because of construction defects when the original cover was in force, but after the reinsurance had expired. The reinsurers denied liability. Phillips J held the brokers were in breach of duty, not only for failing to inform the insurers of the 48-month restriction on the reinsurance at placement, but also in failing to inform them when the reinsurance cover looked likely to terminate before completion of the construction. They had a duty to advise the reinsured to take steps to obtain an extension of the reinsurance (albeit the judge found the insurers to have been 20% contributorily negligent in failing to check themselves).

2.65   As Auld LJ said in *HIH Casualty and General Insurance Ltd v JLT Risk Solutions Ltd*:[115]

> The broker may…effectively devise, structure and establish a scheme, acting together with the insurer and reinsurers in which the insurer is little more than a "'front'" for the reinsurers who shoulder the bulk of the risk.
>
> …
>
> Where a broker has been at the centre of devising and structuring a risky scheme of that sort for insurers and reinsurers…it is plainly a strong candidate for post-placement monitoring obligations of the sort alleged here.

2.66   Therefore an insurance broker who, after placing the risk, becomes aware of information which has a material and potentially deleterious effect on the insurance cover which he has placed is under an obligation to act in his client's best interest by drawing it to the attention of his client and to obtain his instructions in relation to it. The post-placing duty is not restricted to acting merely as a postbox, passing on such information as and when the brokers received it. [116]

---

[113] *HIH Casualty and General Insurance Ltd v JLT Risk Solutions Ltd* [2007] Lloyd's Rep IR 717, para 62.

[114] *Youell v Bland Welch & Co Ltd (The 'Superhulls Cover' Case) (No 2)* [1990] 2 Lloyd's Rep 431.

[115] [2007] Lloyd's Rep IR 717, para 61.

[116] *HIH Casualty and General Insurance Ltd v JLT Risk Solutions Ltd* [2007] Lloyd's Rep IR 717, para 117.

3

THE REINSURANCE CONTRACT—
CONSTRUCTION AND TERMS

A. Construction of Reinsurance Contracts

(1) The Modern Approach to Construction

Reinsurance contracts are subject to the same general principles of contractual con- **3.01**
struction as apply to contracts outside the reinsurance arena. This chapter does not
seek to set out a detailed exposition of that more general terrain, in respect of which
the reader should consult standard texts on contract law, but rather seeks to identify approaches that may be particularly pertinent to the reinsurance practitioner.

In *Arbuthnott v Fagan*[1] Bingham MR stated: **3.02**

> Courts will never construe words in a vacuum. To a greater or lesser extent,
> depending on the subject matter, they will wish to be informed of what may

---

[1] [1996] LRLR 135 cited with approval by Mance J in *Charter Reinsurance Co Ltd v Fagan*
[1997] AC 313.

variously be described as the context, the background, the factual matrix or the mischief. To seek to construe any instrument in ignorance or disregard of the circumstances which gave rise to it or the situation in which it is expected to take effect is in my view pedantic, sterile and productive of error. But that is not to say that an initial judgment of what an instrument was or should reasonably have been intended to achieve should be permitted to override the clear language of the instrument, such that what an author says is usually the surest guide to what he means. To my mind construction is a composite exercise, neither uncompromisingly literal nor unswervingly purposive; the instrument must speak for itself, but it must do so in situ and not be transported to the laboratory for microscopic analysis.

3.03   Steyn LJ emphasized the importance of the purposive rather than literal approach to contractual construction when he said:[2]

> Dictionaries never solve concrete problems of construction. The meaning of words cannot be ascertained divorced from their context. And part of the contextual scene is the purpose of the provision.

Corbin on Contracts (1960) Vol 3, section 545 explains the role that the ascertainment of the purpose of the contract should play in the process of interpretation:

> In order to determine purposes we are obliged to interpret their words in the document of agreement and their relevant words and acts extrinsic to that document. It may seem foolish, therefore, to say that the words of a contract should be interpreted in the light of the purposes that the parties meant to achieve, when we can turn on that light only by process of interpretation. Nevertheless, it is believed that such an admonition serves a useful purpose. As the evidence comes in and as interpretation is in process, the court may soon form a tentative conviction as to the principal purpose or purposes of the parties. As long as that conviction holds … further interpretation of the words of contract should be such as to attain that purpose, if reasonably possible.

In the same section of this seminal work the author added that if the court is convinced that it knows the purpose of the contract, however vaguely expressed and poorly analysed, it should be loath to adopt any interpretation of the language that would produce a different result. In the judgement of the present authors, these observations accurately state the approach to be adopted.

3.04   When construing a contract the court must do so objectively having regard to the material background circumstances of which both parties can be presumed to have been aware.[3]

---

[2] [1996] LRLR 135, 140.

[3] See Lord Wilberforce in *Prenn v Simmonds* [1971] 1 WLR 1381, 1383–1385, and *The Diana Prosperity* [1976] 2 Lloyd's Rep 620, 624–626, cited with approval by Phillips J at first instance in *Youell v Bland Welch* [1990] 2 Lloyd's Rep 423.

In *Investors Compensation Scheme Ltd v West Bromwich Building Society*[4] Lord   **3.05**
Hoffmann set out in some detail the principles by which commercial contracts
should be construed. He set out:

(1) Interpretation is the ascertainment of the meaning which the document
    would convey to a reasonable person having all the background knowledge
    which would reasonably have been available to the parties in the situation in
    which they were at the time of the contract.
(2) The background has been referred to as the 'matrix of fact'. However, this is an
    understated description of what the background may include. Subject to the
    requirement that it should have been reasonably available to the parties, and
    subject to the exception that the law excludes from the admissible background
    the previous negotiations of the parties and their declarations of subjective
    intent (which are only admissible in an action for rectification), it includes
    absolutely everything which would have affected the way in which the lan-
    guage of the document would have been understood by a reasonable man.[5]
(3) The meaning which a document would convey to a reasonable man is not
    the same thing as the meaning of its words. The meaning of words is a mat-
    ter of dictionaries and grammars; the meaning of the document is what the
    parties using those words against the relevant background would reasonably
    have been understood to mean. The background may not merely enable the
    reasonable man to choose between the possible meanings of words which are
    ambiguous, but even to conclude that the parties must, for whatever reason,
    have used the wrong words or syntax.
(4) The 'rule' that words should be given their natural and ordinary meaning
    reflects the common sense proposition that we do not easily accept that peo-
    ple have made linguistic mistakes, particularly in formal documents. On the
    other hand, if one would nevertheless conclude from the background that
    something must have gone wrong with the language, the law does not require
    judges to attribute to the parties an intention which they plainly could not
    have had.[6]

The factual matrix of a reinsurance contract will include any special or peculiar   **3.06**
trade meaning arising from the underlying insurance market that would have been

---

[4] [1998] 1 WLR 896.

[5] More accurately, 'anything which a reasonable man would have regarded *as relevant*' per Lord
Hoffmann in *Bank of Credit and Commerce International SA v Ali* [2002] 1 AC 251, para 39—emphasis in original.

[6] In *Charter Reinsurance Co Ltd v Fagan* [1997] AC 313 Lord Hoffmann stated: 'I think that
in some cases the notion of words having a natural meaning is not a very helpful one. Because the
meaning of words is so sensitive to syntax and context, the natural meaning of words in one sentence
may be quite unnatural in another. Thus a statement that words have a particular natural meaning
may mean no more than that in many contexts they will have that meaning. In other contexts their
meaning will be different but no less natural.'

known to or reasonably available to the parties at the relevant time. In *Gard Marine and Energy Ltd v Tunnicliffe*,[7] the US$400 million insurance of an energy company exploring in the Gulf of Mexico was reinsured against storm risks. The sum insured was stated in the reinsurance policy as 'to pay up to Original Package Policy limits/amounts/sums insured excess of USD250 million (100%) any one occurrence of losses to the original placement'. The meaning of '100%' was disputed. In the insurance the meaning was clear and expressly set out: the figures in the insurance assumed that the energy company owned 100% of the oil well and if it did not, the figures were to be proportionately reduced. Andrew Smith J accepted the expert evidence that in the offshore energy insurance market, the notation '100%' had this special meaning and thus must have been intended to mean the same in the reinsurance.

3.07 It has been suggested that in the context of contracts of insurance the courts have been particularly ready to depart from a literal meaning of the words used in order to produce a result that makes 'commercial sense'. This may be in part due to the tendency of underwriters to use language which is far from clear and in part due to a disinclination on the part of the courts to allow underwriters to take advantage of ill-drafted clauses. Certainly, in the context of reinsurance, in *Teal Assurance Co Ltd v WR Berkley Insurance (Europe) Ltd*,[8] the Court of Appeal commented that the fact that the reinsured's suggested construction of the policies of reinsurance did not lead to a sensible commercial result was an argument against that construction. The reinsurers' construction (that the policies are exhausted in an orderly manner depending on the time when liability is established) did produce a commercially sensible outcome and the more sensible commercial construction was preferred.[9] This is the same touchstone of modern contractual construction alluded to by Lord Collins in *Wasa International Insurance Co v Lexington Insurance Co*[10] when he said that the commercial intentions and expectations of the parties to the reinsurance 'should not be frustrated by allowing reinsurers to take uncommercial and technical points'.

3.08 Fundamentally, a reinsurer cannot be held liable unless the loss falls within the cover of the underlying insurance contract and within the cover created by the reinsurance. What falls within the cover of a contract of reinsurance is a question of construction of that contract.[11] Insurers and reinsurers accept the risk of changes

---

[7] [2012] Lloyd's IR 1.

[8] [2012] Lloyd's Rep IR 315.

[9] Applying *Rainy Sky SA v Kookmin* [2011] 1 WLR 2900, paras 21–30 which was also applied to the construction of employers' liability insurance policies in *Durham v BAI (Run Off) Ltd* [2012] 1 WLR 867. The Court of Appeal's decision in *Teal* is the subject of an outstanding appeal to the Supreme Court.

[10] [2010] 1 AC 180, [2009] 2 Lloyd's Rep 508, para 56.

[11] Lord Collins in *Wasa International Insurance Co v Lexington Insurance Co* [2010] 1 AC 180, [2009] 2 Lloyd's Rep 508 citing *Hill v Mercantile and General Reinsurance Co plc* [1996] 1 WLR 1239.

in the law and cannot complain that the scope of the insured's liability has been increased by judicial decisions.[12]

A purposive or teleological approach is indeed particularly evident in the courts' approach to the construction of reinsurance contracts.[13] This may in large part be due to the fact that reinsurance contracts are often drafted so briefly that their terms are neither clear nor complete, a matter which has led the courts to criticize their drafting on numerous occasions.[14] As stated more recently by Rix LJ: 'insurance and reinsurance provisions are so often dealt with in such brief language, that their construction divorced from a firm understanding of their context can be a dangerous process'.[15] However, seeking to identify the objective intention of the parties can of course be difficult, and there is a need for caution in doing so in the reinsurance context because there may be several parties to the reinsurance slip who become bound by its terms on separate occasions and following separate negotiations; the best evidence of what a reinsurer intended to write may well therefore be what he did write.[16]   **3.09**

In *Charter Reinsurance Co Ltd v Fagan* the House of Lords had to determine (in circumstances where the reinsured had become insolvent) whether the words 'actually paid' in an ultimate net loss clause in an excess of loss reinsurance contract should be construed to impose a requirement that it was a condition precedent that the reinsured had actually paid out money or whether they meant simply that the reinsured had to have established a liability to pay. Prima facie the ordinary and natural meaning of the words suggested prepayment, rather than a liability to pay. However, when set against the landscape of the contract as a whole and its purpose, that was rejected by the House of Lords. Lord Hoffmann pointed out that the London excess of loss reinsurance market operated on the assumption that a   **3.10**

---

[12] *Wasa International Insurance Co v Lexington Insurance Co* [2010] 1 AC 180, [2009] 2 Lloyd's Rep 508.

[13] The parties may also expressly provide that a reinsurance contract should be construed in a way which gives effect to the business realities rather than to the literal meaning of the words used where these conflict, often referred to as an 'honourable engagement' clause. See, for an example, *American Centennial Insurance Co v INSCO Ltd* [1996] LRLR 407. It is noteworthy that in that case, Moore-Bick J stated that even in the absence of such a clause he would need little persuading to adopt that course, stating that it reflected the modern approach to the construction of commercial documents of all kinds.

[14] In *Forsikringsaktieselskapet Vesta v JNE Butcher* [1989] AC 852 Lord Templeman refused to follow a trail of 'insurance jargon in a reinsurance policy and incorporated documents littered with language which is ungrammatical and contradictory'; Lord Griffiths described the policy as 'obscure'. In *Axa Reinsurance (UK) plc v Field* [1996] 1 WLR 1026 Lord Mustill suggested that until disasters emerged in relation to asbestos and pollution damage in the 1980s and 1990s, litigation under reinsurance contracts had been very rare and in the absence of rigorous exposure to scrutiny in the courts, the wording of reinsurance contracts had been allowed to be 'more lax than was healthy'.

[15] Per Rix LJ in *HIH Casualty & General Insurance Ltd v New Hampshire Insurance Co* [2001] Lloyd's Rep IR 596, 606.

[16] See *GE Reinsurance Corp v New Hampshire Insurance Co* [2004] Lloyd's Rep IR 404, para 42.

reinsurance programme would relieve the reinsured of the burden of having to pay claims covered by the reinsured layers and further that the regulation of insurers in this country used a test of solvency which treated reinsurance cover as a proper deduction from the reinsured's liabilities. None of this, he said, would make sense if the reinsured had first to satisfy the claim out of his own resources before he could call upon his reinsurers to pay. Considerations of history, language, and commercial background led him to conclude that the word 'actually' in the ultimate net loss clause was used to emphasize that the loss for which the reinsurer was to be liable was to be net, and that the clause did not restrict liability to the amount by which the liability of the reinsured for the loss had 'actually' been discharged.[17]

3.11 Plainly the words, language, and context are important, but even the headings used in the reinsurance contract can be significant. In *Aegis Electrical and Gas International Services Ltd v Continental Casualty Co*[18] the reinsurance was written subject to some additional conditions which were headed 'Boiler & Machinery Coverage Defined'. On a literal interpretation, they only tinkered with the effect of the follow the terms provision in the reinsurance cover and did not define anything important. The judge used the heading to assist in the exercise of construing the policy, finding that these conditions modified the extent of the reinsurance cover so that the losses were excluded from its scope. He also noted that the admissible factual matrix drove him to the same conclusion, taking into account the fact that the parties were aware that the underwriter had not seen the wording of the direct cover and so concluding that the additional conditions could not have been intended to apply to that, but to the scope of the reinsurance.

(2) Presumption of Co-Extensive Cover

3.12 The purposive approach to construction is evident in what has been described as the 'presumption of co-extensive cover'. The courts have held that as a matter of general principle a policy of *proportional* reinsurance should be construed so that the cover provided under the reinsurance is co-extensive with the cover contained in the primary policies issued by the reinsured; such contracts of reinsurance should, in cases of doubt, accordingly be construed so as to provide back-to-back cover.[19]

---

[17] In *Markel Capital Ltd v Gothaer Allgemeine Versicherung* [2009] Lloyd's Rep IR 433 the Court considered the definition of 'Reinsured' in the slip of a reinsurance of a Directors' and Officers' cover. The defendant's agent was listed as the reinsured, but the Court noted that it was not unnatural for a slip contract to specify that the reinsureds were entering into it through an agent. The Court took into account all the uses of the word 'reinsured' in the slip contract, including the fact that the agreement was to reinsure the 'reinsured's' interest, and the interest was to indemnify 'the Reinsured'. It was the reinsureds and not their agents who were to be indemnified.

[18] [2008] Lloyd's Rep IR 17.

[19] Exceptional cases will, of course, occur. See, eg, *HIH Casualty & General Insurance Ltd v New Hampshire Insurance Co* [2001] Lloyd's Rep IR 96; *Youell v Bland Welch & Co Ltd* [1992] 2 Lloyd's Rep 127; *GE Reinsurance Corp v New Hampshire Insurance Co* [2004] Lloyd's Rep IR 404.

This (rebuttable)[20] presumption has led the courts to lean towards a construction that ensures that a reinsured is not left exposed.

The rationale for this approach is that the reinsurer takes a proportional share of **3.13** the premium and should bear the risk of the same share of any losses. Hence, the presumption is a strong one[21] and the starting point is that the reinsurer and the original insurer enter into a bargain that if the insurer is liable under the insurance contract, the reinsurer will be liable to pay the proportion which it has agreed to reinsure. It is not necessary to characterize the reinsurance policy as liability insurance to achieve this result. It is essentially a question of commercial intentions and expectations. In the usual case, any loss within the coverage of the insurance will be within the coverage of the reinsurance. This will be so whether or not (as is often the case) the reinsurance is put in place before the insurance is put in place or written.

In *Citadel Insurance Co v Atlantic Union Insurance Co SA*, Kerr LJ stated:[22]   **3.14**

> The conditions of the cover were described 'as original' with certain qualifications. This is usual and means no more than that the terms of the reinsurance cover are to be the same as those of the original, ie, reinsured policies.

In *Foskringsaktieselskepat Vesta v Butcher*,[23] Lord Griffiths spoke in even broader   **3.15** terms of reinsurance being 'back to back' with insurance. He said:

> In the ordinary course of business reinsurance is referred to as 'back to back' with the insurance, which means that the reinsurer agrees that if the insurer is liable under the policy the reinsurer will accept liability to pay whatever percentage of the claim he has agreed to reinsure. A reinsurer could, of course, make a special contract with an insurer and agree only to reinsure some of the risks covered by the policy of insurance, leaving the insurer to bear the full cost of the other risks. Such a contract would I believe be wholly exceptional, a departure from the normal understanding of the back to back nature of reinsurance and would need to be spelt out in clear terms. I doubt if there is any market for such a reinsurance.

Vesta v Butcher is an illustration of the general approach to construction which   **3.16** enables a court to resolve ambiguity of wording in a way which it is satisfied that the parties objectively intended. Both insurance and reinsurance contracts contained the same wording, and critically a warranty that a 24-hour watch would be kept over the site insured. A 24-hour watch was not kept, but such a watch would not

---

[20] See, eg, *Youell v Bland Welch* [1992] 2 Lloyd's Rep 127; *Groupama Navigation et Transports v Catatumbo CA Seguros* [2000] 1 Lloyd's Rep 266. See also *Gan Insurance Co Ltd v Tai Ping Insurance Co Ltd* [1999] Lloyd's Rep IR 472 where the Court of Appeal held that where by its express terms the risk presented to reinsurers was materially different from that assumed by the reinsured, it could not reasonably be presumed that the reinsurers intended to afford back-to-back cover.

[21] *Wasa International Insurance Co v Lexington Insurance Co* [2010] 1 AC 180, [2009] 2 Lloyd's Rep 508 per Lord Collins.

[22] [1982] 2 Lloyd's Rep 543, 546.

[23] [1989] AC 852, 895B/C.

have prevented the loss. Under Norwegian law (the law of the original insurance) a breach of warranty could not be relied upon by the direct insurers to avoid liability unless there was a causal link between the breach and the damage. The reinsurers asserted that under English law (the law of the reinsurance contract) the breach of warranty by the insured entitled them to avoid payment. The House of Lords approached their determination on the basis that the cover in the reinsurance was intended to be back-to-back with the underlying insurance and accordingly held that in the absence of any express declaration to the contrary in the reinsurance policy, a warranty must produce the same effect in each policy. The House of Lords accordingly held that the reinsurers could not avoid liability.[24]

3.17   In *Groupama Navigation et Transports v Catatumbo CA Seguros*[25] a similar question arose in circumstances where warranties were stated in the reinsurance itself and had not simply been incorporated into it, and where they were in similar but not identical terms to the warranties in the underlying insurance. As in *Vesta v Butcher* the reinsurers argued that under English law a breach of warranty enabled them to avoid payment even though such a breach was not causative of any loss (contrary to the position under Venezuelan law which governed the underlying policy). The Court of Appeal rejected the reinsurers' approach and held that the warranties should have the same effect in both contracts (ie that the reinsurance warranty should respond to and reflect the interpretation put on the equivalent warranty by Venezuelan law in the original insurance). Although this made the warranties repetitive, this was viewed as being unsurprising in the light of the way wordings were put together in the London market.[26] Tuckey LJ stated:

> I did not understand [counsel] to quarrel with the presumption that in a proportionate reinsurance of the kind with which this case is concerned, there is a presumption that, in the absence of clear words to the contrary, the scope and nature of the cover afforded is the same as the cover afforded by the insurance. That at least I think is the effect of *Vesta* and it makes obvious commercial sense.

3.18   Mance LJ stated that the reinsurers' approach ignored the structure and realities of reinsurance contracts; the basic reality and expectation was that the proportional reinsurance would operate back-to-back with the original insurance. Accordingly the most obvious purpose of including specific warranties in the reinsurance was not to produce a situation where the two contracts were not back-to-back, but rather to specify terms which reinsurers would expect to be included in the original

---

[24] Note that Lord Griffiths said that there may be circumstances in which it would be inappropriate to treat the terms of a contract of insurance as setting out the terms of the contract of reinsurance and indeed on the true construction of the slip he would have so held. His opinion was obiter because at the trial Hobhouse J had refused leave to amend to allow the point to be argued, albeit expressing a different view to Lord Griffiths [1989] 1 AC 852, 894.

[25] [2000] 2 Lloyd's Rep 350; also reported at [2001] Lloyd's Rep IR 141.

[26] Tuckey LJ stated: 'This has been the subject of much uncomplimentary judicial comment in the past which I need not repeat'.

insurance (by amendment if necessary), thus producing what Mance LJ described as a harmonious result, and one that was commercially and legally attractive. He also noted, however, that had the two contracts contained warranties expressed in different and irreconcilable terms, or if the reinsurance had contained a warranty which had in terms no counterpart in the insurance, different considerations would have arisen. It would then be clear that the two contracts were not and could not to that extent be back-to-back. There would be no possibility of reconciling them, or of deriving the meaning or scope of the reinsurance warranty from any equivalent warranty in the original insurance; the reinsurance warranty would in that situation be viewed purely through the eyes of English law.[27]

In both *Vesta* and *Catatumbo* it was possible to identify the foreign law which would govern the insurance. The parties entering into the English law reinsurance could be taken to have had access to what Lord Lowry in the *Vesta* case described as a foreign 'legal dictionary' to interpret the language of the reinsurance. The insurance and reinsurance had like effect because of the circumstances and terms in which they were entered into and not because there is some principle of law that reinsurance is bound to respond to whatever liability the insurers might subsequently be held to incur. This is simply an aspect of the basic principle of contract law that a contract has a meaning which is to be ascertained at the time when it is concluded, having regard to its background and the surrounding circumstances within the parties' knowledge at that time: *Investors Compensation Scheme Ltd v West Bromwich Building Society*.[28] In *Wasa International Insurance Co v Lexington Insurance Co*[29] it was significant that it was not possible to ascertain the legal position under the original insurance contract at the time when the reinsurance was placed. This meant that the circumstances at placement did not suggest back-to-back cover as in the *Vesta* and *Catatumbo* cases.

3.19

Lord Brown of Eaton-Under-Heywood put it this way:[30]

3.20

> The respective contracts are not, of course, back to back as to their governing laws. However powerful and far-reaching the presumption that reinsurance is intended to respond to claims payable under the primary policy, it could not avail Lexington here unless English law were to regard it in effect as tantamount to a rule of law—unless, in short, English law were to dictate that reinsurance must always respond. English law does not, in my opinion, go so far. *Vesta* and *Catatumbo*, clearly the decisions closest in point, are authority for the presumption. They do not warrant

---

[27] And in particular s 33(3) of the Marine Insurance Act which expresses the approach to warranties in English law: 'A warranty...is a condition which must be exactly complied with, whether it be material to the risk or not. If it be not so complied with, then, subject to any express provision in the policy, the insurer is discharged from liability as from the date of the breach of warranty, but without prejudiee to any liability incurred by him before that date.'

[28] [1998] 1 WLR 896.

[29] [2010] 1 AC 180, [2009] 2 Lloyd's Rep 508.

[30] *Wasa International Insurance Co v Lexington Insurance Co* [2010] 1 AC 180, [2009] 2 Lloyd's Rep 508, para 16.

its application in all circumstances, certainly not so as to override so clear a temporal limitation as the reinsurance contracts stipulated here with regard to the risks covered.

3.21 Even a reinsurance which looks to be back-to-back will not follow the underlying insurance if the terms of the reinsurance are clearly different. For example a reinsurance slip will normally include a period of cover and the basic principle is that the reinsurer is liable for a loss actually sustained from a period insured against during the continuance of the risk.[31] Hobhouse LJ summarized the legal principle in *Municipal Mutual Insurance Ltd v Sea Insurance Co Ltd*:[32]

> The judge came to the surprising conclusion that each reinsurance contract covered liability in respect of physical loss or damage whether or not it occurred during the period covered by the reinsurance contract and he went on expressly to contemplate that the same liability for the same physical loss or damage might be covered under a number of separate contracts of reinsurance covering different periods. This is a startling result and I am aware of no justification for it. When the relevant cover is placed on a time basis, the stated period of time is fundamental and must be given effect to. It is for that period of risk that the premium payable is assessed. This is so whether the cover is defined as in the present case by reference to when the physical loss or damage occurred, or by reference to when a liability was incurred or a claim made. Contracts of insurance (including reinsurance) are or can be sophisticated instruments containing a wide variety of provisions, but the definition of the period of cover is basic and clear.

3.22 In *Wasa International Insurance Co v Lexington Insurance Co*[33] the House of Lords (in one of its final decisions before becoming the Supreme Court) considered whether facultative reinsurance should be construed as being back-to-back with the underlying insurance. The reinsurance covered property damage occurring during currency of the reinsurance and was written 'as original' with a follow the settlements clause. The reinsured had provided property cover for a three-year period, but was held by a US court to be liable for property damage dating back 50 years before inception of cover. The question was whether the reinsurers were bound by the settlement reached by the reinsured.

3.23 The underlying insured had incurred pollution losses as a result of being required to fund the clear up of various contaminated sites in the US occupied by it for over 40 years. The reinsured had reached a businesslike $100 million settlement of the US proceedings under its three-year insurance incepting in 1977 in respect of 'all physical loss of, or damage to, the insured property...'. The Supreme Court of the State of Washington had held that the insuring clause was very broad and was not limited by the time of the physical damage, adopting a principle of construction of

---

[31] *Knight v Faith* (1850) 15 QB 649, 667 per Lord Campbell CJ.
[32] [1998] Lloyd's Rep IR 421, 435–436 cited with approval by Lord Mance in *Wasa International Insurance Co v Lexington Insurance Co* [2010] 1 AC 180, [2009] 2 Lloyd's Rep 508.
[33] [2010] 1 AC 180, [2009] 2 Lloyd's Rep 508.

property insurance policies particular to courts of Pennsylvania and a minority of other American states (with its origin in asbestos insurance claims). Any physical damage manifesting itself in 1977 was covered by the policy, including pollution damage starting before the policy inception. The limit of liability was $20 million 'any one loss(es), disasters(s), or casualty(ies) arising out of one event or common cause'. The reinsurance, being on an English form and broked and issued in the London market, was accepted to be governed by English law. The reinsurance expressed the interest to be 'All property of every kind and Description and/or Business Interruption and OPP &/or as original', $20 million each occurrence.

The references in the slip to '&/or as original' under the headings 'Form' and **3.24** 'Interest' were held to incorporate the relevant insurance provisions relating to the subject matter and risks into the reinsurance. The main dispute was whether the cover under this proportional facultative reinsurance contract was co-extensive with the cover under the insurance contract.

The reason why the reinsurance was not back-to-back with the insurance was **3.25** explained in ten steps by Lord Collins:[34]

a. In order to establish liability against a reinsurer, the reinsured has to establish that the loss is within the risk assumed under the underlying insurance contract; and that the relevant risk has been assumed under the reinsurance contract.
b. Whether the relevant risk has been assumed under the reinsurance contract is a question of construction of that contract.
c. In principle the relevant terms in a proportional facultative reinsurance—and in particular those relating to the risk—should be construed so as to be consistent with the terms of the insurance contract on the basis that the normal commercial intention is that they should be back-to-back.
d. Where the insurance contract and the reinsurance contract are governed by different laws, it remains a question of construction of each contract under its applicable law as to what risk is assumed, and there is no special rule of the conflict of laws which governs the consequences of any inconsistency.
e. Both the insurance contract and the reinsurance contract were 'losses occurring during' (or 'LOD') policies (or 'occurrence policies' as they are known in the United States), which in English law means that a reinsurer is liable to indemnify the reinsured in respect of loss or damage which occurs during the policy period.
f. When the insurance contract and the reinsurance contract were concluded, there was no identifiable system of law applicable to the insurance contract which could have provided a basis for construing the contract of reinsurance in a manner different from its ordinary meaning in the London insurance market.

---

[34] [2010] 1 AC 180, [2009] 2 Lloyd's Rep 508, para 58.

g. The effect of the decision of the Supreme Court of Washington is to impose liability on the insurer under the contract of insurance for loss and damage which occurred both before and after (as well as during) the policy period in the reinsurance contract.

h. Under English law an insurer or reinsurer would not be liable for losses occurring before and after the policy period.

i. Although normally any loss within the coverage of the insurance will be within the coverage of the reinsurance, there is no rule of construction, and no rule of law, that a reinsurer must respond to every valid claim under the insurance irrespective of the terms of the reinsurance.

j. The reinsurance contract cannot reasonably be construed to mean that it would respond to any liability which 'any court of competent jurisdiction within the United States' (the phrase in the service of suit clause) would impose on the insurer irrespective of the period of cover in the reinsurance contract.

3.26 The way in which reinsureds can avoid such a mismatch is for the reinsurance to specify that for the purposes of any claim for indemnity under the reinsurance, it should be construed in the same manner as the insurance would be construed under whatever law is applicable to the insurance for the purposes of the claim against the reinsured for which indemnity is sought.

3.27 Even where the insurance and reinsurance are back-to-back, it must be borne in mind that this is only for the purpose of ensuring a corresponding scope of cover. In *Home Insurance Co of New York v Victoria-Montreal Fire Insurance Co*[35] the Privy Council were faced with a case in which reinsurers denied liability to meet a reinsurance claim on the ground that a condition in the original policy had been incorporated into the reinsurance policy and resulted in the reinsurance claim being time-barred. The reinsurance contract had been created by amending the original policy by insertion of the word 're' before the word 'insure'. Reinsurers argued that all the terms of the original policy were thus terms of the reinsurance contract and that they were entitled to repudiate because of a breach of a time clause in the original policy which provided that no claim could be brought unless commenced within 12 months of the relevant event. The insurance claim had taken time to investigate and settle and therefore the claim was not made against reinsurers until more than 12 months had elapsed. The Privy Council rejected the reinsurers' defence and declined to regard the time bar as incorporated into the reinsurance. Lord McNagthen, giving the opinion of the Privy Council, stated:

> It is difficult to suppose that the contract of re-insurance was engrafted on an ordinary printed form of policy for any purpose beyond the purpose of indicating the origin of the direct liability on which the indirect liability, the subject of re-insurance, would depend, and setting forth the conditions attached to it.

---

[35] [1907] AC 59.

…according to the true construction of this instrument, so awkwardly patched and so carelessly put together, the condition in question is not to be regarded as applying to the contract of re-insurance. *To hold otherwise would…be to adhere to the letter without paying due attention to the spirit and intention of the contract* [emphasis added].

The presumption of back-to-back cover where the reinsurance is proportionate can- **3.28** not be extended to all reinsurance. In particular it is not apt to apply the presumption to excess of loss (ie non-proportional) reinsurance contracts where the insurance and reinsurance may or may not in any real sense be back-to-back. If a party to an excess of loss reinsurance contract wants to ensure that the provisions in the underlying policy and the reinsurance policy are construed in the same way, he should make sure that the clauses are the same. Thus in *Axa Reinsurance (UK) plc v Field*[36] the House of Lords rejected the contention that there was an assumption that where a direct insurer had taken out excess of loss reinsurance, and where both policies contained provisions enabling the amount of losses to be aggregated, the parties were likely to have intended their effect to be much the same.[37] Similarly, the House of Lords rejected an argument that (save perhaps where the direct and reinsurance policies were intended to be back-to-back) limiting terms in reinsurance contracts should not readily be found to operate more stringently than those in the underlying policy.[38]

In *Municipal Mutual Insurance Ltd v Sea Insurance Co Ltd*[39] there was a mismatch **3.29** between the reinsured's inward and outward contracts not so much in their wording as in the way in which they chose to place and operate them. The reinsured chose to enter into distinct and independent *annual* excess of loss reinsurance contracts with different reinsurers who took different proportions of the risk from year to year. However, the underlying policy contemplated annual renewal and because there was no annual limit it did not matter as between the underlying insured and the reinsured when a liability was incurred provided that it preceded the lapsing of the policy; in practice this rendered the distinction between one year and another irrelevant. Damage occurred to machinery that was the subject of the insurance and reinsurance over a period of 18 months (straddling different reinsurance contracts) as a result of a succession of individual acts of pilferage and vandalism. Reinsurers argued that there was therefore a succession of losses each subject to a separate excess. The Court of Appeal[40] held that it was wrong in principle to apply

---

[36] [1996] 1 WLR 1026. The House of Lords reversed the decisions of Phillips J at first instance and the Court of Appeal [1996] 1 Lloyd's Rep 436 to the contrary effect.

[37] Lord Mustill stated that if the syndicate had wished to secure identical measures of loss for its inward and outward contracts it would have negotiated with the reinsurers to that end and taken the obvious course of using the same words in each. However, they chose not to do so, and thereby accepted the possibility that although in some combinations of facts the outcomes might be the same, in others they might not (at 1036).

[38] See *Axa Reinsurance (UK) plc v Field* [1996] 1 WLR 1026, 1034A–1035A.

[39] [1998] Lloyd's Rep IR 421.

[40] Allowing an appeal from the decision of Waller J [1996] 1 Lloyd's Rep 265.

the presumption of back-to-back cover so as to distort or disregard the terms of the reinsurance contracts in order to make them fit in with a different position under the original cover. The words 'conditions as underlying' could not contradict either the period or excess of loss limit provisions of the individual reinsurance contracts. It was incumbent upon the judge to give effect to the annual nature of each reinsurance contract and to ask whether the relevant loss or damage occurred during the relevant period of cover.[41]

(3) Full Reinsurance Clause

3.30 Reinsurance contracts may contain as a condition wording such as 'full reinsurance clause'. That expression when used in a contract of reinsurance introduces into the contract (at least) the following words:

> Being a reinsurance of and warranted same gross rate, terms and conditions as and to follow the settlements of the assured.

In *Toomey v Banco Vitalicio de España*[42] Andrew Smith J held that the clause has the effect of incorporating into the contract of reinsurance, with or without a degree of manipulation, all those terms of the underlying insurance that regulate the scope of the cover. By agreeing to it the insurer agrees that all the relevant and applicable terms of the contract of insurance become terms of the reinsurance, and in return the reinsurer agrees to follow the settlements made by the insured (made properly and in good faith).[43] This construction gives the full reinsurance clause the meaning that it is generally understood to have in the market and accords with the ordinary presumption that facultative reinsurance is intended to be back-to-back with the underlying policy.[44] In taking this approach, Andrew Smith J departed from the view expressed by Lord Griffiths in *Forsikringsaktieselskapet Vesta v JNE Butcher* when considering the words 'being a reinsurance of and warranted same . . . terms and conditions as and to follow the settlements of the company'. Lord Griffiths said:

> For my part, I would be reluctant to read these contractual documents as making the terms of the contract of insurance terms of the contract of reinsurance. Although the wording is archaic and difficult to comprehend I understand the phrase 'warranted same gross rate, terms and conditions' as a warranty given by

---

[41] Hobhouse LJ stated that the US cases that he had been referred to, which adopted a different approach, were of no assistance and arose from the special problems of liability for asbestosis claims arising from long periods of potential exposure and were clearly governed by policy considerations relevant to special factors affecting the insurance market in the United States. In that context the House of Lords' decision in *Fairchild v Glenhaven Funeral Services Ltd (t/a GH Dovener & Son)* [2003] 1 AC 32 is of some note.

[42] [2004] Lloyd's Rep IR 354. On appeal Thomas LJ said that 'this difficult issue' did not arise and so he indicated that he expressed no view and the issue remained open for decision (*Toomey v Banco Vitalicio De Espana Sa De Seguros Y Reasseguros* [2005] Lloyd's Rep IR 423).

[43] Per Andrew Smith J, in *Toomey v Banco Vitalicio de España* at paras 86–87.

[44] See *Toomey v Banco Vitalicio de España*. Andrew Smith J did not follow the dicta of Lord Griffiths in *Forsikringsaktieselskapet Vesta v JNE Butcher* [1989] AC 852, 896C/D.

the company, ie the insurer, that he has placed the risk on the same terms that he has disclosed to the reinsurers. This view is I think strongly supported by the fact that the policy is attached to the slip against the heading 'Infn' which is clearly an abbreviation of the word 'Information' and shows that at the time that the slip is completed the policy terms are available to the reinsurer to show the nature of the risk that he is accepting. The warranty in the insurance is that the policy has been or will be written in those terms.

Andrew Smith J set out that the other members of the House of Lords did not agree with that part of Lord Griffiths' speech, and although it was cited uncritically by Beldam LJ in *Gan Insurance Co Ltd v Tai Ping Co Ltd*[45] that should not be read as indicating acceptance of what Lord Griffiths had said about the reinsured giving a warranty. He considered that: (a) his approach was consistent with the ordinary presumption that facultative reinsurance is intended to be back-to-back with the underlying policy; (b) it was difficult to read the words of the full reinsurance clause as expressing the meaning that Lord Griffiths suggested and that on any view the clause did not refer to the terms of the original insurance being disclosed to the reinsurers; and (c) although a full reinsurance clause might sometimes import the warranty suggested by Lord Griffiths it would not invariably do so (and it was not clear that Lord Griffiths intended his observations to apply to any case other than that before him—where not only were the terms of the original insurance disclosed to the reinsurers, but it was stated on the slip that they were—a matter to which Lord Griffiths had attached importance).[46] A warranty in the reinsurance contract that terms would be the same as those of the underlying insurance policy will not assist an argument that the parties intended to incorporate ancillary provisions as well as terms that are germane to the subject matter of the insurance.[47]

(4) Slip as an Aid to Construction of Policy

In the absence of a policy which has been agreed either expressly or by implication or inference, a Market Reform Contract (MRC) or a slip signed or initialled by the reinsurers will be the document which records the contractual terms. The requirement for there to be an MRC rather than a slip was introduced into the London market in November 2007. An MRC resembles a slip but the most important difference is that in addition to setting out the most important details of the risk as a slip would, an MRC must also specify the terms of the policy, either by setting them out or by expressly referring to standard market clauses or form of policy. The purpose of the requirement for an MRC is to ensure contract certainty as at the time of placement and to avoid the problems that arose in relation to slips. However, there may still in the future be disputes in relation to risks that were placed using

3.31

---

[45] [1999] Lloyd's Rep IR 472, 479.
[46] At paras 78–91.
[47] Per Andrew Smith J in *Prifti v Musini Sociedad Anonima de Seguros y Reaseguros* [2004] Lloyd's Rep IR 528, para 17.

slips prior to the introduction of the MRC or which are placed in other markets but subject to English law. Therefore some of the issues that can arise in relation to slips are referred to below.

3.32　In a number of cases the courts had held that where a reinsurance slip was followed by a formal policy, the slip was inadmissible as an aid to construction of the policy because of the application of the parol evidence rule.[48]

3.33　That orthodoxy was, however, undermined in *HIH Casualty & General Insurance Ltd v New Hampshire Insurance Co.*[49] In that case, Rix LJ stated that in principle it is always admissible to look at a prior contract as part of the matrix or surrounding circumstances of a later contract, and that the parol evidence rule cannot exclude prior contracts (as distinct from mere negotiations)—although in practical terms the earlier contract would, in most cases, be of no assistance as an aid to construing the latter. Where it is not common ground that the later contract is intended to supersede the earlier one then prima facie it would not be permissible to exclude reference to the earlier contract. Rix LJ identified three possibilities:

(1)　the later contract is intended to supersede the earlier, in which case it is unlikely that the earlier contract will be of any assistance;

(2)　the later contract is intended to live together with the earlier contract, to the extent that that is possible, but where it is not possible it may well be proper to regard the later contract as superseding the earlier; or

(3)　the later contract is intended to be incorporated into the earlier contract, in which case it is prima facie the second contract which may have to give way to the first in the event of inconsistency.

In the reinsurance context, where a slip is followed by a policy there will usually be an intention to supersede the slip by the policy.[50] Furthermore, the fact that slips customarily set out the contract in shorthand in a way that is neither clear nor complete will in general promote and underline the inutility of seeking to find in the slip an aid to the construction of the policy.[51]

---

[48] In *Youell v Bland Welch & Co Ltd* [1990] 2 Lloyd's Rep 423 Phillips J held that the slip was rendered *inadmissible* by the parol evidence rule. He stated that the strict application of that rule had a particular justification in the context of reinsurance because a slip customarily set out a shorthand version of the contract of insurance in terms which may be neither clear nor complete and the slip had expressly provided for the formal wording to be agreed in due course. In the Court of Appeal Beldam LJ held that the slip was inadmissible, but Staughton LJ held that the slip was of no assistance, whether or not it was actually admissible. In *Punjab National Bank v de Boinville* [1992] 1 Lloyd's Rep 7 Hobhouse J followed the approach taken by Phillips J in *Youell v Bland Welch*. See also *St Paul Fire & Marine Insurance Co (UK) Ltd v McDonnell Dowell Constructors Ltd* [1993] 2 Lloyd's Rep 503.

[49] [2001] Lloyd's Rep IR 596.

[50] Rix LJ stated that in the insurance market it may well be possible to talk of a general presumption that a policy is intended to supersede a slip.

[51] See *HIH Casualty & General Insurance Ltd v New Hampshire Insurance Co* [2001] Lloyd's Rep IR 596, paras 84–85.

A slip will often have been the culmination of negotiations between the parties and sometimes there will have been a sequence of agreements culminating in the final form of the slip. The slip may also contain text which has been deleted. This situation arose in the insurance case of *Mopani Copper Mines plc v Millenium Underwriting Ltd.*[52] In that case, the parties negotiated insurance cover for new copper smelting facilities. They started with a slip limited to 'Construction/Erection All Risks'. They then moved on to discussing the inclusion of operational cover, beyond the limited operational cover provided by the testing and commissioning provision, in respect of elements of the project that became operational before the project as a whole was complete. A second slip was presented headed (against the word 'Type') 'Construction/Erection and Operational All Risks' which contained a condition including provision for operational cover for completed phases up until the final handover certificate. That slip was scratched by the insurer but the words in the condition providing for operational cover were struck through in pencil and the underwriter wrote 'TBA MLM' against the condition to signify that those words had not yet been agreed. The final contract was contained in (1) an amended version of the second slip, in which the words struck through in pencil were struck through in ink but the heading to the slip remained as it was; and (2) an email exchange relating to one of the elements of the project (the Oxygen Plant) which recorded that it would not be operational after testing and commissioning. This was subsequently corrected and varied by an endorsement which gave specific but limited operational cover in relation to the Oxygen Plant and associated plant.

3.34

On the question whether the second slip gave more general operational cover, as its title suggested, Christopher Clarke J held that, whilst mere negotiations were inadmissible, it was permissible to look at the sequence of agreements because they shed light on the final agreement. He took into account the fact that the first slip did not extend to operational cover and that the pencilling out of the relevant words in the second slip and the annotation next to them indicated that operational cover had not yet been agreed. He also took into account the inking out of those words in the final form of the second slip as underscoring the fact that the parties were not agreeing additional operational cover on all items until final handover. In that context, the word 'Operational' against the word 'Type' in the second slip did not carry with it an intention to provide general operational cover as that reference had only been introduced as part of a 'yet to be agreed' means of providing additional operational cover. In *Markel Capital Ltd v Gothaer Allgemeine Versicherung*[53] the Court considered the definition of 'Reinsured' in the slip of a reinsurance of a Directors' and Officers' cover. The defendant's agent was listed as the reinsured, but the Court noted that it was not unnatural for a slip contract to

3.35

---

[52] [2009] Lloyd's Rep IR 158. On the admissibility of deleted text, see also *Punjab National Bank v de Boinville* [1992] 3 All ER 104.
[53] [2009] Lloyd's Rep IR 433.

specify that the reinsureds were entering into it through an agent. The Court took into account all the uses of the word 'reinsured' in the slip contract, including the fact that the agreement was to reinsure the 'reinsured's' interest, and the interest was to indemnify 'the Reinsured'. It was the reinsureds and not their agents who were to be indemnified.

B. Incorporation

3.36 Reinsurance contracts are rarely voluminous documents. As set out in Chapter 2,[54] although on occasion a policy will set out express terms in some detail, more often it specifies little more than that the terms and conditions of the reinsurance are to be found in a standard Lloyd's or other form, or simply that the terms and conditions are those of the underlying insurance by use of phrases such as 'terms and conditions as original' or 'as underlying'.[55] Terms may also be incorporated into a reinsurance contract when the slip is scratched by reference to some other document.

3.37 Against such a background it is not surprising that the reinsurance arena has spawned numerous and varied disputes about whether and to what extent terms have been incorporated into the reinsurance contract.

3.38 It is axiomatic that if an underlying document is to be incorporated into the reinsurance contract then it must be properly identified. Absent such an identification it may simply be impossible to conclude that the parties intended to incorporate the document.[56] The same principle applies to the incorporation of any particular term. In *HIH Casualty & General Insurance Ltd v New Hampshire Insurance Co* a reinsurance slip included the following term: 'Cancellation Clause as Original Policy'. The Court of Appeal held that the clause was effectively meaningless because no such clause could be identified in the underlying insurance; it accordingly failed to have any content.

3.39 There can be little doubt that words such as 'all terms, clauses and conditions as original' in a reinsurance slip frequently cannot mean what they say. There are many provisions in an underlying contract which may well be wholly inappropriate for incorporation into any contract of reinsurance. The question of whether terms have actually been incorporated, notwithstanding an apparent statement that they have,

---

[54] See paras 2.27–2.34.
[55] Retrocessions may contain similar wording (eg 'as original'). It has been held that this is a reference to the original insurance rather than the original reinsurance (see *Pine Top Insurance Co Ltd v Unione Italiana Anglo Saxon Reinsurance Co Ltd* [1987] 1 Lloyd's Rep 477).
[56] This was the position in *Cigna Life Insurance Co of Europe SA-NV v Intercaser SA de Seguros y Reaseguros* [2001] Lloyd's Rep IR 821.

and what meaning and effect they have if incorporated, is essentially therefore a question of construction.[57]

In *HIH Casualty & General Insurance Ltd v New Hampshire Insurance Co*[58] David   **3.40** Steel J set out that incorporation of a specific term can only be achieved if:

(1) the term makes sense, subject to permissible manipulation, in the context of the reinsurance;
(2) the term is apposite for inclusion in the reinsurance;
(3) the term is germane to the reinsurance, rather than being merely collateral to it;
(4) the term is consistent with the express terms of the reinsurance.

It may transpire, therefore, that even where there is a specific reference to a term or   **3.41** condition it will be incapable, on a proper construction, of being incorporated.

(1) Does the Clause Make Sense Without Undue Manipulation?

The first rule of incorporation is to test the allegedly incorporated term in the con-   **3.42** text of the incorporating document by writing it out verbatim in the latter.[59] In that context the question may immediately arise as to whether it should be manipulated. The Court of Appeal in *HIH* suggested that there was nothing unusual about such manipulation, provided that it could be done simply and deftly as a matter of language, where everything pointed to the incorporation of the term in question. Such manipulation was approved in *CNA International Reinsurance Co Ltd v Tranquilidade SA*,[60] where Clarke J held that terms of the insurance contract should be treated as terms of the reinsurance, but that each term should then be considered in order to see whether it was applicable in the context of the reinsurance, with manipulation if necessary (for example, references to 'the underwriters' being manipulated to read 'reinsurers' and 'assured' to read 'reassured'). He did so in order to maintain what he regarded as essentially a fronting arrangement in good back-to-back order. In *HIH* Rix LJ stated that where a clause was specifically incorporated there was pressure to see that it worked if at all possible and if necessary by appropriate manipulation.[61]

---

[57] Per Clarke J in *CNA International Reinsurance Co Ltd v Companhia de Seguros Tranquilidade SA* [1999] Lloyd's Rep IR 289, 299.

[58] [2001] Lloyd's Rep IR 224.

[59] Per Rix LJ *in HIH Casualty & General Insurance Ltd v New Hampshire Insurance Co* [2001] Lloyd's Rep IR 596, see also para 3.40.

[60] [1999] Lloyd's Rep IR 288.

[61] Per Rix LJ in *HIH Casualty & General Insurance Ltd v New Hampshire Insurance Co* [2001] Lloyd's Rep IR 596, para 148. In that case he held that a waiver of defences clause could not be incorporated in manipulated form because in such form it did not make sense, could not be successfully manipulated, and was 'contrary to the reason of the thing' at para 172. He stated also that in manipulated form the clause would not be consistent with either the letter or the spirit of the express terms of the reinsurance. He noted that *Miramar Maritime Corp v Holborn Oil Trading Ltd (The Miramar)* [1984] AC 676 was a warning that the need to manipulate in uncertainly apposite circumstances is a pointer against incorporation.

(2) Is the Clause Germane?

3.43 General incorporating clauses only bring with them terms which are germane to the proper subject matter of the incorporating contract. Clauses which are central to the risk or material to the nature and scope of the risk are likely to be viewed as germane. Collateral clauses will not be so viewed.[62] In *HIH Casualty & General Insurance Ltd v New Hampshire Insurance Co* there was a waiver of defences clause in the original insurance policy, whereby the reinsured waived its rights to avoid or rescind the contract or reject any claim or to seek any remedy in relation to any non-disclosure or misrepresentation by the original insured. The reinsurance slip provided that the reinsurance was 'subject to all terms, clauses and conditions as original and to follow the placement in all respects'. A number of the reinsurers argued that the waiver of defences clause was not incorporated by those general words; alternatively that if it was incorporated its effect was not to waive the reinsurers' right to avoid or rescind the contract or reject any claim or to seek any remedy in relation to any non-disclosure or misrepresentation by its own reinsured, but rather to emphasize that the reinsurers could not complain if HIH paid a claim in circumstances where in the absence of the waiver of defences clause no claim would have been payable at all.[63] In relation to their primary argument, the reinsurers asserted that the clause was not germane to the reinsurance because it did not relate directly to the scope of cover and that it should therefore be considered as a collateral provision that should not be incorporated. The Court of Appeal held that the clause was germane to the reinsurance contract and to the scope of the risk accepted by the reinsurer. Rix LJ, with whom the other members of the Court agreed, set out the reasons for taking that approach as follows. The reason why an insurer is entitled to avoid his contract of insurance for material non-disclosure or misrepresentation is that he calculates the risk that he is prepared to run and the premium that he stipulates for running that risk on the basis of the information he is given. Accordingly, clauses affirming that common law position, or altering it, are germane to the risk covered, even though they do not seek to define that risk. The reinsurers themselves appeared to recognize that the clause was a form of 'follow the settlements' clause, and Rix LJ stated that nothing could be more germane to a reinsurance contract than such a clause.[64]

(3) Is the Clause Consistent?

3.44 A strong pointer against incorporation is the fact that the incorporated term contradicts express provisions of the reinsurance policy,[65] whether in spirit or

---

[62] See in particular paras 3.51–3.56 on arbitration clauses, jurisdiction clauses, and choice of law clauses.

[63] See para 3.48 regarding the Court of Appeal's approach to the alternative argument advanced by the reinsurers.

[64] See *HIH Casualty & General Insurance Ltd v New Hampshire Insurance Co* [2001] Lloyd's Rep IR 596.

[65] See *Australian Widows' Fund Life Assurance Society Ltd v National Mutual Life Association of Australasia Ltd* [1914] AC 634; *Home Insurance Co of New York v Victoria-Montreal Fire Insurance Co* [1907] AC 59.

letter.[66] The exclusion of a standard and important common law obligation should not easily be regarded as incorporated by merely general words.[67]

(4) Is the Clause Otherwise Inapposite?

This criterion overlaps considerably with the question as to whether a clause makes **3.45** sense. Nonetheless the criterion affords the courts the ability to have regard to the general purpose and commercial realities of a contract in determining whether a clause should be deemed to be incorporated.

(5) Unusual Clauses

Questions have arisen as to whether unusual clauses should be incorporated **3.46** into the reinsurance contract. In *HIH*[68] the reinsurers asserted that the waiver of defences clause[69] was unusual and that it should not therefore be regarded as incorporated by words of general incorporation. At first instance David Steel J held that as a matter of general principle the test to be applied to this question was whether the term was so unusual or uncommon that it would be unfair in all the circumstances to hold the party to it. He found that although the clause was not standard or customary, it was in no sense unique and in all the circumstances it was fair to regard it as incorporated. In the Court of Appeal the reinsurers, in support of their argument that the judge was wrong to take the approach that he had done, relied on a section in *MacGillivray on Insurance Law* (9th edn, 1997) paras 33–52 headed 'Unusual terms':

> It has been held that a reinsurer is not bound by the incorporation of terms unless they are well known and in common use. The reasoning is that the reinsurer may not be entitled to see, or will not in practice be aware of, the precise terms of the underlying insurance. It is submitted that the fact that a clause is highly unusual may be relevant to the question of whether the parties intended the clause to be incorporated into their contract. A different way of approaching the problem is that, while the actual incorporation of the term does not necessarily depend upon how unusual it is, this factor is relevant to the question of whether the term ought to have been disclosed to the reinsurer.

The reinsurers relied on a number of cases in support of their proposition. In *Marten v Nippon Sea and Land Insurance Co Ltd*,[70] Bigham J had to consider the term 'subject to the same terms and conditions as original policy' and a well-known

---

[66] See *HIH Casualty & General Insurance Ltd v New Hampshire Insurance Co* [2001] Lloyd's Rep IR 596.

[67] *HIH Casualty & General Insurance Ltd v New Hampshire Insurance Co* [2001] Lloyd's Rep IR 596, para 185.

[68] *HIH Casualty & General Insurance Ltd v New Hampshire Insurance Co* [2001] Lloyd's Rep IR 596, para 185.

[69] See para 3.43.

[70] (1898) 3 Com Cas 164.

warehouse to warehouse clause. He said that the latter was so common that the reinsurers ought to have known that it was in the original policy. He found that the clause was customary and should be read into the reinsurance. The Court of Appeal in *HIH* held that this (ie whether the clause was well-known and/or in common use) was not the proper test for incorporation.[71] In *Charlesworth v Faber*[72] the facts were similar and the clause in question was found to be in 'common use', and the reinsurer either knew or should have known that the clause was probably in the original policy. The effect of the incorporation was to extend the 12-month term of the reinsurance to beyond 12 months because the term was a continuation clause which provided for the insured to be covered if the ship insured was at sea at the expiration of the policy. The reinsurers also relied on the case of *Interfoto Picture Library Ltd v Stiletto Visual Programme Ltd*,[73] in which a defendant was held not to be bound by a term described as 'very onerous' and 'unreasonable and extortionate' and which he had neither signed nor read but which had appeared in some printed conditions on a delivery note. The Court of Appeal doubted whether the *Interfoto* approach was helpful or was of any assistance in circumstances where the contract had actually been signed, and noted also that the *Interfoto* case was essentially concerned with a question of notice rather than construction, and that the question of notice was more akin to the question of knowledge (actual or constructive), which would have to be determined at trial.

3.47 The Court of Appeal approved the test adopted by David Steel J in relation to the incorporation of unusual clauses[74] but stated that the question of knowledge could not sensibly be separated from the question of whether there had been a fair presentation of the risk[75] and that the two issues should therefore be considered together. Rix LJ stated that he was not persuaded that the *Interfoto* case applied to a term that was merely unusual, particularly in the context of a binding incorporation clause. He further stated that in circumstances where the term of the reinsurance slip policy provided that the reinsurance was subject to all terms as original together with an invitation to consult the information held on the brokers' file, a burden was placed on the reinsurers to show that the waiver of defences clause was not incorporated or that the proposal was unfairly presented. The Court of Appeal further held that the judge was entitled to come to the view that such clauses were sometimes agreed and were not to be categorized as unconscionable or extortionate.

---

[71] [2001] Lloyd's Rep IR 596, para 207.
[72] (1900) 5 Com Cas 508.
[73] [1989] QB 433.
[74] No party had sought to argue that the test was wrong.
[75] The remedy for the case of notice which is insufficient because of unfairness will be that the term in question does not become part of the contract; however, the remedy for a case of an unfair presentation of a reinsurance proposal is avoidance of the contract.

(6) Effect of Incorporation

The real battleground between parties regarding the incorporation of a term may **3.48** not be the fact of incorporation, but rather the effect of the incorporated term. This was the case in *HIH Casualty & General Insurance Ltd v New Hampshire Insurance Co* where a question arose as to whether the waiver of defences clause that was incorporated into the reinsurance contract served merely to emphasize the follow the settlements provisions of the contract or whether it was independent so that the reinsurer was held to have waived defences as between itself and its reinsured. If the clause was fully incorporated so as to operate independently at the reinsurance level, then the reinsurers could not complain about non-disclosure or misrepresentation as between themselves and their reinsured. If, however, the effect of the incorporation was merely to bind the reinsurers to a payment made by their reinsured where only the reinsured's defences under the original contract were in issue, then the reinsurers remained free at the reinsurance level to refuse payment to their reinsured where there was a separate ground of avoidance in the circumstances of the placement of the reinsurance. The Court of Appeal held that the clause was intended to operate as a follow the settlements clause, so that the reinsurer could not rely on the fact that the reinsured would, absent the clause in the underlying policy, have had a good defence to a claim by its underlying insured.

(7) Reinsured's Ability to Amend Insurance

Limitations are also placed on the reinsured in circumstances where reinsurance is **3.49** effected on the basis that it is on the same terms as the original. In *HIH Casualty & General Insurance Ltd v New Hampshire Insurance Co*[76] David Steel J at first instance stated that the only commercially realistic construction of a clause providing that the reinsured should obtain the reinsurers' agreement to all amendments to the original policy was that it excluded from its application amendments which did not affect the sense or substance of the underlying policy in a manner potentially prejudicial to the reinsurer. This resulted in the amendment clause being categorized as a warranty. David Steel J held that this gave contractual substance to the position at common law.

In fact, as the Court of Appeal in *HIH*[77] recognized, the common law position is **3.50** rather more stringent. In *Norwich Union Fire Insurance Society v Colonial Mutual Fire Insurance Co Limited*[78] it was held that the variation of the original policy without the consent of the reinsurer discharged the latter. McCardie J referred to the decision of the Court of Appeal in *Lower Rhine and Wurtemberg Insurance Association v Sedgwick*[79] and Rigby LJ's statement that there was no half-way house

---

[76] [2001] Lloyd's Rep IR 596.
[77] [2001] Lloyd's Rep IR 596.
[78] [1922] 2 KB 461.
[79] [1899] 1 QB 179.

between a right to alter the underlying policy without consent and an absence of a right to do so. Either it could be altered or not. If it could not be altered then the only sound rule was that the original policy could only be altered with the consent of the reinsurer. He applied by analogy the rule in contracts of guarantee that the court will not entertain any discussion about the materiality of the variation in the contract of guarantee and unless it is self-evident that it is not material or prejudicial to the surety he is left to be the sole judge as to whether he will consent to remain liable. Rigby LJ stated that if a direct policy could be altered without the consent of the reinsurer, he would 'be thrown into a position of danger, difficulty and doubt'.

(8) Arbitration Clauses

3.51 In a number of cases the courts have refused to incorporate arbitration clauses into either a reinsurance or a retrocession by way of general words of incorporation (such as 'as original'). In reviewing a number of authorities in *HIH*,[80] the Court of Appeal held that an arbitration clause is patently an ancillary or collateral provision which is personal to the parties: arbitration is private and confidential and cannot be conjoined with another arbitration without the express consent of the parties. This is equally true of retrocession agreements. In *Pine Top Insurance Co Ltd v Unione Italiana Anglo Saxon Reinsurance Co Ltd*[81] Gatehouse J held that in a retrocession contract the words 'all terms and conditions as original' did not have the effect of incorporating an arbitration clause in the standard form primary policy either directly or via a general incorporation clause in the reinsurance contract thus retroceded. He held that the effect of the incorporating words was confined to the scope of the cover, and that in the absence of express words of incorporation the arbitration clause was not incorporated.

(9) Exclusive Jurisdiction Clauses

3.52 The courts have taken a similar approach to jurisdiction clauses, holding that general words of incorporation in a reinsurance contract will not ordinarily incorporate jurisdiction clauses from the primary policy because they are not germane to the primary risk insured, to the substance of the underlying policy or to the reinsurance policy, but are merely ancillary provisions which the parties to the reinsurance would not normally intend to incorporate.[82] This approach does not

---

[80] Including *Pine Top Insurance Co Ltd v Unione Italiana Anglo Saxon Reinsurance Co Ltd* [1987] 1 Lloyd's Rep 477; *Aughton Ltd v MF Kent Services Ltd* [1991] 31 Con LR 60; *Excess Insurance Co Ltd v Mander* [1997] 2 Lloyd's Rep 119. See also *Trygg Hansa v Equitas* [1998] 2 Lloyd's Rep 439, endorsed by Morison J in *Cigna Life Insurance Co of Europe SA-NV v Intercaser SA de Seguros y Reaseguros* [2001] Lloyd's Rep IR 821.

[81] Gatehouse J held that there was no reference to the arbitration clause in the slip and if it was to be included by reason of the general conditions it would not bind the retrocessionaires to arbitrate disputes with the reinsurers.

[82] See *Assicurazioni Generali SpA v Ege Sigorta AS* [2002] Lloyd's Rep IR 480. A further reason for non-incorporation was that neither the leading underwriter nor any of the following underwriters

depend upon the particular language of the clause, but rather on its essential nature. The approach is consistent with European Community law[83] which also regards jurisdiction clauses as ancillary to the substantive provisions of the contract for the purpose of Article 17 of the Brussels Convention. The following principles about the incorporation of jurisdiction clauses through reference to a body of terms were set out by Gross J in *Siboti v BP France*[84] in considering the application of principles of Community law to jurisdiction clauses:

(1) Community law recognizes the validity of incorporation by reference, provided that the body of terms to be incorporated is clearly identified and whether or not it was available to the parties at the time of entry into the contract.

(2) Community law, like English law, regards jurisdiction clauses as ancillary to the substantive provisions of the contract. In many cases, general words of incorporation will only suffice to incorporate terms germane to the subject matter of the contract and not terms ancillary thereto. The reason is that in the absence of specific language, the court may not be able to conclude that the parties have demonstrated clearly and precisely the existence of a consensus to incorporate clauses which are ancillary to the subject matter of the contract.

(3) While in Community law the language of the contract is emphasized rather than extrinsic matters, this does not entail ignoring the commercial background. On the contrary, in each case the court must construe the language of the contract in context and inquire whether a consensus on the subject

---

agreed that the reinsurance would incorporate anything except what was referred to in the slip, namely a standard form agreement which included a UK jurisdiction clause. The tendering by the brokers of the form which included a Turkish jurisdiction clause was an error which reinsurers negligently failed to pick up. However, the variation of the wording did not lead to a variation in the slip for the simple reason that the tendering by the broker to the underwriter of the wording was a purely ministerial exercise. Unless expressly indicated by the broker as containing matters inconsistent with the pre-existing slip the tender of wording would not be construed as an offer to vary the contract and the signature of the broker would not be understood as an acceptance of an offered variation. If both the brokers' staff and the underwriters' staff incorrectly agreed that the wording was accurate, what had been accomplished was not an amended contract but a wording inaccurately reflecting the true contract; *OK Petroleum AB v Vitol Energy SA* [1995] 2 Lloyd's Rep 160; *AIG Europe (UK) Ltd v Anonymous Greek Insurance Co of General Insurances (The Ethniki)* [1999] Lloyd's Rep IR 221, [2000] Lloyd's Rep IR 343; *AIG Europe SA v QBE International Insurance Ltd* [2002] 1 Lloyd's Rep IR 22.

[83] See *Benincasa v Dentalkit Srl* [1997] ECR I-3767, cited with approval in *AIG Europe SA v QBE International Insurance Ltd* [2002] Lloyd's Rep IR 22, para 26.

[84] [2003] 2 Lloyd's Rep 364, cited with approval by Andrew Smith J in *Prifti v Musini Sociedad Anónima de Seguros y Reaseguros* [2004] Lloyd's Rep IR 528 when considering arguments relating to Art 23 of the Brussels Convention as to whether the parties had agreed that the courts of a particular Member State had jurisdiction to settle any disputes between them. In such cases the court must first consider whether the clause conferring jurisdiction was in fact the subject of a consensus between the parties which was clearly and precisely demonstrated (see *Salotti v RUWA Posteriemaschinen GmbH* [1976] ECR 1831).

matter of the jurisdiction clause has been clearly and precisely demonstrated. It was, however, to be kept in mind that the commercial background could not always be relied upon to make good deficiencies in the language that the parties had chosen to use.

(10) Choice of Law Clauses[85]

3.53   In *Forsikringsaktieselskapet Vesta v JNE Butcher*[86] Hobhouse J said:

> Where a contract such as the present provides that its terms and conditions are to be the same as those of another contract and where its clear commercial purpose is to provide corresponding cover to that provided by the other contract then unless some other powerful consideration is to intervene the conclusion must be that there is an intention that both contracts are to be governed by the same law. However, there remains something surprising and improbable about the conclusion that the Lloyd's slip and the Lloyd's policy are governed by anything other than English law.

He concluded that the legal effect of the clauses defining the cover should be the same in the reinsurance and the original insurance but declined to hold that the relevant law (Norwegian) was intended to be the proper law of the reinsurance contract. On appeal, the Court of Appeal rejected as unrealistic the suggestion that the whole contract should be governed by Norwegian law. The House of Lords, whilst confirming that cover under the two policies was intended to be back-to-back and describing the reinsurance as 'the English contract of reinsurance', did not give any detailed consideration of the issue of whether English law was the proper law of the reinsurance contract.

3.54   In *Gan Insurance Co Ltd v Tai Ping Insurance Co Ltd*[87] a question arose as to whether the use of the words 'as original' in the reinsurance slip resulted in the reinsurance contract being governed by Taiwanese law (as under the underlying policy). The Court of Appeal held that it was not possible to infer that the parties intended to effect such a result. A departure from the usual course of business on the London market could only be justified if the terms of the reinsurance agreement unequivocally pointed to an intention that the proper law of the contract should be Taiwanese law.

3.55   These presumptions regarding the non-incorporation of particular terms are not inflexible rules of construction.[88] There may be cases in which it would be unrealistic to restrict the scope of incorporation so as to exclude a jurisdiction or arbitration clause.

---

[85] See also paras 7.05–7.15.
[86] [1986] 2 Lloyd's Rep 179, 193.
[87] [1999] Lloyd's Rep IR 472.
[88] Per Colman J in *AIG Europe (UK) Ltd v Anónymous Greek Insurance Co of General Insurances (The Ethniki)* [1999] Lloyd's Rep IR 221.

A warranty in the reinsurance contract that terms would be the same as those of the   **3.56**
underlying insurance policy did not assist an argument that the parties intended
to incorporate not only the terms that were germane to the subject matter of the
insurance, but also ancillary provisions.[89]

(11) Errors and Omissions Clauses

Errors and omissions clauses are near universal features of modern treaties. They   **3.57**
generally provide that the reinsured should not be prejudiced by an inadvertent
omission or error. In *Highlands Insurance Co v Continental Insurance Co*[90] Steyn J
held that the language of the clause in that case was not sufficient for it to be incorporated into the reinsurance contract as it was applicable to the original insurance
only but he also held that even if it were to be incorporated it would not apply to a
pre-contractual material misrepresentation which would entitle the reinsurers to
avoid on the grounds of misrepresentation.[91]

C. Implied Terms[92]

As with the implication of terms into any contract, the basis upon which the court   **3.58**
will imply a term will depend upon the nature of the contract. A term can be
implied as a necessary legal incident to a particular type of contract[93] or on the basis
that it is necessary to imply the term to give the contract business efficacy,[94] or by
reason of an invariable custom and general usage or custom of any trade.[95]

(1) Businesslike Obligations

In *Phoenix General Insurance Co of Greece SA v Halvanon Insurance Co Ltd*[96]   **3.59**
Hobhouse J held that facultative/obligatory reinsurance, which imposes no

---

[89] Per Andrew Smith J in *Prifti v Musini Sociedad Anónima de Seguros y Reaseguros* [2004] Lloyd's
Rep IR 528, a case in which the incorporation of an exclusive jurisdiction clause into a reinsurance
contract was rejected.

[90] [1987] 1 Lloyd's Rep 109, 117.

[91] Steyn LJ took a similar approach in *Pan Atlantic Insurance Co Ltd v Pine Top Insurance Co Ltd*
[1993] 1 Lloyd's Rep 496.

[92] For a fuller treatment of implied terms generally the reader should consult the standard works
on contract law.

[93] *Liverpool City Council v Irwin* [1977] AC 239; *The Moorcock* (1889) 14 PD 64.

[94] *The Moorcock* (1889) 14 PD 64; *Shirlaw v Southern Foundries* (1926) [1939] 2 KB 306.

[95] See *Liverpool City Council v Irwin* [1977] AC 239. In *Friends Provident Life & Pensions v Sirius
International Ins* [2006] Lloyd's Rep IR 45 Mance LJ commented that reasonableness was not a basis
for implication of terms in to an insurance contract.

[96] [1985] 2 Lloyd's Rep 599, 613. Note that this was a case in which the contractual material was
sparse and where the true contractual intention of the parties had to be inferred or implied. In many
cases, therefore, matters will be dealt with expressly and there will be no need to imply such a term
or terms. Hobhouse J stated that this term (or terms) was (or were) innominate and therefore the
consequences of any breach for any particular cession or any individual claim or for the contract as

restriction on the reinsured's right to choose whether or not to cede without giving the reinsurer any equivalent right, necessitated the implication of a term, or terms, that the reinsured should conduct the business involved in the cession prudently, reasonably carefully and in accordance with the ordinary practice of the market. Hobhouse J accordingly accepted the duties required of the reinsured pleaded by the reinsurer pursuant to the implied term,[97] namely:

(a) to keep full and proper records and accounts of all risks accepted or premiums received and receivable and all claims made or notified;

(b) to investigate all claims and confirm that they fell within the terms of the contract and were properly payable before accepting them;

(c) properly to investigate risks offered to them before acceptance and closings relating thereto subsequently;

(d) to keep full and proper accurate accounts showing at all times the accounts due and payable by the reinsured to the reinsurers and by the reinsurers to the reinsured under the contracts;

(e) to ensure that all amounts owing to them were collected promptly when due and entered forthwith in their accounts, and all balances owing to the reinsurers were likewise paid promptly when due;

(f) to obtain, file or otherwise keep in proper manner all accounting, claims and other documents and records and make these reasonably available to the reinsurers.[98]

Hobhouse J stated that the obligations under sub-paras (a), (d), and (f) above could be said to be the obligations of an 'accounting party'; such terms had to be implied primarily to ensure that the reinsured conducted his business in a proper and businesslike fashion and so that the reinsurer was able to find out what his rights were, what credits he was entitled to, whether the business was profitable or not, etc. There is little reason to suppose that these duties would not be of more general application and thus, in the absence of express terms, implied into most treaty reinsurance contracts. Hobhouse J further found that the necessity for the duty set out at sub-para (b) arose from the provision of the contract that the reinsurers

---

a whole must depend on the nature and gravity of the relevant breach—at 614. Note further that the decision of Hobhouse J was overturned by the Court of Appeal, but not in respect of the matters set out above, in *Phoenix General Insurance Co of Greece SA v Administratia Asigurarilor de Stat* [1986] 2 Lloyd's Rep 552. The existence of a duty of care owed by reinsureds to reinsurers would seem inconsistent with *Sphere Drake v EIU* [2003] 1 Lloyd's Rep IR 525 in which Thomas J trenchantly commented that if the reinsured had made proper disclosure then the reinsurer could not complain about the nature of the business written. In other words, the reinsured owed no contractual duties to write prudent business. Note also the approach of Mance LJ in *Friends Provident Life & Pensions v Sirius International Ins* [2006] Lloyd's Rep IR 45 to implication of terms.

[97] [1985] 2 Lloyd's Rep 599, 613.

[98] The Court had two expert witnesses before it and both thought these implied terms were appropriate. Hobhouse J held that although the opinion of the witnesses as to what was appropriate and reasonable did not itself suffice to show that such terms should be implied, he was satisfied that such terms were necessary in the transaction in issue.

would 'follow the settlements' of the reinsured. As such it would appear that that duty should apply to all reinsurance contracts which contain a 'follow the settlements' clause and is reflected in subsequent decisions on such clauses.[99] However, sub-para (e) above is unlikely to be of much consequence in reinsurance litigation, and it is uncertain to what extent sub-para (c) would be regarded as necessary, insofar as it relates to underwriting, where there is an obligation to cede qualifying risks, because it would be open to the reinsurer to stipulate for a minimum retention in order to keep the reinsured's attention sufficiently focused.

The Court of Appeal in *Bonner v Cox*[100] held that non-proportional reinsurance was **3.60** not subject to such implied terms. They expressly refused to rule on whether it was necessary to imply such terms into the proportional facultative obligatory treaty which was at issue before Hobhouse J. However if such a duty is to be implied into all proportional reinsurance it is surprising that claims are not commonplace as many unprofitable treaties could be alleged to have been negligently written. The market reality is perhaps better reflected by the 'law of the jungle' approach taken by Thomas J in *Sphere Drake Insurance v Euro International Underwriting Ltd*:[101]

> No other participant in a market owes a duty to protect those who knowingly enter a market but who do not understand it, are imprudent, or who miscalculate; indeed, it is likely that a person who is imprudent or foolish or who miscalculates in any market will be ruthlessly exploited by those who understand the market; he is at risk of having dumped on him, risks which no one else wants.

This would seem to be in accordance with cases which suggest that the law can **3.61** leave such matters to be governed by market reputation. In *Glasgow Assurance v Symondson*,[102] Scrutton J said that an reinsured must have confidence in every open cover where he reinsures part of risks of which he knows nothing except that they are to be written by someone else. He said that no one suggested that the assured owes any duty in law to the underwriter, but that commercial confidence would suggest that a reinsurer would need to exhibit prudent if it wanted its contracts to be renewed. Certainly in the case of non-proportional reinsurance the reinsured and the reinsurer have adverse and competing interests and there can be no necessity for implying a term that one of the parties owes some sort of duty to protect the interests of the other. In such reinsurance the Court of Appeal decided that there was no implied duty on a reinsured to act 'prudently' or 'reasonably carefully' or

---

[99] See paras 4.13 et seq and also 5.46 et seq. Tuckey J followed *Phoenix v Halvanon* in *Economic v Le Assicurazioni d'Italia* (unreported, 27 November 1996) in the case of a proportional reinsurance where all risks were being shared between reinsured and reinsurer. Cover holders had written bonds for a pool of insurers which included Economic. Later the bonds were written solely for Economic who then ceded them under what was in effect a quota share reinsurance to itself (notionally) and to the other pool members. Tuckey J held that Economic owed a duty to the other insurers to conduct the business prudently.
[100] [2006] Lloyd's Rep IR 385.
[101] [2003] 1 Lloyd's Rep IR 525.
[102] (1911) 16 Com Cas 108.

even limit its risks to those that the leading underwriter would write in the ordinary course of business.[103] It would appear that any duty is limited to avoiding dishonesty or recklessness.[104]

3.62   Where there is a follow the settlements clause, but no claims co-operation clause, the obligation to follow the settlements of the reinsured is subject to an implied proviso that the insurers must have acted both honestly and in a proper and businesslike manner in the settlement.[105] In this situation the insurer is responsible for the whole handling of the settlement, but the settlement imposes liability on the reinsurer. As set out by Mance LJ in *Gan Insurance Company Ltd v Tai Ping Insurance Company Ltd (Nos 2 and 3)*,[106] the rationale of the proviso is to protect B in circumstances where A is able to bind B's financial interest. Mance LJ suggested that the concept of a proper and businesslike settlement must contemplate that insurers will have regard to the prospects and risks attaching to the claim as a whole, whether it is wholly or partly reinsured.

(2) Retention

3.63   The courts have rejected the contention that there is an implied term that the reinsured should retain some part of the risk on the grounds that an element of retention is part of the essential nature of a contract of reinsurance. In *Phoenix General Insurance Co of Greece SA v Halvanon Insurance Co Ltd*,[107] Hobhouse J held that 'as a matter of reinsurance law there is no inconsistency between the idea of reinsurance and a nil retention'.[108] In a later case,[109] Hobhouse J stated that if a reinsurer wished to have the benefit of his reinsured retaining some part of the risk, he could effect this by inserting a retention warranty.[110] In a proportional treaty reinsurance it may of course be particularly important to the reinsurer to know the amount of the reinsured's retention, and also whether any such retention is protected by other reinsurance. The rationale for this has been explained by Moore-Bick J:[111]

> [T]he underwriter who is thinking of becoming a reinsurer under a quota share treaty invariably wants to know what proportion of the risks being ceded the reinsured intends to retain for his own account. He regards retention as of considerable

---

[103]   *Bonner v Cox* [2006] Lloyd's Rep IR 385.

[104]   See s 55(2)(a) of the Marine Insurance Act 1906.

[105]   See *Insurance Co of Africa v Scor (UK) Reinsurance Co Ltd* [1985] 1 Lloyd's Rep 312.

[106]   [2001] Lloyd's Rep IR 667.

[107]   [1985] 2 Lloyd's Rep 599, 612. In this case the standard full reinsurance clause was used but with the amount of the retention left blank. Hobhouse J refused to fill in the blank by way of an implied term that there should be a reasonable retention.

[108]   [1985] 2 Lloyd's Rep 599, 611.

[109]   *Iron Trades Mutual Insurance Co Ltd v Companhia de Seguros Imperio* [1991] 1 Re LR 213, 226.

[110]   The full reinsurance clause referred to above includes a provision for a retention but if the reinsurer does not stipulate the amount that the reinsured should retain, then it will not be implied that the reinsured should have retained any part of the risk.

[111]   In *Kingscroft Insurance Co v Nissan Fire & Marine* [1999] Lloyd's Rep IR 603, 622.

importance because it provides a measure of the reinsured's confidence in the business he is writing and provides a continuing incentive to underwrite responsibly. The greater the retention, the greater the confidence the reinsurer can have in the quality of the business that will be ceded to him and if nothing is said about the retention he will ask about it. Because quota share reinsurance effectively involves transferring a share of the business, both premiums and claims, to the reinsurer, it reduces to a corresponding extent the reinsured's liability for each loss that occurs and so reduces his interest in each risk written. Non-proportional reinsurance, typically in the form of excess of loss reinsurance, is different in that the reinsured remains liable for all losses up to a certain amount and to that extent he retains a direct economic interest in each risk underwritten.

However, there is no implied term that the reinsured's retention is unprotected by other reinsurance, and if the reinsurer wants to ensure that the reinsured should actually be exposed to a real level of risk on the business he will have to specify that in the contract.[112]

(3) Withholding Approval of Settlements[113]

In *Gan Insurance Co Ltd v Tai Ping Insurance Co Ltd (Nos 2 and 3)*[114] the court was **3.64** concerned with a facultative reinsurance, the terms of which included a claims co-operation clause that provided, inter alia, that 'no settlement and/or compromise shall be made and liability admitted without the prior approval of reinsurers'.[115] Gan asserted that two terms should be implied into the contract: (a) that reinsurers would not withhold approval of a settlement unless there were reasonable grounds for doing so; and (b) that reinsurers would respond with reasonable promptness to a request for the approval of a settlement. At first instance, Longmore J held that a term should be implied that reinsurers should have reasonable grounds for withholding approval of a settlement. He stated that 'a right arbitrarily to refuse approval of a settlement would defeat the purpose of the reinsurance contract, which was to indemnify the reinsured in respect of his actual liability to his underlying insured, not to give the reinsurer an option to indemnify the reinsured if he felt like it, but not if he did not feel like it'.[116] Longmore J adjudged that the implication was necessary to give business efficacy to the contract as a whole because to force the reinsured to litigate his liability to his underlying insured to the point of judgment was 'so uncommercial and so unbusinesslike that it cannot have been the parties' intention'.[117]

---

[112] See, eg, *Great Atlantic Insurance Co v Home Insurance Co* [1981] 2 Lloyd's Rep 219; *Kingscroft Insurance Co v Nissan Fire & Marine* [1999] Lloyd's Rep IR 603, 622; *GE Reinsurance Corp v New Hampshire Insurance Co* [2004] 1 Lloyd's Rep 404. See also para 6.18 on materiality of retention clauses.
[113] See also paras 4.42 et seq and 5.42 et seq.
[114] [2001] Lloyd's Rep IR 667.
[115] See para 5.17 et seq.
[116] [2001] Lloyd's Rep IR 291, 308.
[117] [2001] Lloyd's Rep IR 291, 308.

3.65   The Court of Appeal[118] set aside that decision. However, it nonetheless held that there was a limitation on reinsurers' ability to withhold approval. Mance LJ held that it could not have been contemplated that Tai Ping should be exposed to having judgments given against it at the instance of third parties, unless Gan genuinely determined this to be appropriate having regard to the characteristics of the particular claim, and therefore accepted a general qualification:

> [t]hat any withholding of approval by reinsurers should take place in good faith after consideration of and on the basis of the facts giving rise to the particular claim and not with reference to considerations wholly extraneous to the subject matter of the particular reinsurance.[119]

Mance LJ had in mind reinsurers refusing approval not for any reason connected with the claim but as part of an attempt to influence an insurer's attitude in relation to a matter arising under another quite separate reinsurance or to harm an insurer as a competitor in respect of other business or in the eyes of a local regulator. Although the right to withhold approval was provided for reinsurers' protection, that did not necessarily mean that they could exercise it solely with their own 'sectional interests' in mind. Mance LJ further stated that:

> If there is any further implication, it is along the lines that the reinsurer will not withhold approval arbitrarily, or (to use what I see as no more than an expanded expression of the same concept) will not do so in circumstances so extreme that no reasonable company in its position could possibly withhold approval. This will not ordinarily add materially to the requirement that the reinsurer should form a genuine view as to the appropriateness of settlement or compromise without taking into account considerations extraneous to the subject matter of the reinsurance. But I would for my part be prepared to accept this further qualified limitation— since the stringency of the [clause referred to above] . . . seems to require it, both as a matter of necessity and to give the sub-clause business efficacy in the rare cases in which it could be material.[120]

Sir Christopher Staughton was somewhat critical of the approach taken by Mance LJ (with whom Latham LJ had agreed on this issue). He rejected the term contended for by Tai Ping on the grounds that it was not necessary for business efficacy and was not so obvious that it went without saying. He posed the question whether it would be unreasonable to require the insured to go into the witness box and give evidence of his loss on oath (in other words to force the reinsured to litigate a dispute with his underlying insured). If the parties believed that the market would welcome the implied term proposed, or any other implied term, they had only to persuade the market to adopt it.

---

[118] [2001] 2 Lloyd's Rep IR 667.
[119] [2001] 2 Lloyd's Rep IR 667, 697.
[120] [2001] 2 Lloyd's Rep IR 667, 699.

(4) Provision of Documents and Information

Where there is a 'follow the settlements' clause and in the absence of a claims co-   **3.66**
operation clause to similar effect, a reinsurer has the implied right[121] to require the
reinsured to provide documents and information showing (although not necessarily in detail) the claim that was made by its underlying insured, how the claim was
dealt with (for instance, whether by the appointment of loss adjusters, or in-house,
or by both means), if by appointment of loss adjusters, who they were, sight of all
their reports, and the answers to any relevant questions the answers to which might
reasonably enable the reinsurer to *contend* that the loss adjusters had not adjusted
or that the reinsured had not settled the claim in a businesslike way. However, the
right does not extend to the provision of answers to enable the reinsurer to satisfy
himself that the claim has been adjusted and settled in a businesslike way; for if the
reinsurer was to be entitled to that information he would, in effect, be entitled to
require his reinsured to prove both liability and the precise reasons why the claim
had been adjusted and settled in the way in which it had been.[122] In the absence of
a claims co-operation clause, reinsurers are not entitled to be involved in or consulted about the steps taken to settle the claim or the amount at which it should be
settled.[123]

(5) Costs of Defending, Investigating or Settling Claims[124]

In *Scottish Metropolitan Assurance Co Ltd v Groom*,[125] the Court of Appeal refused   **3.67**
to imply a term enabling a reinsured to recover from its reinsurers the costs and
expenses that it had incurred in successfully defending a claim brought by its
insured. In *Insurance Co of Africa v Scor (UK) Reinsurance Co Ltd*[126] proceedings
by an insured seeking payment under a fire policy were unsuccessfully defended
by insurers and they were ordered, inter alia, to pay to their insured costs of
$58,000. They sought, inter alia, to recover those costs from their reinsurers. At
first instance,[127] the court held that the insurers could recover the costs under an
implied term of the reinsurance contract. The basis for the implication was that
there was a provision in the reinsurance contract which conferred a right on the
reinsurers to withhold their approval of settlement. The Court of Appeal (by a
majority) overturned that decision,[128] holding that there was no basis for the implication of such a term.

---

[121] *Charman v Guardian Royal Exchange Assurance plc* [1992] 2 Lloyd's Rep 607. See also paras
5.45 et seq for the reinsurer's right to inspect the reinsured's documents generally.
[122] Per Webster J at 614.
[123] For claims co-operation clauses see paras 4.42 et seq.
[124] See also paras 5.21 et seq in relation to when reinsurers have withheld approval for costs.
[125] (1924) 19 Ll L Rep 131, 20 Ll L Rep 44.
[126] [1985] 1 Lloyd's Rep 312.
[127] [1983] 1 Lloyd's Rep 541—judgment of Leggatt J.
[128] [1985] 1 Lloyd's Rep 312.

3.68   In *Baker v Black Sea & Baltic General Insurance Co Ltd*[129] the House of Lords had to consider the question as to whether a term should be implied into a contract of quota share or other proportional reinsurance that an insurer could recover a proportion of costs incurred by him in investigating, settling or defending claims by his insured (ie not in respect of third party claims which are often recoverable from the reinsurer as one of the risks insured under the underlying policy). It was argued by the reinsured that the nature of proportional reinsurance, the essential characteristic of which was the sharing of underwriting fortunes both as to risk and premium, was such that a term should be implied. The House of Lords rejected the implication of such a term on this basis. Lord Lloyd set out that the reinsured's argument would have been a strong one if proportional reinsurance was in the nature of a partnership (but it was not) or if the profits on the business ceded to Black Sea were to be shared equally (which they were not). However, the House of Lords remitted the case for further consideration to be given to the question of whether a term could be implied on the basis of trade practice or usage in proportional reinsurance contracts that such costs were shared on a pro rata basis.

(6) Obligation to Follow Judgment Entered Against the Reinsured

3.69   In *Commercial Union Co v NRG Victory Reinsurance Ltd*[130] Potter LJ accepted obiter the implication of a term into a contract of reinsurance that the reinsurer would treat the decision of a foreign court of competent jurisdiction as to the liability of the reinsured to his underlying insured as binding, subject only to reversal on appeal and the following limits:

(1) that the foreign court should in the eyes of the domestic court be a court of competent jurisdiction;
(2) that judgment should not have been obtained in the foreign court in breach of an exclusive jurisdiction clause or other clause by which the underlying insured was contractually excluded from proceeding in that court;
(3) that the reinsured took all proper defences; and
(4) that the judgment was not manifestly perverse.

Potter LJ suggested that the policy reasons for the implication of such a term were that 'it would be quite impracticable, productive of endless dispute, and against the presumed intention of the contract of insurance (absent contrary or special provision of a kind which does not exist in this case) for an English Court trying a dispute concerning the reinsurers' liability not to treat the judgment of a foreign

---

[129] [1998] 1 WLR 974.
[130] [1998] 2 Lloyd's Rep 600, 610–611. See also paras 4.08 et seq.

Court as to the reinsured's original liability as decisive and binding, save within the most circumscribed limits'.[131]

However in *Wasa International Insurance Co v Lexington Insurance Co*[132] a certain **3.70** amount of judicial doubt was poured on this proposition. It was argued that, even without a follow the settlements clause, reinsurers would, as a matter of contractual implication, have been bound by the court's interpretation of the scope and application of the original cover, citing the obiter remarks in the *Commercial Union Assurance* case. Lord Mance[133] was distinctly lukewarm about such submissions although he said that it was unnecessary to decide the point. He noted however that there was no suggestion in *Scor*[134] that such a judgment against the insurer could be binding under the reinsurance in the absence of a follow the settlements clause. He went on to say that the basis for such a contractual implication has been questioned by a 'powerfully constituted' Bermudian arbitration panel.[135]

---

[131] [1998] 2 Lloyd's Rep 600, 610. Saville J was rather more reluctant to make such a finding in *Hayter v Nelson and Home Insurance Co* [1990] 2 QB 265, referring the issue to an arbitrator to determine.

[132] [2010] 1 AC 180; [2009] 2 Lloyd's Rep 508.

[133] At para 37.

[134] [1985] 1 Lloyd's Rep 312 (where there was such a judgment).

[135] In an interim award dated 12 December 2000 in *Gold Medal Insurance Co v Hopewell International Insurance Ltd*. He also noted it was also criticized by O'Neill & Woloniecki, *The Law of Reinsurance in England and Bermuda*, 2nd edn (2004), 191–193. It should also be noted that, in *Omega Proteins Ltd v Aspen Insurance UK Ltd* [2011] Lloyd's Rep IR 183, Christopher Clarke J was unwilling to apply what had been said in the *Commercial Union Assurance* case to insurance and held that it was open to the insurer and indeed the insured to re-open the basis of the insured's liability to a third party notwithstanding what had been said in the judgment against the insured in favour of the third party for which indemnity was being sought.

4

OBLIGATIONS OF THE REINSURER

A. Reinsurer's Obligation to Indemnify the Reinsured

4.01 A reinsurer is obliged to indemnify its reinsured where a loss falls within the cover of the policy reinsured and within the cover created by the reinsurance.[1] In the absence of any express provision in the reinsurance policy to the contrary, the burden of proof is on the reinsured to prove that the underlying insured's loss fell as a matter of law within the risks covered and that it was as a matter of fact liable to the underlying insured in respect of that loss.[2]

---

[1] *Hill v Mercantile & General Reinsurance Co Plc* [1996] LRLR 341, 350.
[2] The importance of this is illustrated by the litigation arising out of the Exxon Valdez disaster: *King v Brandywine Reinsurance Co Ltd* [2005] 1 Lloyd's Rep 655 (relating to a claim for an indemnity from the reinsurer in respect of certain claims settled for oil pollution clean-up expenses and whether such expenses fell within the relevant section of cover provided to the underlying insured, Exxon).

4.02   It is not sufficient for the reinsured to establish that any settlement was business-like and sensible.[3] It must prove the loss in the same manner as the underlying insured must have proved it against the reinsured, and the reinsurer can raise all the defences which were open to the reinsured against the underlying insured.[4] The fact that the reinsurer has previously paid a claim under similar circumstances does not stop him from requiring the reinsured to prove its liability.[5]

4.03   Consequently, in *Commercial Union Assurance v NRG Victory Reinsurance*[6] the Court of Appeal held that the judge had erred in finding that the reinsured had proved the loss by adducing evidence from a local lawyer as to the likely outcome of the trial based on his previous experience of the local courts. The correct enquiry was to find the answer which application of the law and appropriate rules of construction would produce. Potter LJ said that whilst the lawyer's predictions 'might appropriately have been directed to the decision of the insurers to settle in the light of their predictions, it did not bite on the question of whether the evidence demonstrated legal liability under the insurance contract' which the reinsurer, in response to the reinsured's claim for indemnity, had the 'right' to require the reinsured to establish.[7]

4.04   A reinsurer is not obliged to pay its reinsured more than the reinsured has paid its underlying insured. Consequently, where a reinsured compromises a claim on a 66% basis he cannot issue proceedings and claim against his reinsurer on the basis that he, the reinsured, was, in fact, 100% liable to his underlying insured and seek to recover from his reinsurer on a full liability basis: the reinsured cannot make a profit out of the reinsurance.[8]

4.05   A reinsurance contract may cover losses occurring during the period of the underlying insurance, or may be itself written on a 'loss occurring' basis so that it covers loss and damage occurring between two dates specified in the reinsurance contract itself. Under such a reinsurance, a reinsurer is obliged to pay its share of the loss suffered by the reinsured if and to the extent that it occurred during the period when the reinsurance contract was in force.[9] Not only must the reinsured prove the loss and that it fell within the cover of the insurance, but it must prove that the loss fell within the period specified in the reinsurance.

4.06   A difficulty that arises is a potential mismatch between the periods of cover in the insurance contract and the reinsurance contract. In *Municipal Mutual Insurance*

---

   [3]   *Commercial Union Assurance Co v NRG Victory Reinsurance Ltd* [1998] 2 Lloyd's Rep 600.
   [4]   *Re London County Commercial Reinsurance Office Ltd* [1922] 2 Ch 67, 80.
   [5]   *London and Manchester Plate Glass Co Ltd v Heath* [1913] 3 KB 411.
   [6]   [1998] 2 Lloyd's Rep 600.
   [7]   [1998] 2 Lloyd's Rep 600, 612.
   [8]   *British Dominions General Insurance Co Ltd v Duder* [1915] 2 KB 394, 402–403.
   [9]   *Balfour v Beaumont* [1984] 1 Lloyd's Rep 272, 274, per Donaldson MR; *Youell v Bland Welch & Co Ltd* [1992] 2 Lloyd's Rep 127, 131, per Staughton LJ; *Wasa International Insurance Co v Lexington Insurance Co* [2010] 1 AC 180, [2009] 2 Lloyd's Rep 508.

Ltd v Sea Insurance Co Ltd[10] the reinsurance did not have to respond to the insurance because the vandalism for which the insurers had indemnified the insured port authority had occurred outside the policy period in the reinsurance. The importance of the period of cover was emphasized by Hobhouse LJ:

> It is wrong in principle to distort or disregard the terms of the reinsurance contracts in order to make them fit in with what may be a different position under the original cover…When the relevant cover is placed on a time basis, the stated period of time is fundamental and must be given effect to. It is for that period of risk that the premium payable is assessed. This is so whether the cover is defined as in the present case by reference to when the physical loss or damage occurred, or by reference to when a liability was incurred or a claim made. Contracts of insurance (including reinsurance) are or can be sophisticated instruments containing a wide variety of provisions, but the definition of the period of cover is basic and clear. It provides a temporal limit to the cover and does not provide cover outside that period; the insurer is not then 'on risk'.[11]

The leading authority on the need to prove the occurrence of loss during the **4.07** period of the reinsurance contract is *Wasa International Insurance Co v Lexington Insurance Co*.[12] The underlying property damage insurance policy with a term of three years from 1977 offered cover up to US$20 million any one occurrence. There was no choice of law clause, but there was a US service of suit clause. The reinsurance slip also expressly provided cover for the same three years. It had a full reinsurance clause which 'warranted same gross rate, terms and conditions as and to follow the settlements of the Company' but was governed (impliedly) by English law. The insured sued Lexington in the State of Washington which decided that the law of Pennsylvania must be applied in construing the insurance contract. The Washington Supreme Court found that as some portion of property damage occurred during the insured years (although the pollution started in the 1940s) the insurer was liable for the whole of the loss including pollution damage which occurred before the policy inception. Therefore the insurance contract was construed, in accordance with its applicable law, to cover loss outside the three years of express cover. Lexington paid US$103 million, but its reinsurers refused to indemnify Lexington on the basis that the reinsurance, as a matter of English law, only covered property damage during the period of cover stipulated in the reinsurance. The House of Lords agreed. The reinsurance contract provided different cover to the insurance contract as English law applied and under English law the reinsurance covered only damage to property occurring during the period of the cover.[13] There was no need for the reinsurance to respond in the same way as the insurance

---

[10] [1998] Lloyd's Rep IR 421.

[11] [1998] Lloyd's Rep IR 421, 435–436; cited with approval by Lord Collins in para 77 of *Wasa International Insurance Co v Lexington Insurance Co* [2010] 1 AC 180, [2009] 2 Lloyd's Rep 508.

[12] [2010] 1 AC 180, [2009] 2 Lloyd's Rep 508.

[13] [2010] 1 AC 180, [2009] 2 Lloyd's Rep 508, para 39. It was said to be a basic principle of property insurance law, that the insurer is liable for a loss actually sustained from a peril insured against during the continuance of the risk: *Knight v Faith* (1850) 15 QB 649.

as a contract of reinsurance was one in which the reinsurer reinsured the property that was the subject of the primary insurance and was not a contract under which the reinsurers agreed to indemnify the reinsured in relation to any liability that it might incur under the primary policy. A reinsured must therefore establish both its liability under the terms of the insurance and its entitlement to indemnity under the terms of the reinsurance. There may be a strong presumption under a proportional facultative reinsurance that it was co-extensive with the insurance, but it depends on the wording of the reinsurance.[14]

B. Obligation to Follow any Judgment Entered Against the Reinsured

4.08 In *Commercial Union Co v NRG Victory Reinsurance Ltd*[15] Potter LJ said that 'it would be quite impracticable, productive of endless dispute, and against the presumed intention of the contract of insurance (absent contrary or special provision of a kind which does not exist in this case) for an English Court trying a dispute concerning the reinsurer's liability not to treat the judgment of a foreign court as to the reinsured's original liability as decisive and binding, save within the most circumscribed limits'.[16] The same reasoning would be applicable to domestic judgments and arbitration awards obtained against the reinsured by the underlying insured.

4.09 Potter LJ rejected the reinsurer's argument that the decision of a court should be no more than evidence, albeit in many cases conclusive evidence, of the occurrence of a loss through the operation of an insured peril which ultimately falls to be determined by the court deciding the dispute as to the liability of the reinsurer to the reinsured.

4.10 He said that, absent any provision to contrary effect, there is an implied term in a contract of reinsurance that the reinsurer will treat the decision of a foreign court as to the liability of the reinsured to his underlying insured as binding, subject only to reversal on appeal and the following limits: (1) the foreign court must (in the eyes of the domestic court) be a court of competent jurisdiction; (2) judgment should not have been obtained in breach of an exclusive jurisdiction clause or other clause by which the underlying insured was contractually excluded from proceeding in the foreign court; (3) the reinsured took all proper defences; and (4) the judgment was not manifestly perverse.

4.11 As is clear from the passage in the judgment set out at para 4.08, Potter LJ was clearly concerned by the practical implications of allowing the issue of the reinsured's

---

[14] [2010] 1 AC 180, [2009] 2 Lloyd's Rep 508, para 116.
[15] [1998] 2 Lloyd's Rep 600, 610–611.
[16] [1998] 2 Lloyd's Rep 600, 610.

liability to be re-litigated. However, his conclusion (which was obiter) constitutes a relaxation of the requirement that the reinsured should prove the loss in the same manner as the underlying insured must have proved it against them and a restriction on the reinsurer's right to raise all the defences which were open to the reinsured against the underlying insured and has been doubted.[17]

C. Loss Settlements Clauses

Insurers have over the years sought (with varying degrees of success) to relieve themselves of the responsibility of proving that they were as a matter of fact liable to their underlying insured and of proving the quantum of such liability by inserting in policies of reinsurance a clause requiring the reinsurer to follow the settlements or fortunes of the reinsured.   **4.12**

D. Follow the Settlements

The effect of a clause binding reinsurers to 'follow the settlements' of the reinsured is that the reinsurers are obliged to indemnify the reinsured in the event that they settle a claim by their underlying insured provided that the claim as recognized by them falls within the risks covered by the policy of reinsurance as a matter of law, and provided also that in settling the claim, the reinsured has acted honestly and has taken all proper and businesslike steps in making the settlement.[18] As Lord Mance said:[19]   **4.13**

> ...an insurer seeking indemnity under a reinsurance must, in the absence of special terms, establish both its liability under the terms of the insurance and its entitlement to indemnity under the terms of the reinsurance. In practice, the former task is eased by express terms in a proportional reinsurance: originally, these took the form of a provision 'to be paid as may be paid', but courts gave this a limited interpretation which confined it to questions of quantum, so that it would only assist insurers once they had proved that they had some liability to their insured; there thus developed 'follow the settlements' clauses or the 'full reinsurance' clause appearing in the present reinsurance. As interpreted by the Court of Appeal,[20] the effect of these clauses is to bind the reinsurer to follow settlements of the insurer

---

[17] *Re London County Commercial Reinsurance Office Ltd* [1922] 2 Ch 67, 80. The existence or necessity of the implied term was not obvious to Saville J in *Hayter v Nelson and Home Insurance Co* [1990] 2 Lloyd's Rep 265, 271. For the doubts about this, see *Wasa International Insurance Co v Lexington Insurance Co* [2010] 1 AC 180, [2009] 2 Lloyd's Rep 508, para 37 per Lord Mance.

[18] *Insurance Co of Africa v Scor (UK) Reinsurance Co Ltd* [1985] 1 Lloyd's Rep 312, 330 per Goff LJ and 334 per Fox LJ.

[19] In *Wasa International Insurance Co v Lexington Insurance Co* [2010] 1 AC 180, [2009] 2 Lloyd's Rep 508, para 35.

[20] *Insurance Co of Africa v Scor (UK) Reinsurance Co Ltd* [1985] 1 Lloyd's Rep 312.

(whether made by admission or compromise or, as in the *Scor* case itself, following a judgment against the insurer). The Court of Appeal in the *Scor* case identified two provisos: the first, that the claim so recognised falls within the risk covered by the policy of reinsurance and, the second, that the insurers acted honestly and took all proper and business-like steps in making the settlement.

4.14   The starting point is that a reinsurer is not liable to pay the reinsured until the amount of the reinsured's liability has been ascertained by judgment, award or settlement.[21] The fact that the reinsured has paid under the underlying insurance policy does not enable the reinsured to substantiate its claims against the reinsurer.[22] Subject to any provision to the contrary in the reinsurance policy the reinsured, in order to recover from the reinsurer, must prove the loss in the same manner as the original insured must have proved it against the reinsured, and the reinsurer can raise all defences which were open to the reinsured against the original assured.[23] Where a reinsured seeks to recover under a policy of reinsurance, the reinsurer cannot be held liable unless the loss falls within the cover of the policy reinsured and within the cover created by the reinsurance.[24] The effect of a clause binding reinsurers to follow settlements of the reinsured is that the reinsurer agrees to indemnify the reinsured in the event that the reinsured settles any claim by their assured (whether by admission or compromise) provided that the claim falls within the risks covered by the policy of reinsurance as a matter of law and that in settling the claim the reinsured has acted honestly and has taken all proper and business-like steps in reaching the settlement.[25]

4.15   *Hill v Mercantile & General Reinsurance Co plc*[26] addresses the proper analysis of the two provisos in a double proviso follow the settlements clause. The first proviso is that settlements of losses by the insurer must be within the terms and conditions of the original policies. The second proviso is that they must be within the terms and conditions of the reinsurance. Lord Mustill said:[27]

> There are only two rules, both obvious. First, that the reinsurer cannot be held liable unless the loss falls within the cover of the policy reinsured and within the cover created by the reinsurer. Second, that the parties are free to agree on ways of proving whether these requirements are satisfied. Beyond this, all problems come from the efforts of those in the market to strike a workable balance between conflicting practical demands and then to express the balance in words.

---

[21] *Versicherungs and Transport A/G Daugava* v *Henderson* (1934) 49 Ll L Rep 252, 254 per Scrutton LJ.

[22] For a helpful summary of the principles see Cresswell J in *CGU International Insurance plc v Astra Zeneca Insurance Co Ltd* [2006] Lloyd's Rep IR 409, paras 95–98 cited with approval by Gloster J in *English and American Insurance Co Ltd v Axa Re SA* [2007] Lloyd's Rep IR 359.

[23] *Re London County Commercial Re-Insurance Office Ltd* (1992) 10 Ll L Rep 370, 371.

[24] *Hill v Mercantile and General Reinsurance Co plc* [1996] 1 WLR 1239, 1251.

[25] *Insurance Co of Africa v Scor (UK) Reinsurance Co Ltd* [1985] 1 Lloyd's Rep 312, 330.

[26] [1996] 1 AC 1239.

[27] [1996] 1 AC 1239, 1251F.

Lord Mustill did not address what the standard of proof was upon the insurer to **4.16** establish compliance with the first and second provisos. Gross J in *Equitas Ltd v R & Q Reinsurance Co (UK) Ltd*[28] concluded that compliance with both provisos had to be proved on the balance of probabilities. He said:

> *Hill v Mercantile* essentially stands as authority for the proposition that the Settlements Clause requires the insurer/reinsured to satisfy both provisos...or, in other words, to satisfy Lord Mustill's 'first rule'. The burden is on the insurer/ reinsurer to do so, to a standard of a balance of probabilities. This issue is one of law, so that if the insurer/reinsurer fails to satisfy either or both provisos...the reinsurer/retrocessionnaire will not be liable.

On that basis he held that a reinsurer was entitled to use actuarial models to prove **4.17** losses sustained under contracts of retrocessional excess of loss reinsurance written within the London Market Excess of Loss spiral. The LMX market had initially wrongly aggregated a number of large losses and included some irrecoverable losses. The reinsurer proved its losses, on the balance of probabilities, by applying actuarial modelling techniques to the spiral to strip out the wrongly aggregated or irrecoverable elements, leaving a minimum recoverable amount properly due under each of the reinsurance contracts. The retrocessionaires' argument that the reinsurer had to prove more specifically that the sums claimed were properly due was rejected. The modelled output permitted conclusions to be drawn, with confidence and to the requisite standard of proof, as to the recoverable losses for each syndicate. They provided answers that were representative of the actual position.

Lord Mustill pointed out in *Hill v Mercantile & General Reinsurance Co plc*[29] the **4.18** conflict between avoiding the investigation of the same issues twice (and a second investigation by a disadvantaged reinsurer) and ensuring that the reinsurer's bargain is not eroded by an agreement over which he has had no control. This conflict is not problematic when the insurance and the reinsurance are on the same terms (participatory reinsurance or facultative reinsurance with a large retention) as the interests of the insurers and the reinsurers are broadly the same. It is not imprudent for the reinsurers to put themselves in the hands of the reinsured for the settlement of claims. However problems arise where the terms of the policies are not the same.[30]

In *Aegis Electrical and Gas International Services Ltd v Continental Casualty Co*[31] the **4.19** reinsurance contained an exclusion in respect of explosion. The reinsured argued (citing *Scor*)[32] that as they had settled the claim on the basis that the proximate

---

[28] [2010] Lloyd's Rep IR 600.
[29] [1996] 1 AC 1239.
[30] He gave the example of 'constructive total loss' cases like *Chippendale v Holt* (1895) 1 Com Cas 197, where a claim under the direct policy does not require the determination of issues which are crucial to liability under the reinsurance. That was also the case in *Hill v Mercantile* itself where the loss fell within the direct contracts, but not necessarily within the reinsurances.
[31] [2008] Lloyd's Rep IR 17.
[32] *Insurance Co of Africa v Scor (UK) Reinsurance Co Ltd* [1985] 1 Lloyd's Rep 312.

cause was not explosion, the follow the settlements clause meant that the reinsurer was confined to arguing that upon that factual basis, the loss, as a matter of law, did not fall within the reinsurance cover. The follow the settlements clause provided that the reinsurer should follow the 'settlements of the original policy wording as far as applicable hereto'. The reinsured's argument was rejected, obiter, by Andrew Smith J holding that *Scor* concerned back-to-back reinsurance, where the reinsurers agreed that if the reinsured settled a claim, the reinsurers would not dispute the settlement provided it was made honestly and in a proper and businesslike manner. In such a case, they implicitly agreed not to challenge the factual basis for it. He found that where reinsurance was not back-to-back it does not follow from the fact that a loss falls within the original cover that it falls within the reinsurance and the natural meaning of the qualification 'as far as applicable hereto' is that the follow the settlement provision applied when the risk is one covered by the reinsurance. The reinsurer had agreed to follow settlements, not the basis of settlements or the reinsured's reasons for settlements.

(1) Burden of Proof

4.20 Provided the reinsured can establish (a) that it has paid its underlying insured; and (b) that its claim against the reinsurer falls within the reinsurance policy, the burden of proof lies on the reinsurer to displace the reinsured's right to rely on the 'follow the settlements' clause, ie to prove an absence of good faith or the fact that the settlement was not made in a businesslike fashion.[33] In this regard, a reinsurer has a right to require the reinsured to provide him with information and documents showing that the claim was made and how it was handled and settled.[34]

4.21 Thus the proof on the balance of probabilities is that the original claim (ie the arguable claim as accepted by compromise), fell within the terms of the insurance. This is reinforced by the words of Tuckey LJ who said:[35]

> . . . the reinsurer cannot require the insurer to prove that the assured's claim was in fact covered by the original policy, but requires him to show that the basis upon which he settled it was one which fell within the terms of the reinsurance as a matter of law or arguably did so.

(2) Risks Covered by the Reinsurance Policy

4.22 A reinsurer is only required to 'follow the settlements' of claims which, as a matter of law, fall within the policy of reinsurance. In determining whether a claim, as a matter of law, is covered where coverage is back-to-back, the court is concerned

---

[33] *Charman v Guardian Royal Exchange Assurance Plc* [1992] 2 Lloyd's Rep 607, 613; *Gan Insurance Co Ltd v Tai Ping Insurance Co Ltd (No 2)* [2001] Lloyd's Rep IR 667, 676.
[34] *Charman v Guardian Royal Exchange Assurance Plc* [1992] 2 Lloyd's Rep 607, 614. See also para 3.66.
[35] *Assicurazioni Generali SpA v CGU International Insurance plc* [2004] Lloyd's Rep IR 457.

with the basis on which the claim has been settled (which may not necessarily be the same as the underlying insured's original formulation of the claim). The reinsured must prove that the claim was disposed of by admission or compromise on a basis which, if and assuming it to be valid, falls or arguably falls within the risks covered by the contract of reinsurance as a matter of law.[36]

In *Assicurazioni Generali SpA v CGU International Insurance Plc*,[37] Gavin Kealey   **4.23** QC (sitting as a Deputy High Court Judge), at first instance, said:

> ...the identification of the loss, the circumstances in which it came to occur, the causes of it, whether and how particular terms of the contract of insurance which could impact upon its recoverability were considered, might all be matters relevant to the identification of the real basis on which the claim was settled; and thus to ascertaining whether the claim recognized by the insurers, when by admission or compromise they came to settle it, falls within the reinsurance as a matter of law.[38]

A claim may fall outside the risks covered by a contract of reinsurance, as a matter   **4.24** of law, even if it falls within the risks covered by the insurance, if there are limitations on the extent of the reinsurance cover provided, for example, if it falls outwith the chronological and geographical extent of the reinsurance policy, the types of casualty insured under the reinsurance, the boundaries of the reinsured layer, the mode of calculating the loss and any exclusion clauses contained in the contract of reinsurance.[39]

However, as regards limitations on cover in the original insurance that were applic-   **4.25** able equally to the reinsurance, in *Assicurazioni Generali SpA*, Gavin Kealey QC said[40] that if, for example, the reinsured had considered the application of an exclusion clause and determined both on the facts and on the law that it did not apply or arguably did not apply to exclude the loss, the real basis on which the claim will have been recognized in those circumstances will have been that the loss was not excluded. Therefore the claim so recognized would fall within the risks covered by the contract of reinsurance as a matter of law, and save for the purpose of challenging the businesslike nature of the settlement, the reinsurers would not be entitled to re-open the issue.[41]

---

[36] *Assicurazioni Generali SpA v CGU International Insurance Plc* [2004] Lloyd's Rep IR 457, 464.
[37] *Assicurazioni Generali SpA v CGU International Insurance Plc* [2003] Lloyd's Rep IR 725.
[38] *Assicurazioni Generali SpA v CGU International Insurance Plc* [2003] Lloyd's Rep IR 725, 737.
[39] See para 4.12f.
[40] *Assicurazioni Generali SpA v CGU International Insurance Plc* [2003] Lloyd's Rep IR 725, 738.
[41] The Court of Appeal, whilst approving the principle that the reinsured need only show that the claim as accepted arguably fell within the contract of reinsurance, declined to comment on the correctness of the judge's hypothetical examples. It noted that the parties disputed the application of the judge's conclusions to the examples he gave. However, it deemed it unwise for it 'to be drawn into controversy about the application of principle to hypothetical facts': *Assicurazioni Generali SpA v CGU International Insurance Plc* [2004] Lloyd's Rep IR 457, 464–465.

4.26 Similarly, in *Hiscox v Outhwaite (No 3)* Evans J said that a reinsurer may well be bound to follow the insurer's settlement of a claim which arguably, as a matter of law, is within the scope of the original insurance, regardless of whether the court might hold, if the issue was fully argued before it, that as a matter of law the claim would have failed.[42]

4.27 If, however, there was no dispute, or could not have been any realistic dispute, that the losses in question did not fall within the risks covered or if the reinsured waived reliance on, for example, an exclusion clause or overlooked its existence, the reinsurer will not be precluded from disputing its liability on the basis that the claim so recognized by the reinsured did not fall within the risks covered by the contract of reinsurance as a matter of law.[43]

4.28 Lord Mance in *Wasa International Insurance Co v Lexington Insurance* Co[44] cited *Assicurazioni Generali* as authority for how the principle in the *Scor* case might apply when the relevant terms of the insurance and reinsurance are identical and in particular how the second proviso applied to an insurer who, acting honestly and taking all proper and businesslike steps, settled an insurance claim under insurance terms which were identical to those of the reinsurance. He confirmed that the insurer remained obliged to show that the basis on which the claim had been settled was 'one which fell within the terms of the reinsurance as a matter of law or arguably did so'.[45] Lord Mance said that the last three words must be read in the context of that case, where the insurance and reinsurance incorporated materially identical terms with materially identical effect (and the issue was whether and on what basis the facts fell within such terms). He questioned whether they could apply in the *Wasa* case where the like terms in the insurance and reinsurance had different effects due to the application of different governing laws.

4.29 A reinsurer may not be bound by its reinsured's determination of the scope and application of the insurance policy if the follow the settlements clause is qualified. For example, in *Hill v Mercantile and General Reinsurance Co Plc*[46] the relevant clause provided that settlements were to be binding on the reinsurers only 'providing that such settlements are within the terms and conditions of the original policies and/or contracts and within the terms and conditions of this reinsurance'. The House of Lords held that the effect of the proviso was to prevent 'even an honest and conscientious appraisal of the legal implications of the facts embodied in an agreement between parties down the chain to impose on the reinsurers risks

---

[42] [1991] 2 Lloyd's Rep 524, 530. This passage from the judgment of Evans J was cited with approval by the Court of Appeal in *Assicurazioni Generali SpA v CGU International Insurance Plc* [2004] Lloyd's Rep IR 457, 464.

[43] *Assicurazioni Generali SpA v CGU International Insurance Plc* [2003] Lloyd's Rep IR 725.

[44] [2010] 1 AC 180, [2009] 2 Lloyd's Rep 508.

[45] Per Tuckey LJ at para 18.

[46] [1996] LRLR 341.

beyond those which they have undertaken and those which the reinsured have undertaken'.[47]

(3) Ex Gratia Payments

A 'settlement' is a concluded agreement between the original insurer and its insured **4.30** that cannot be reconsidered at a later stage by the parties and it does not need any particular formality.[48] It would include a 'without prejudice' settlement made without admission of liability on the part of the insurer under the underlying policy to indemnify the insured. However an 'ex gratia' settlement is one where there is a payment of money by the insurer to the insured where there was no liability under the policy to indemnify him.[49] Sometimes payments are made by the reinsured to its underlying insured in circumstances where it is under no obligation to do so (perhaps for commercial reasons). Reinsurers are however entitled to insist that the reinsured must prove that there was liability under the original policy.[50] And whether such ex gratia payments will be covered by a follow the settlements clause will depend on its express terms. Unless the clause refers to ex gratia payments, the reinsurer will not be obliged by a 'follow the settlements' clause to indemnify the reinsured in respect of such settlements, however reasonable and businesslike the payments may have been. In *Hiscox v Outhwaite (No 3)*[51] a 'follow the settlements' clause that did encompass ex gratia payments was held not to extend to payments into a facility that included non-insureds amongst its beneficiaries.

The addition to a 'follow the settlements' clause of a specific exclusion in respect of **4.31** without prejudice and ex gratia settlements has been held to indicate to the reinsured that if it is not prepared to make any admission of liability when entering into the settlement, it must prove that it was liable in order to recover under the reinsurance, the rationale for the exclusion being that it was an encouragement to the reinsured to give proper and businesslike consideration to its liability to the underlying insured and to act honestly in settling the claim.[52] If all that was done, there was no reason not to admit liability to that extent and thereby come within the ambit of the follow the settlements clause.

---

[47] [1996] LRLR 341, 351 per Lord Mustill.

[48] *Faraday Capital Ltd v Copenhagen Reinsurance Co Ltd* [2007] Lloyd's Rep IR 23, para 45.

[49] For the distinction between without prejudice and ex gratia settlements, see *Faraday Capital Ltd v Copenhagen Reinsurance Co Ltd* [2007] Lloyd's Rep IR 23, para 46 applying the dicta of Gavin Kealey QC in *Assicurazioni Generali SpA v CGU International Insurance Plc* [2003] Lloyd's Rep IR 725.

[50] *Faraday Capital Ltd v Copenhagen Reinsurance Co Ltd* [2007] Lloyd's Rep IR 23.

[51] [1991] 2 Lloyd's Rep 524.

[52] *Faraday Capital Ltd v Copenhagen Reinsurance Co Ltd* [2007] Lloyd's Rep IR 23, paras 46 and 47. The settlement between Faraday and Nevada Power was held to fall within the definition of 'Without Prejudice... Settlement'. The settlement agreement was made on the basis that there was no admission by the insurers of the existence of any liability to indemnify the insured under the terms and conditions of the underlying policy.

(4) Proper and Businesslike Steps

4.32   A reinsured does not discharge its businesslike obligation simply by appointing a competent loss adjuster. The reinsured's obligation extends to the conduct of its loss adjusters and any other agents it employs for the purpose of making the settlement. Thus to comply with the businesslike obligation the reinsured is under an obligation to appoint its loss adjusters in a businesslike way, its loss adjusters must then adjust the claim in a businesslike way and the reinsured must then settle the claim in a businesslike manner.[53]

4.33   Mance LJ in *Gan Insurance Ltd v Tai Ping Insurance Co Ltd (No 2)*[54] said that in reaching a 'proper and businesslike settlement' the insurer must have regard to the prospects and risks attaching to the claim as a whole, ie it cannot settle a claim without real regard to its merits simply because it will be covered by reinsurance.

4.34   It has been held that the reinsured is not relieved of the businesslike obligation even where the 'follow the settlements' clause is followed by the words 'whether liable or not liable'[55] or 'without question'.[56] Similarly in *Hiscox v Outhwaite (No 3)* the clause made the insurers' settlements 'in every respect … unconditionally binding', but the requirement was still held to apply. This is not to say that it would be impossible to draft a clause which excluded the obligation, but clear words would be required to do so.[57]

(5) Fraudulent Claim

4.35   The obligation to follow settlements extends to settlement of a fraudulent claim. If the reinsured has settled a claim, acting honestly and in a proper and businesslike manner, then the fact that the reinsurer may thereafter be able to prove that the claim was fraudulent does not of itself entitle the reinsurer not to follow the settlement of the reinsured.[58]

4.36   The reinsurer may, however, have recourse to a right of subrogation, arising upon payment of the claim under the policy of reinsurance, in order to seek to rescind the settlement with the underlying insured and to recover the money paid by the insurers under the settlement.

(6) Commutation Agreements

4.37   A commutation is an agreement between a reinsurer and his reinsured under which the reinsured releases the reinsurer from all further liability under the reinsurance

---

[53]   *Charman v GRE Assurance Plc* [1992] 2 Lloyd's Rep 607, 612.
[54]   [2001] Lloyd's Rep IR 667, 691.
[55]   *Charman v GRE Assurance Plc* [1992] 2 Lloyd's Rep 607, 612.
[56]   *Assicurazioni Generali SpA v CGU International Insurance Plc* [2004] Lloyd's Rep IR 457, 465.
[57]   *Assicurazioni Generali SpA v CGU International Insurance Plc* [2004] Lloyd's Rep IR 457, 465 per Tuckey LJ.
[58]   *Insurance Co of Africa v Scor (UK) Reinsurance Co Ltd* [1985] 1 Lloyd's Rep 312.

policy in consideration for a specified payment. The release will often apply not only to claims which have already been made and paid by the reinsured (accrued claims) but also to claims which have been notified to the reinsured but had yet to become payable by the reinsured (outstanding claims) or are believed to have been incurred but have not been reported (IBNRs).

An interesting but as yet unresolved issue is whether a retrocessionaire is bound **4.38** to indemnify a reinsurer under a retrocession agreement which contains a 'follow the settlements' clause, in respect of sums paid by the reinsurer in commutation of outstanding claims and/or IBNRs, ie claims in respect of which, at the time of the commutation, the loss (if any) has not yet crystallized.

The issue was considered by the High Court of Singapore in *Overseas Union* **4.39** *Insurance Ltd v Home and Overseas Insurance Co Ltd*.[59] The judge expressed the obiter view that a retrocessionaire is not bound, by a 'follow the settlements' clause, to indemnify the reinsurer in respect of sums paid under a commutation agreement whether it includes IBNRs or not. He said a commutation agreement is not a settlement within the meaning of the clause, 'it is a separate agreement over and above a reinsurance contract'.[60] While accepting that a commutation agreement does, in a sense, include the settlement of losses he said the reasons for settlement are quite different to a normal settlement because the reinsurer has another priority besides merely settling the individual losses. Accordingly a reinsurer may be prepared to pay a premium over and above what it would otherwise have agreed to in the usual settlement of the loss. The judge concluded that as the commutation agreement is entered into to serve the reinsurer's own purpose he cannot impose such an agreement on the retrocessionaire unilaterally.

The judge noted that if the reinsurer takes the position that it did not take into **4.40** account any consideration other than the settlement of the loss, then it is open to him to make his claim against his retrocessionaire on the basis that he has settled a loss rather than on the basis of the commutation agreement. This will be difficult where the 'losses' which were settled included claims the value of which was still uncertain at the date of the commutation agreement.

If this view is correct, the reinsurer who wishes to bind his retrocessionaire by enter- **4.41** ing into a commutation agreement will need to provide for such an eventuality in the retrocession agreement or involve the retrocessionaire in his negotiations with the reinsured for a commutation agreement and try and obtain the retrocessionaire's agreement.[61] In view of the potential problems, great care is necessary in structuring commutation arrangements in such a way as to enhance the prospects of recovery.

---

[59] [2002] 4 SLR 104.
[60] [2002] 4 SLR 104, 116, but see *IRB Resseguros SA v CX Reinsurance Co Ltd* [2010] Lloyd's Rep IR 560 where an arbitral tribunal decided that a follow settlements clause covered an insurance policy buyback which included future potential claims.
[61] As suggested by Evans J in *Hiscox v Outhwaite (No 3)* [1991] 2 Lloyd's Rep 524, 532.

(7) Effect of a Claims Co-operation Clause

4.42   In *Scor* the Court of Appeal considered the effect on a 'follow the settlements' clause of a claims co-operation clause which provided that 'no settlement shall be made without the approval' of the reinsurer. Goff LJ concluded that:

> In my judgment the undertaking by the insurers not to make a settlement without the prior approval of reinsurers must have been intended to circumscribe the powers of the insurers to make settlements binding upon reinsurers, so that reinsurers would only be bound to follow a settlement when it had received their approval...This effectively emasculates the follow the settlements clause, but it is nevertheless, in my judgment, what the parties to a policy in this form have agreed.[62]

4.43   If the claims co-operation clause is a condition precedent[63] to the reinsurer's liability under the contract of reinsurance then, in the event of non-compliance with the clause, the reinsurer will not be liable to indemnify the reinsured even if it can prove that the claim paid by it fell within the original insurance policy.[64] If, as in *Scor*, the reinsurer's approval of any settlement is not a condition precedent, it will be open to the insurer to recover under the contract of reinsurance by proving its legal liability under the original insurance to the underlying insured.

4.44   In *Eagle Star Insurance Co Ltd v JN Cresswell*[65] the claims co-operation clause provided that the reinsured agreed that the reinsurers:

> ...shall control the negotiations and settlements of any claims under this Policy. In this event the Underwriters [Reinsurers] hereon will not be liable to pay any claim not controlled as set out above.

At first instance, Morison J stated that a condition precedent needs to be clearly spelt out and that therefore this claims co-operation clause was not a condition precedent to the reinsurer's liability to the reinsured. This conclusion was reversed on appeal. Longmore LJ said:[66]

> The question then arises whether it is a condition precedent to reinsurers' liability that the opportunity to control negotiations or settlements should be afforded to them. The answer to this question is 'Yes', because the clause says in terms that in the event of there being negotiations or settlements reinsurers will not be liable to pay any claim not controlled by them. The judge was able to avoid this conclusion by (*inter alia*) pointing out the clause did not use the term 'condition precedent' as such, whereas the deleted clause did use that term. As to that, it is not essential that the very words 'condition precedent' be used to achieve the result that reinsurers will not be liable unless a certain event happens. Other words can be used, if they are clear. Other words have been used which in my view are clear.

---

[62]   [1985] 1 Lloyd's Rep 312, 331. Fox LJ reached the same conclusion at 334.
[63]   On condition precedents generally see paras 6.58 et seq.
[64]   *Gan Insurance Co Ltd v Tai Ping Insurance Co Ltd (No 2)* [2001] Lloyd's Rep IR 667, 688; see also *Eagle Star Insurance Co Ltd v JN Cresswell* [2004] Lloyd's Rep IR 537.
[65]   [2004] Lloyd's Rep IR 537.
[66]   *Eagle Star Insurance Co Ltd v JN Cresswell* [2004] Lloyd's Rep IR 537, 544.

Rix LJ noted that whilst the words 'condition precedent' were absent, the language **4.45** of 'will not be liable to pay any claim' were strong words, 'if not the language of condition precedent, at any rate the language of exclusion'.[67] Consequently, unless some reason[68] was shown for excusing the fact that the reinsurers did not control the negotiations or settlement, the clause amounted to an exclusion of the reinsurer's liability to indemnify the reinsured.[69] The distinction between 'exclusion' and 'condition precedent' would appear to be semantic rather than substantive since in either case the reinsurer will not be obliged to indemnify the reinsured.

E. 'Pay as may be Paid Thereon'/'Pay as may be Paid Thereon and to Follow their Settlements'

Where the contract of reinsurance provides that the reinsurer is obliged to 'pay as **4.46** may be paid thereon' the reinsured is not relieved of its obligation to prove that the underlying claim fell as a matter of fact, as well as law, within the cover of the original policy.[70] The effect of this clause is that if the reinsured proves its liability under the original policy and has taken all proper and businesslike steps to have the amount of it fairly and carefully ascertained it will not have to prove the quantum of that liability: 'So long as liability exists, the mere fact of some honest mistake having occurred in fixing the exact amount of it would afford no excuse for not paying. He [the reinsurer] has promised to "pay as may be paid thereon".'[71]

The addition of the words 'and to follow their settlements' will have the effect of **4.47** precluding the reinsurer from requiring the reinsured to prove that it was in fact liable under the original policy.[72]

F. Follow the Fortunes

American authorities suggest that the inclusion of a clause requiring the reinsurer **4.48** to 'follow the fortunes' of its reinsured will have the same effect as a 'follow the settlements' clause.[73] Hoffmann, in his comparative analysis, notes that the American

---

[67] *Eagle Star Insurance Co Ltd v JN Cresswell* [2004] Lloyd's Rep IR 537, 548.

[68] eg, if the reinsurers simply refuse to exercise control there remains the argument of waiver; or if, while exercising or refusing to exercise control the reinsurers act in bad faith, capriciously or arbitrarily, that would be in breach of the implied term found by the majority in *Gan Insurance Co v Tai Ping Insurance Co (No 2)* [2001] Lloyd's Rep IR 667, 693, discussed at paras 5.42–5.44.

[69] [2004] Lloyd's Rep IR 537, 550.

[70] *Chippendale v Holt* (1895) 1 Com Cas 157.

[71] Per Bigham J in *Western Assurance Co of Toronto v Poole* [1903] 1 KB 376, 386.

[72] *Excess Insurance Co Ltd v Matthews* (1925) 23 Ll L Rep 71.

[73] WC Hoffmann, 'Common Law of Reinsurance Loss Settlement Clauses: A Comparative Analysis of the Judicial Rule Enforcing the Reinsurer's Contractual Obligation to Indemnify the Reinsured for Settlements' [1994] LMCLQ 47.

courts have developed a 'follow the fortunes doctrine' which is often applied even where the 'loss settlements' clause in question contains neither 'follow' nor 'fortune'.[74] He notes that the effect of these clauses is to bind the 'reinsurer generally by the reinsured's disposition of claims unless: (1) the settlement was for a loss that did not fall within the scope of the reinsurance or of the original insurance as a matter of law;[75] or (2) the reinsured settled the claim fraudulently, collusively or in bad faith; or (3) the reinsured failed to ascertain the loss by a proper investigation'.[76]

4.49   In *CGU International Insurance v Astrazeneca Insurance Co*[77] there was a follow the fortunes clause in the reinsurance which provided:

> The reinsurer agrees to follow in all respects the fortunes of the reinsured. Reinsurers hereunder will, however, have the right to and shall be given the opportunity to associate with the reinsured in the defence and control of any claim, suit or proceedings relative to any loss where the claim or suit involves or appears relatively likely to involve reinsurers hereunder.

The reinsurance was expressly governed by English law. The original policy was issued by an English captive to the English parent company of a group of companies but the insured group of companies had worldwide activities and included subsidiaries in the United States. There was a US service of suit for US claims. The reinsured settled a claim with one of the US subsidiaries by reference to its exposure to liability to the subsidiary under Iowa law, the law of the subsidiary's principal place of business, on the basis that if it had not settled it would have been successfully sued in Iowa under the service of suit clause. In circumstances where there was no judgment against the reinsured and the reinsured was seeking to require the reinsurer to follow its settlement without the benefit of a 'follow the settlements' clause, the 'follow the fortunes' clause was not relied upon by the reinsured as giving rise to a free-standing right to indemnity either at the original arbitration hearing or on appeal (as is recorded in the judgment on the appeal). However, the 'follow the fortunes' clause was relevant to the reasoning of the majority of the arbitration panel, being the lay arbitrators. They held (applying their commercial experience) that where, as in the case before them, the terms of the direct policy were incorporated into the reinsurance, the extent of the reinsurers' obligations to the reinsured was to be construed as having the same meaning as that in the direct policy, the presence of the 'follow the fortunes' clause in the reinsurance was a factor reinforcing this conclusion and the inclusion of such a clause made little sense

---

[74]   An example is *American Insurance Co v North American Co for Property and Casualty Insurance* 697 F 2d 79 where the 'follow the fortunes' clause provided that 'all claims involving this reinsurance, when settled by the company, shall be binding on the reinsurer'.

[75]   See *American Insurance Co v North American Co for Property and Casualty Insurance* 697 F 2d 79 where it was held that the 'follow the fortunes' clause only bound the reinsurer to pay when the reinsured settled a claim covered by the underlying policy and not when the reinsured made ex gratia payments outside the scope of the policy.

[76]   Hoffmann, n 43, at 55.

[77]   [2006] Lloyd's Rep IR 409.

if reinsurers could rely on English law to assert that they were not liable to provide an indemnity under the reinsurance. On appeal, Cresswell J held that the scope of cover under the original insurance and under the reinsurance was governed by English law and that this could not be variable according to the circumstances of a particular claim against a particular insured. He agreed with the dissenting arbitrator that if the scope of cover under the reinsurance was to vary depending on (1) the identity of the insured company, (2) the court in which the claim against the reinsured would have been pursued if not settled, and (3) the law which that court would have applied, that would not be 'back-to-back' reinsurance but 'back-to-front'. He held that such a conclusion would be contrary to English conflicts rules and would involve a commercially uncertain and unworkable answer.[78] The presence of the 'follow the fortunes' clause in the reinsurance did not dissuade him from that conclusion.

G. Diminution of the Loss

The extent of the reinsurer's obligation to indemnify its reinsured may be affected **4.50** by payments received by the reinsured from third parties. In *Merrett v Capitol Indemnity Corp*[79] the arbitrators found as a fact that the reinsured was entitled to recover from its reinsurer losses totalling around US$113,000. However, they disallowed the sum of US$45,000 which the reinsured had received from its brokers. The brokers had been under no legal obligation to pay the US$45,000 but had made this payment for their own commercial purpose, namely to save themselves work and to keep the reinsured's goodwill.

On appeal Steyn J held that, since the contracts of reinsurance are contracts of **4.51** indemnity, the critical question was whether the payment by the brokers diminished the loss.[80] Not every gift to a reinsured by his broker diminishes his loss. It is a question of fact in each case whether a gift has or has not been paid in diminution of the loss. Steyn J said that if it is established that the payment was intended solely for the benefit of the reinsured it will not have been paid in diminution of the loss. In *Merrett* the arbitrators had made primary findings of fact that the payment was made to retain the reinsured's goodwill and that the brokers expected to be reimbursed by the reinsurer. It followed inexorably that the payment was made solely for the benefit of the reinsured and not for the benefit of the reinsurer and therefore should have been disregarded in assessing the reinsured's recoverable loss.[81]

---

[78] *CGU International Insurance plc v AstraZeneca Insurance Co Ltd* [2006] Lloyd's Rep IR 409, para 128.
[79] [1992] LRLR 46.
[80] [1992] LRLR 46, 48.
[81] [1992] LRLR 46, 48.

H. Aggregation

4.52 The extent of the reinsurer's obligation to indemnify its reinsured will be affected by the wording of any aggregation clause contained in the policy. An aggregation clause enables two or more separate losses covered by the policy to be treated as a single loss for deductible or other purposes when they are linked by a unifying factor of some kind. Such a clause may assist a reinsured to pierce the limits of its deductible so as to call on his reinsurer; however, in the event that the reinsurance is limited, as is ordinarily the case, he runs the risk of exceeding the cover provided by the reinsurance. For example, a natural disaster may give rise to a large number of individual losses, some small, some large, which cumulatively (ie in aggregate) give rise to a very large total liability. Under an aggregation clause any excess or limit might fall, depending on the unifying factor, to be applied to the aggregate of the claims, not to the individual claims.[82]

4.53 In whose interests it will be to seek to aggregate losses will depend on the profile of the losses and the structure of the cover. For example, it will be in the reinsured's interests to aggregate a number of small claims, the individual value of which falls below the deductible; whilst it will be in the reinsurer's interests to aggregate a number of large claims if the reinsurance permits the payment of multiple limits of indemnity for separate losses.

4.54 The unifying factor is often a common origin in some act or event or cause, as specified by the aggregation clause. The choice of language by which the parties designate the unifying factor in an aggregation clause is very important. The more general the description of the unifying factor the wider the scope of the aggregation clause.[83] Examples of unifying factors commonly used are an 'event', 'occurrence', 'originating cause', and 'one source or original cause'.[84]

(1) One Event/One Occurrence

4.55 One of the narrower aggregation clauses used in the reinsurance market is 'Each and every loss or series[85] of losses *arising from one event*'. An 'event' is something which happens at a particular time, at a particular place, in a particular way.[86] A state of affairs or omission cannot constitute an event,[87] thus the lack of research

---

[82] For the reinsurance consequences of incorrect aggregation see *Equitas v R&Q Reinsurance* [2010] Lloyd's Rep IR 600.

[83] *Lloyds TSB General Insurance Holdings Ltd v Lloyds Bank Group Insurance Co Ltd* [2003] 4 All ER 43, 48 per Lord Hoffmann.

[84] Sometimes, there may simply be an overall aggregate limit on the deductible and/or the limit of indemnity, eg 'each and every loss or claim and in all in any one policy year'.

[85] To form part of a series there must be some connecting factor that links losses which would otherwise be separate: *Countryside Assured Group Plc v Marshall* [2003] Lloyd's Rep IR 195.

[86] *Axa Reinsurance (UK) Plc v Field* [1996] 1 WLR 1026, 1035G per Lord Mustill.

[87] *Scott v Copenhagen Reinsurance Co (UK) Ltd* [2003] Lloyd's Rep IR 696, 713.

of a Lloyd's underwriter was not an 'event' giving rise to losses under 32 separate policies which he had written on behalf of various syndicates. The relevant event from which each loss arose was the writing of the individual policies; there were, therefore, 32 events.[88] In the same vein, the installation of windows with a common defect was not an event where poor workmanship was to blame for various defects and the mistakes were not attributable to a single event such as giving faulty instructions [89]

The parties must ask themselves the question 'is there one event which should be **4.56** regarded as the cause of these losses so as to make it appropriate to regard these losses as constituting for the purposes of aggregation under this policy one loss?'[90] The event does not need to be the proximate or immediate cause of the loss but the causative link must be significant.[91] This link can be tested by reference to 'unities' such as locality, time, and the intentions of human agents.[92]

The 'unities' test was developed by Mr Kerr QC sitting as an arbitrator in *Dawson's* **4.57** *Field Arbitration Award*.[93] That award arose out of the hijacking of four aircraft in 1970 by members of the Popular Front for the Liberation of Palestine (PFLP). One was destroyed at Cairo and three at Dawson's Field. The question was whether the loss of the three aircraft at Dawson's Field arose out of 'one event'. Mr Kerr concluded that the planes were not lost when hijacked but when destroyed. If the hijacking had been the cause he said the losses could not be aggregated because the aircraft were hijacked by different persons in widely separate localities. However, he then said:

> In my view there was one occurrence, one event, one happening: the blowing up of three aircraft in close proximity, more or less simultaneously, within the time span of a few minutes, and as a result of a single decision to do so without anyone being able to approach the aircraft between the first explosion and their destruction.

In the absence of unity in time or place, unity of intent or central orchestration is **4.58** probably not sufficient. In *Mann v Lexington Insurance*[94] the deliberate orchestration

---

[88] *Scott v Copenhagen Reinsurance Co (UK) Ltd* [2003] Lloyd's Rep IR 696, 713. See also *Caudle v Sharp* [1995] LRLR 433. Cf the similar case of *Cox v Bankside* [1995] CLC 180 discussed at para 4.64.

[89] *Seele Austria GmbH & Co KG v Tokio Marine Europe Insurance Ltd* [2008] Lloyd's Rep IR 739.

[90] *Scott v Copenhagen Reinsurance Co (UK) Ltd* [2003] Lloyd's Rep IR 696, 714.

[91] *Scott v Copenhagen Reinsurance Co (UK) Ltd* [2003] Lloyd's Rep IR 696, 714.

[92] In *IRB Brasil Resseguros Sa v CX Reinsurance Co Ltd* [2010] Lloyd's Rep IR 560 Burton J upheld the arbitrators' award which had concluded that the determination of the insured each year to carry out its asbestos insulation installation activities was an annual aggregating event (applying *Axa Reinsurance (UK) Plc v Field* [1996] 1 WLR 1026) and met the test of unity in *Kuwait Airways Corporation v Kuwait Insurance Co SAK* [1996] 1 Lloyd's Rep 664 and that, in any event, as a finding of fact, in the context of the excess of loss of reinsurance written by IRB the claim was settled by CX Re as a single loss.

[93] *Dawson's Field Arbitration Award* (29 March 1972).

[94] [2001] 1 Lloyd's Rep 179.

of civil unrest by the government which resulted in riot damage to 22 supermarket stores in Jakarta was not sufficient for the total riot damage to constitute one occurrence.[95] Since the losses occurred at different locations over a wide area, at different times over two days, there was no unity in time or place. Relying on Mr Kerr's rejection of the orchestration of the hijackings as being a sufficiently unifying factor in *Dawson's Field*, Waller LJ doubted whether the riot damage could be said to have resulted from one occurrence. In *Kuwait Airways Corporation v Kuwait Insurance Co SAK*[96] Rix J, having reviewed the authorities, said that an 'occurrence' was not materially different from an 'event'.

(2) Originating Cause/One Source or Original Cause

4.59 A wider aggregation clause used by the market defines the relevant unifying factor by reference to the originating cause or original cause of the losses. In *Axa Reinsurance (UK) Plc v Field* Lord Mustill, in contrasting an 'originating cause' from an 'event', said:

> A cause is to my mind something altogether less constricted. It can be a continuing state of affairs; it can be the absence of something happening. Equally, the word 'originating' was in my view consciously chosen to open up the widest possible search for a unifying factor in the history of the losses which it is sought to aggregate.[97]

4.60 However, it is still necessary for there to be some causative link between the originating cause and the loss and there must also be some limit to the degree of remoteness that is acceptable.[98]

4.61 The wider scope of an 'originating cause'/'original cause' aggregation clause is demonstrated by the decision of the Court of Appeal in *Municipal Mutual Insurance Ltd v Sea Insurance Ltd*.[99] In that case a large piece of machinery had been left unguarded and unprotected on the dockside for some 18 months and was progressively stripped during that period by a number of individuals or groups acting independently of one another. Hobhouse LJ noted that if the relevant clause was an 'any one event' clause each act of pilferage or vandalism could be said to have been a distinct event. However, under the 'original cause' clause the losses fell to be aggregated because the acts of pilferage and vandalism which occurred over the 18-month period were a series of occurrences attributable to a single source or cause, namely the inadequacy of the port's system for protecting the goods of which it was bailee.

---

[95] The relevant clause provided for the aggregation of claims arising from 'any one occurrence'.
[96] [1996] 1 Lloyd's Rep 664, 686. In *Dawson's Field* Mr Kerr concluded that the two words were more or less interchangeable.
[97] [1996] 1 WLR 1026, 1035G.
[98] *American Centennial Insurance Co v Insco* [1996] LRLR 407, 414 per Moore-Bick J.
[99] [1998] Lloyd's Rep IR 421.

As Lord Hoffman commented in *Lloyds TSB General Insurance Holdings v Lloyds* **4.62**
Bank Group Insurance Co Ltd:[100]

> The more general the description of the act or event, the wider the scope of the
> clause. For example, in *Municipal Mutual*…the unifying clause was expressed in
> very general terms: '…all occurrences of a series consequent on or attributable to
> one source or original cause…' This meant that as long as one could find any act,
> event or state of affairs which could properly be described as a cause of more than
> one loss, they formed part of a series for the purposes of the aggregation clause.

Christopher Clarke J pointed out in *Beazley Underwriting v The Travelers Companies* **4.63**
Inc[101] the particular factors that led to this conclusion. He noted that the clause was
concerned with occurrences attributable to one source or original cause, which he
said involves a considerably looser causal connection than proximate cause. The
words 'attributable to' on their own could, he thought, import a test of proximate
cause.[102]

In *Cox v Bankside Members Agency Ltd*[103] the negligent approach to underwriting **4.64**
of a Lloyd's underwriter was held to be the 'originating cause' of the losses arising
from a number of separate policies he had written on behalf of various syndicates.[104]
However, the scope of the clause was not sufficiently wide to encompass the situation where a number of underwriters adopted the same negligent approach when
writing a number of separate policies. Since there were three underwriters there
were three originating causes. However, where several people reach a common
culpable misunderstanding as the result of discussions between them on which
they all subsequently act it might be possible, depending on the facts of the case, to
find in their discussions a single originating cause of the negligent acts.[105]

In *Countryside Assured Group Plc v Marshall*[106] the lack of proper training of the **4.65**
selling agents was held, on the assumed facts, to be the original cause of the pen-
sion mis-selling claims. The lack of training was a consistent and necessary factor
which allowed the mis-selling to occur. The activities of individual salesmen were
also causative but Morison J said that the aggregation clause entitled him to move
back and find a single source or original cause.

---

[100] [2003] Lloyd's Rep 623, paras 15 and 16.
[101] [2012] Lloyd's Rep IR 78.
[102] He referred on this point to *Corporation of the Royal Exchange Assurance Co v Kingsley
Navigation Co* [1923] AC 235, 244. He also noted that the strength of the causal connection required
in a clause can differ according to the context in which the question is asked. In *Beazley* the clause
was dealing with loss arising out of events attributable to or arising out of negligent acts. He noted
that if the loss did not arise out of the relevant event, the question of what the event is attributable
to did not arise.
[103] [1995] 2 Lloyd's Rep 437.
[104] [1995] 2 Lloyd's Rep 437, 455. This can be contrasted with the result in *Axa Reinsurance*,
discussed at para 4.59, where similar losses did not fall to be aggregated under an 'arising out of one
event' clause.
[105] *American Centennial Insurance Co v Insco* [1996] LRLR 407, 414 per Moore-Bick J.
[106] [2003] Lloyd's Rep IR 195.

(3) Binding the Reinsurer to the Reinsured's Determination on Aggregation

4.66 In *Brown (RE) v GIO Insurance Ltd*[107] the Court of Appeal considered the effect of the following two clauses in contracts of reinsurance:

> The Reassured shall be the sole judge as to what constitutes each and every loss and/or one event.
>
> The Reassured's definition of each and every loss and/or events shall be final and binding on the Reinsurers.

4.67 The Court held that the effect of the clauses was such as to leave to the reinsured, subject to considerations of good faith and reasonableness, the power to decide, in making a claim against his reinsurer, whether, as a matter of fact and construction of the reinsurance contract, losses arose from one or more events for the purpose of aggregation.

4.68 It is not sufficient for a reinsurer challenging the reinsured's decision to show that the decision was incorrect in law; he must go further and demonstrate that the reinsured asked himself the wrong question, ie that he misdirected himself in law.[108] Consequently, provided the reinsured has addressed his mind to the correct question, ie out of how many events did the losses arise, the reinsurer will be bound by his construction even if it turns out to have been wrong as a matter of law. However, Waller LJ was prepared to accept that if a decision was taken which was not even arguable, at the time the decision was made, then that would provide a basis for challenge on the grounds of reasonableness.[109]

(4) Different Aggregation Clauses in the Direct Insurance and Reinsurance Policies

4.69 In *Axa Reinsurance v Field*[110] the reinsured provided professional indemnity insurance for underwriting agents at Lloyd's; the reinsurer provided a layer of reinsurance for the reinsured. The reinsurance policy contained an 'arising out of one event' clause whereas the professional indemnity insurance contained an 'originating cause' clause. The underwriting agents were successfully sued for negligence and breach of contract arising out of the negligent underwriting of three syndicate underwriters and in other proceedings it was held that there were three originating causes under the professional indemnity policy. The question then arose whether, in aggregating claims for losses arising out of one event under the reinsurance policy, the parties were bound by the finding on the differently worded underlying insurance.

---

[107] [1998] Lloyd's Rep IR 201.
[108] [1998] Lloyd's Rep IR 201, 207 per Waller LJ, and 209, per Chadwick LJ.
[109] [1998] Lloyd's Rep IR 201, 207.
[110] [1996] 1 WLR 1026.

The Court of Appeal held that the test in the originating cause clause in the under- **4.70**
lying insurance was to be applied to the aggregation clause in the reinsurance policy in determining the common cause of losses which were to be aggregated for the
purposes of determining liability under the reinsurance policy. This decision was
overturned by the House of Lords. Lord Mustill, giving the leading speech, noted
that where a direct insurer took out reinsurance and both policies contained provisions enabling the amount of losses to be aggregated, it was not to be assumed that
the parties intended their effect to be the same. For example, if the reinsurer wrote
an excess of loss treaty for only a layer of the whole account of the reinsured rather
than providing proportionate reinsurance under which he shared the risk assumed
by the reinsured, the insurances were not in any real sense back-to-back and there
was no reason to assume that the clauses in both policies were intended to have the
same effect if they were expressed differently. Consequently the aggregation clauses
were to be construed separately and so a finding that certain losses arose from one
originating cause for the purpose of the direct insurance was not determinative of
the question whether those same losses had arisen out of one event for the purpose
of the reinsurance policy.[111]

(5) 'Conditions as underlying'

Similarly, in *Municipal Mutual Insurance Ltd v Sea Insurance Ltd* Hobhouse LJ **4.71**
stated that it was wrong in principle to distort or disregard the terms of the reinsurance contracts in order to make them fit in with what may be a different position
under the original cover.[112] The court, in that case, held that the words 'conditions
as underlying' cannot contradict either the period or limit provisions of a contract
of reinsurance.

In *Municipal Mutual* the discrepancy between the reinsured's inward and outward **4.72**
contracts was not so much in the wording but in the way the reinsured chose to
place and operate them. The reinsured chose to enter into distinct and independent
annual reinsurance contracts with different reinsurers, whereas in their dealings
with the underlying insured the reinsured chose effectively to disregard policy
years. The Court of Appeal held that it was incumbent upon the judge, in considering claims by the reinsured against different reinsurers in respect of losses alleged to
have been incurred over a three-year period, to give effect to the essentially annual
character of each reinsurance contract. It therefore overruled the trial judge who,
having construed the reinsurance contracts as being back-to-back with the original insurance, had concluded that each reinsurance contract covered liability in
respect of loss or damage whether or not it occurred during the 12-month period
covered by the reinsurance contract.

---

[111] [1996] 1 WLR 1026, 1035–1036. However, the position may be affected by the presence of an
aggregate extension clause in the reinsurance contract, as discussed at paras 4.75 et seq.
[112] [1995] LRLR 433.

I. Losses Discovered or Claims Made Clause

4.73   The issue of the extent to which a reinsurer's liability may be extended to cover losses occurring outside the policy year was also considered in *Caudle v Sharp*.[113] In that case the reinsured relied on a 'Losses Discovered or Claims Made Clause' in the contract of reinsurance to argue that its reinsurers, who were on risk under the reinsurances only for the calendar year 1985, were liable not only for claims first notified in 1985 but also claims first notified in 1987. All of the claims arose out of the negligent writing of 32 contracts of reinsurance in 1982; the underlying insureds were various agencies that had placed Names on the syndicate that wrote the 32 contracts. The Losses Discovered or Claims Made Clause provided:

> It is understood and agreed that as regards losses arising under policies and/or contracts covering on a 'losses discovered' or 'claims made' basis, that is to say, policies and/or contracts in which the date of discovery of the loss or the date when the claim is made determines under which policy or contract the loss is collectible, such losses are covered hereunder irrespective of the date on which the loss occurs provided that the date of the discovery of the loss, in respect of policies and/or contracts on a 'losses discovered' basis or the date the claim is made, in respect of policies and/or contracts on a 'claims made' basis, falls within the period of this reinsurance.

The judge held that the effect of this clause was that where an event gives rise to a series of losses under a claims made policy, for the purposes of the reinsurance contract those losses are to be treated as occurring when the first claim is made in respect of one loss arising from that event. Consequently, he held that the reinsured was entitled to recover in respect of the losses arising from the 1987 claims because they were part of a series of losses (all arising from the negligent underwriting in 1982) which began when the first claims were made, in 1985, during the period of the reinsurance.

4.74   However, the Court of Appeal[114] held that the claims made clause only renders reinsurers liable for the whole of the loss established in respect of a claim made or loss discovered during the period of the reinsurance. The clause did not extend the cover to include claims made or losses discovered after that period had expired. Consequently, the reinsured could not recover against its 1985 reinsurers in respect of any losses arising from the 1987 claims.

---

[113] [1998] Lloyd's Rep IR 421, 435. For a discussion generally on the relationship between terms in the contract of reinsurance and the underlying contract of insurance see Chapter 3.
[114] [1998] Lloyd's Rep IR 421, 442.

J. Aggregate Extension Clauses

The reinsurer's obligation to indemnify may also be affected by the presence of **4.75** an aggregate extension clause in the contract of reinsurance. This clause operates to extend the reinsurance cover where the reinsured is covering aggregated losses exceeding certain limits. It is found, for example, in the products liability field where a producer may take out products liability insurance to cover itself against the risk of having to pay out more than a certain sum in the aggregate in respect of claims arising out of a particular product risk (for example, from the bursting of a defective soft drinks bottle). Under this type of cover, once the aggregate excess has been reached, the insurer becomes liable to pay every claim that comes in during the relevant period (possibly subject to an overall policy limit). The existence of an aggregate extension clause in the contract of reinsurance enables the insurer to pass on those liabilities, in the aggregate, to the reinsurer. It carries through into the reinsurance policy the same principle of aggregation as exists in the original policy which has been written 'on an aggregate basis'.

An aggregate extension clause has the effect of circumventing the discrepancy illus- **4.76** trated by the *Axa Reinsurance v Field* case.[115] If the original cover defined related losses or claims in wider terms than the reinsurance contracts, then a result of the inclusion of the aggregate extension clause would be that the reinsured would be entitled to treat those claims that were aggregated under the original cover as an aggregated claim for the purpose of the reinsurance contract.[116]

In *Denby v English and Scottish Maritime Insurance Co*[117] the Court of Appeal con- **4.77** sidered the scope of an aggregate clause which provided that:

> As regards liability incurred by the Reinsured for losses on risks covering on an aggregate basis, this Agreement shall protect the Reinsured excess of the amounts as provided for herein in the aggregate any one such aggregate loss up to the limit of indemnity as provided for herein in all any one such loss.

The Court had to determine whether the policies issued by the reinsured to the **4.78** various original underlying insureds (the accountancy firms) were written on an aggregate basis so that the reinsured, having paid unrelated claims under those original policies, was entitled under the aggregate extension clause to combine or aggregate those sums so as to result in a larger ultimate loss claim upon the reinsurers which would then exceed the deductible and give a recovery from the reinsurers. The unrelated claims were made under original policies which provided coverage

---

[115] [1996] 1 WLR 1026, see also at paras 4.59 and 4.69.
[116] Per Hobhouse LJ in *Denby v English and Scottish Maritime Insurance Co Ltd* [1998] Lloyd's Rep IR 343.
[117] Per Hobhouse LJ in *Denby v English and Scottish Maritime Insurance Co Ltd* [1998] Lloyd's Rep IR 343.

on an occurrence basis and contained 'each and every loss' deductibles and limits; the only element of aggregation relied on was that the policies were subject to an overall aggregate limit or included some initial aggregate retention.

4.79 The court rejected the reinsured's argument that any element of aggregation was sufficient to bring the unrelated claims within the aggregate extension clause; the clause required the basis of the cover provided by the reinsured to the underlying insured to have been 'on an aggregate basis'. Hobhouse LJ said that cover which requires criteria to be applied to each and every loss and imposes an each and every loss excess and limit cannot be said to be cover provided on an aggregate basis. This, however, may be overridden as regards the application of some other provision, in the original insurance, which expressly provides for the aggregation of claims in one respect or another or in one situation or another, for example a related losses clause.

4.80 In *American Centennial Insurance Co v Insco Ltd*[118] Moore-Bick J considered the following paragraph[119] of an aggregate extension clause:

> 4. Furthermore, in circumstances in which one event or occurrence or series of events or occurrences originating from one cause affects more than one policy or contract issued to different insureds or reinsureds, then in such circumstances, a series of policies or contracts so issued shall be deemed to constitute one aggregate risk for the purpose of this reinsurance, provided that each policy or contract has inception during the period of this reinsurance.

Moore-Bick J said that the 'fundamental purpose' of this provision:

> ...is to allow aggregation where several different claims are made against the reinsured arising out of the same event. It is concerned, therefore, with a situation in which something has happened to cause the reinsured to incur liability under the underlying policies. In this context the natural meaning of 'affects' is 'gives rise to a liability under' since it is only when an event has that effect that it affects a policy in a relevant way... [the relevant paragraph in the aggregate extension clause set out above] is only concerned with events or occurrences which give rise to a liability under underlying policies.

4.81 In *American Centennial*, Insco reinsured an original insurance covering, inter alia, the liabilities of 14 directors of an American financial institution, Farmers, which collapsed in 1985. A claim was made against the 14 directors which was settled for US $60 million (when claiming against Insco the insurer split the claims against the directors). Insco had also directly insured Farmers' auditors against whom a claim was also made which was settled. Insco, when claiming against its reinsurer, American Centennial, sought to aggregate the claims made in respect of both the directors and the auditors on the basis that 'the collapse of Farmers was a single

---

[118] [1996] LRLR 407.
[119] Identical paragraphs were contained in the aggregate extension clauses considered in *Denby v English and Scottish Maritime Insurance Co Ltd* [1998] Lloyd's Rep IR 343.

financial "event" within the meaning of the expression "one event or occurrence"' as used in the aggregate extension clause and that it 'affected' the policies issued by Insco so as to allow aggregation under that clause.

Moore-Bick J held that Insco were not entitled to aggregate the claims since the collapse of Farmers did not give rise to liability under the underlying policies. Insco's liability to its insureds depended in each case on the acts or omissions of the persons concerned. These caused the collapse of Farmers which followed some time later and precipitated claims against Insco, but it was the acts or omissions of the directors and auditors, not the subsequent collapse of Farmers, which rendered Insco liable. An event which precipitated claims under the underlying policies was not sufficient to 'affect' them within the meaning of the aggregate extension clause.[120] **4.82**

Insco settled with its reinsured on the basis of 14 separate claims in respect of the liabilities of the Farmers' directors. Moore-Bick J held that Insco was precluded from presenting those claims to its reinsurer on a different basis from that which it had settled with its insured as a result of the following provisions in the contract of reinsurance: **4.83**

> V.3. The liability of the Reinsurer hereunder shall, in all instances, follow the liability of the Reinsured for business the subject matter hereof.
>
> XIX.1. The liability of the Reinsurer shall follow that of the Reinsured in every case and shall be subject in all respects to the general and special stipulations, clauses, waivers and modifications of the Reinsured's policy.

Moore-Bick J said that: **4.84**

> One of the primary purposes of these articles is to bind the reinsurer to the acceptance by the reinsured of liabilities under the underlying policies. A liability does not exist in a vacuum, however; it is owed to a particular person or persons and arises out of particular facts. If the reinsured has accepted or settled a claim on a particular basis, art XIX makes that binding as between him and the reinsurer; it is not open to the reinsured to pursue a claim against the reinsurer on the basis that the liability was incurred on a different basis.[121]

K. Limitation[122]

(1) When does the Reinsurer's Liability to Indemnify its Reinsured Arise?

Section 5 of the Limitation Act 1980 requires a reinsured to bring an action against its reinsurer within six years from the date on which the reinsured's action accrues. **4.85**

---

[120] [1996] LRLR 407, 413.
[121] [1996] LRLR 407, 412–413.
[122] On limitation generally, see also paras 6.85 et seq.

Traditionally,[123] the reinsured's cause of action has been held to arise when its underlying liability is ascertained by judgment, arbitration award or binding settlement: 'ascertainment of liability is a pre-condition to the accrual of insurers' rights against reinsurers'.[124] Recovery under a reinsurance contract is not dependent on payment having been made by the reinsured, provided his liability to pay has been ascertained.[125]

4.86   This traditional approach seems equivalent to treating the reinsurer as in effect insuring the liability of the reinsured, ie the relevant loss which gives rise to the cause of action is not the occurrence of the insured peril but the crystallization of the financial liability of the reinsured.

4.87   This approach does not strictly tie in with the analysis of reinsurance being the insurance of an insurable interest in the subject matter of the original insurance and not a form of liability insurance.[126] On that basis, the cause of action under both the insurance and reinsurance policies should accrue at the same time, ie on the occurrence of the insured peril and loss. However, the limitation problems that this approach would involve have resulted in the adoption of the rule that the limitation period begins to run from the crystallizing of the liability of the reinsured.

4.88   The situation may arise where following the reinsured giving notice of a possible claim to the reinsurer the latter denies liability or otherwise seeks to avoid the policy before the reinsured's cause of action accrues. In such a case, the limitation period will only start to run at an earlier date than judgment, arbitration or settlement if the reinsured takes the exceptional course of accepting the reinsurer's repudiation. If the reinsured accepts the reinsurer's repudiation and terminates the policy on the basis of the anticipatory repudiatory breach, limitation runs from the date of termination even though the reinsured's liability may not yet have been ascertained and the reinsured will have to commence proceedings for damages against the reinsurer.

(2) Excess of Loss Reinsurance

4.89   In *North Atlantic Insurance Co Ltd v Bishopsgate Insurance Ltd*[127] Timothy Walker J held that the point when the aggregate excess point is reached, in that case £2.5 million, should be determined by reference to the date the reinsured's liability is

---

[123] *Versicherungs Und Transport A/G Daugava v Henderson* [1934] 49 Lloyd's Rep 252, 253–254 per Scrutton and Maugham LJJ.
[124] *Gan Insurance Co Ltd v Tai Ping Insurance Co Ltd (No 2)* [2001] Lloyd's Rep IR 667, 690; see also *Halvanon Insurance Ltd v Companhia de Seguros do Estado de Sao Paulo* [1995] LRLR 303, 306.
[125] *North Atlantic Insurance Co Ltd v Bishopsgate Insurance Ltd* [1998] 1 Lloyd's Rep 459, 462.
[126] *Toomey v Eagle Star* [1994] 1 Lloyd's Rep 516. See further paras 1.20 et seq.
[127] [1998] 1 Lloyd's Rep 459.

ascertained (for example when he has made settlements in the sum of £2.5 million), not at the date the reinsured has actually paid out £2.5 million.[128]

The reinsurance contract in that case also contained a variable excess clause which **4.90** provided that the excess point should be increased if the net premium income exceeded the estimated income. Timothy Walker J rejected the submission that the reinsured's cause of action did not arise until it was possible to ascertain if there had been any increase in the excess point. Whilst the inclusion of the variable excess point gave the reinsurer protection in the event that the reinsured chose to write business above the estimated net premium income, it did not postpone the reinsured's right to be paid: 'once £2.5 million in settlement has been reached, the reinsurer must pay leaving the final accounting to be done afterwards'.[129]

(3) 'Actually paid'

As stated at para 4.85, in principle the liability of the reinsurer is wholly unaffected **4.91** by whether the reinsured has satisfied the claim under the original insurance. This result can be altered by express provision, but clear words would be required as demonstrated by the decision of the House of Lords in *Charter Reinsurance Co Ltd v Fagan*.[130] In *Charter Re* the contract of reinsurance provided that '[t]he Reinsurers shall only be liable if and when the Ultimate Net Loss sustained by the Reinsured' exceeded £3 million. It further provided that 'the term "[Ultimate][131] Net Loss" shall mean the sum actually paid by the Reinsured in settlement of losses or liability'.

The House of Lords held that in the context of the particular reinsurance contract **4.92** in issue, payment by the reinsured was not a condition precedent to the reinsurer's liability. Lord Hoffmann said that the context pointed to an intention, by the use of the words 'actually paid', to emphasize the net character[132] of the reinsurer's liability as opposed to what, under the terms of the policies, the liability might have been. In this regard, Lord Mustill said that properly understood the policy required:

> ... the satisfaction of only two conditions before an indemnity falls due. First, that an insured event shall have occurred within the period of the policy, and second that the event shall have produced a loss to Charter [the reinsured] of a degree sufficient, when ultimately worked out, to bring the particular layer of reinsurance into play ... the purpose of 'the sum actually paid' in clause 2(c) is not to impose an additional condition precedent in relation to the disbursement of funds, but to

---

[128] [1998] 1 Lloyd's Rep 459, 462.
[129] [1998] 1 Lloyd's Rep 459, 463.
[130] [1997] AC 313.
[131] Lord Mustill said that the omission of the word 'ultimate' was clearly a mistake, [1997] AC 313, 385.
[132] ie that there was to be a netting-down for recoveries, salvage and the like when ascertaining whether, and if so by how much, the relevant liabilities of the reinsured cross the boundary into the layer covered by the reinsurance: per Lord Mustill at 385.

emphasize that it is the ultimate outcome of the net loss calculation which determined the final liability of the syndicates under the policy. In this context, 'actually' means 'in the event when finally ascertained', and 'paid' means 'exposed to liability as a result of the loss insured under clause 1'. These are far from the ordinary meanings of the words, and they may be far from the meanings which they would have had in other policies, and particularly in first-tier policies of reinsurance.[133]

(4) 'Pay to be paid'

4.93   An example of wording which might be sufficient to alter the point in time at which the reinsurer's liability arises may be found in the rules of the P and I club considered by the House of Lords in *Firma C-Trade SA v Newcastle Protection and Indemnity Association*.[134] Under the rules the club undertook to: 'Protect and indemnify members in respect of losses which they as owners of the entered vessel shall have become liable to pay and shall have in fact paid'. The House of Lords held that under this provision, known as a 'pay to be paid' provision, the members were not entitled to be indemnified by the club in respect of liabilities to third parties which they had incurred unless and until the members had first discharged those liabilities themselves.

---

[133] [1997] AC 313, 386.
[134] [1991] 2 AC 1.

5

RIGHTS OF THE REINSURER

A. Payment of Premium

As outlined in Chapter 2, the premium is the consideration for the contract which **5.01** proceeds from the reinsured to the reinsurer in return for coverage according to the policy terms. The reinsured's agreement to pay the premium is normally sufficient as the payment itself may follow some time later. A reinsurer has the right to treat the contract of reinsurance as discharged upon non-payment of the premium if the contract contains an express right to cancel for non-payment of premium (for example under a premium warranty clause). In the absence of such an express clause, cancellation may be justified if it is an implied condition of the contract that the premium would be paid in advance or on the grounds that the reinsured has repudiated the contract by evincing an intention not to pay the premium.[1]

---

[1] *Pacific & General Insurance Co Ltd v Hazell* [1997] 1 LRLR 65, 82. Moore-Bick J held that the broker was not itself liable to the reinsurer for non-payment of the premium. In contrast it has been long held that the position is different in marine reinsurance (*Universo Insurance Co of Milan v Merchants Marine Insurance Co* [1897] 2 QB 93, 96 and also s 53(1) of the Marine Insurance Act 1906: 'Unless otherwise agreed, where a marine policy is effected on behalf of the assured by a broker, the broker is directly responsible to the insurer for the premium . . .').

(1) Premium Warranty Clause

5.02 A reinsurer may reserve to itself the right to treat the contract of reinsurance as at an end on non-payment of the premium by the inclusion of a premium warranty clause.[2] However, the reinsurer may be precluded from relying on a breach of the premium warranty clause if it acts in a way, following breach, which is only consistent with an intention to continue with the contract. In *Compagnia Tirrena Di Assicurazioni SpA v Grand Union Insurance Co Ltd*[3] the reinsurer, following the failure of the reinsured to pay the premium on time, made demands for premiums as they fell due. Waller J held that the demands for premiums which were only due on the basis that the contract continued were unequivocal acts affirming the contract. From the moment of their communication they affirmed the contract and both parties were bound by that election. Further, Waller J said that where, following the reinsurer's demand, the reinsured tenders payment, he doubted whether the reinsurer would have any entitlement to reject the payment tendered. If there was such an entitlement, Waller J said that any rejection of that payment is required within a reasonable time if that too is not to be taken as an act affirming the contract.[4]

(2) Implied Term

5.03 In *Pacific & General Insurance Co Ltd v Hazell*[5] the contract provided for a minimum and deposit premium expressed to be payable 'in four equal instalments in advance'. Moore-Bick J held that it would require very much clearer language than this to give rise to an implication that payment on a due date is a condition of cover under the contract.[6] He said that the stipulation for payment in advance in the contract was merely intended to establish that instalments of premium fell due at the beginning rather than at the end of the relevant period and did not make prompt payment a condition of the contract so that any breach would entitle the reinsurer to treat it as discharged. Similarly, he rejected the argument that the provision for payment of instalments of premium in advance was sufficient to make payment of the premium a condition precedent to the reinsurer's liability under the contract.[7] *Hazell* suggests that a court will be reluctant to imply a term making prompt payment of premium a precondition to the reinsurer being on risk.

(3) Repudiation

5.04 A failure to pay premium will not usually of itself amount to a repudiation of the contract of reinsurance.[8] In *Fenton Insurance Co Ltd v Gothaer Verischerungsbank*

---

[2] See paras 6.74 et seq for breach of warranty generally.
[3] [1991] 2 Lloyd's Rep 143.
[4] [1991] 2 Lloyd's Rep 143, 154.
[5] [1997] LRLR 65.
[6] For the implication of terms generally see paras 3.58 et seq.
[7] *Pacific & General Insurance Co Ltd v Hazell* [1997] LRLR 65, 82.
[8] *Pacific & General Insurance Co Ltd v Hazell* [1997] LRLR 65, 82.

VvaG[9] Potter J pointed out that in the context of insurance business in which accounts are rendered and balances paid through brokers and underwriting agents and where delays in payment are not infrequent, it would rarely be possible to infer an intention not to perform the contract from a simple failure to pay balances. However, he did recognize that different considerations might apply to a persistent failure to pay despite demands or protests.[10] In *Hazell*, the reinsured's failure to pay the first two instalments of premium coupled with the clear statement that no funds would be made available for the payment of premium in the future was held to be sufficient to amount to a repudiation of the contract of reinsurance.[11]

If the reinsured has evinced an intention no longer to be bound by the contract, in order to discharge the contract of reinsurance the reinsurer will need to accept the repudiatory breach. No particular form of words is necessary; all that is required is that the reinsurer's intention to treat the contract as discharged is effectively communicated to the reinsurer.[12] Any such acceptance will only discharge the parties from their obligations prospectively.[13] **5.05**

(4) 'Premiums and claims to be settled in account'

In *Compagnia Tirrena Di Assicurazioni SpA v Grand Union Insurance Co Ltd*[14] the relevant clause provided for 'Premiums and claims to be settled in account. Premium warranty on due dates.' Waller J held that on the true construction of this clause the reinsured was entitled to pay the premium by rendering an account showing claims in excess of premium. **5.06**

B. Claims Co-operation Clause/Claims Control Clause

A reinsurer can circumscribe the power of the reinsured to make settlements or other decisions which are binding on it by the use of a claims co-operation clause. This clause gives the reinsurer the right to be involved in the investigation and settlement of the underlying loss. A claims control clause gives a reinsurer even more influence in the handling of the original claim by the underlying insured. There are many forms of these clauses in use, each of which varies in the level of involvement given to the reinsurer from a right merely to be consulted to the right to exercise full control in respect not only of negotiations and settlement but also of the defence of the claim. **5.07**

---

[9] [1992] LRLR 37.
[10] [1992] LRLR 37, 46. Moore-Bick J expressed his agreement with this reasoning in *Pacific & General Insurance Co Ltd v Hazell* [1997] LRLR 65, 82.
[11] *Pacific & General Insurance Co Ltd v Hazell* [1997] LRLR 65, 83.
[12] *Pacific & General Insurance Co Ltd v Hazell* [1997] LRLR 65, 83.
[13] *Fenton Insurance Co Ltd v Gothaer Verischerungsbank VvaG* [1992] LRLR 37, 46.
[14] [1991] 2 Lloyd's Rep 143.

5.08   Standard clauses such as claims control clauses and claims co-operation clauses in reinsurance contracts should receive a uniform construction, whoever proposed them, ie the *contra proferentem* rule does not apply.[15]

(1)   Typical Features of Claims Co-operation/Control Clauses

(a) Notification of loss[16]

5.09   Notification of loss clauses are not commonly found in contracts of reinsurance but a requirement to notify the reinsurer of a loss or claim may be included as part of claims co-operation/control clauses. Notification can trigger the exercise of the reinsurer's rights under the claims co-operation/control clauses, ie once notified of a claim the reinsurer can then decide whether it wants to exercise its right under a claims control clause to control the investigation and settlement of the claim. The requirement to notify the reinsurer does not generally impose any obligation upon the reinsured to take positive steps to acquire the relevant knowledge. However, once it has actual knowledge of a claim then the obligation to advise reinsurers is triggered.

5.10   Where the subject of the reinsurance is the legal liability of the underlying insured for financial loss suffered by third parties the relevant 'loss', in a clause requiring notification upon knowledge of any loss which may give rise to a claim, will be that of the third party claimant rather than that of the underlying insured.[17] Once the reinsured has actual knowledge of a 'claim' against the underlying insured it knows that a third party claimant *may* have suffered an actual loss, which may give rise to a claim by the underlying insured against the reinsured, which *may* give rise to a claim on the reinsurance. If and when the reinsured obtains actual knowledge that the third party claimant against the underlying insured has suffered an actual loss, then the reinsured will have actual knowledge of a loss which may give rise to a claim under the reinsurance and his duty to notify under such a clause will then be triggered.[18]

5.11   In *Royal & Sun Alliance Insurance plc v Dornoch*[19] the claims co-operation clause required notification within 72 hours of knowledge of a loss which might give rise

---

[15]   Mance LJ in *Gan Insurance Co Ltd v Tai Ping Insurance Co Ltd (No 2)* [2001] Lloyd's Rep IR 667, 686.

[16]   On notification clauses see paras 6.78 et seq.

[17]   In *Royal & Sun Alliance Insurance plc v Dornoch* [2004] Lloyd's Rep IR 826 at first instance, Aikens J at para 62 considered the various possibilities as to whose loss was being referred to: (i) the losses of claimants against the original insured; (ii) losses of the original insured, which occur when they have been held liable to the third party claimants and which are recoverable under the original insurance; and (iii) losses of the original insurer, because it has become liable to pay the insured. The judge (affirmed on appeal) concluded at para 86 that the words 'loss or losses' 'refer to the actual loss or losses of third party claimants against the original insured'.

[18]   *Royal & Sun Alliance Insurance plc v Dornoch* [2004] Lloyd's Rep IR 826 for an extensive discussion by Aikens J of the concept of actual knowledge in a claims co-operation clause.

[19]   [2005] Lloyd's Rep IR 544.

to a claim. The Court of Appeal held that the relevant loss was that of the third party claimant seeking to recover from the original insured. However it also held that no loss would be 'known' until the insured settled the claim. Before the settlement the loss was an alleged loss and would not, therefore, be known to be a loss. The reinsurers argued that such a conclusion rendered the clause entirely useless in the very circumstances when it should be operative but the Court of Appeal held that the reinsured could not know that there had been a loss before it was ascertained by the fact of settlement.[20]

Often the reinsured will only have actual knowledge of an actual loss once it has been proved or admitted in court or arbitration proceedings or accepted as part of a settlement. The reinsured could attain actual knowledge of an actual loss prior to the conclusion of proceedings by receiving that information from an external source. An example is the reinsured who learns from Lloyd's List that a ship has sunk. In those circumstances, the reinsured would have actual knowledge of an actual loss of the underlying insured owner of the ship because the probability is that Lloyd's List is accurate and the loss has, in fact, occurred. **5.12**

At first instance *Royal & Sun Alliance Insurance Plc v Dornoch*[21] Aikens J held that objective knowledge was enough so that the reinsured must be deemed to know what any reasonable insurer would have known in the circumstances of this case. This was the submission of the reinsurers in *AIG Europe (Ireland) Ltd v Faraday Capital Ltd*.[22] Longmore LJ held that it was unnecessary for that question to be addressed commenting: **5.13**

> I am far from saying Aikens J was wrong, but I would prefer to decide the question in a case where it mattered. Since insurers are, of course, knowledgeable people it will be a rare case indeed in which an insurer did not know of a loss in circumstances when any knowledgeable insurer would have done.

---

[20] The facts are of some note. It was alleged that the directors of a company insured under an E & O policy had made false statements which caused the value of company shares to be artificially inflated. When the falsity of the statements was discovered, shareholders brought a claim. The company denied making any false statements and asserted that the loss in value of the shares was caused by ordinary market fluctuations. The Court of Appeal held that in these circumstances, the reinsured could not have knowledge of any loss and the claims co-operation clause was not triggered.

[21] [2004] Lloyd's Rep IR 826

[22] [2008] Lloyd's Rep IR 454. Note the similarity to the facts in *Royal & Sun Alliance Insurance v Dornoch* [2005] Lloyd's Rep IR 544, where shareholders alleged that the directors of a company had made false statements which caused the value of the shares to be artificially inflated. The Court of Appeal held that the relevant losses under contemplation in the claims co-operation clause were those of the third party claimant seeking to recover from the original insured; but that there was no actual loss until it had been established that the value of the shares had been artificially inflated on account of the directors' false statements. In *AIG*, the Court of Appeal distinguished *Dornoch*, holding that the shareholders had suffered a loss as a result of a sharp fall in the company's share price. A third case in this vein is *Stonebridge Underwriting Ltd v Ontario Municipal Insurance Exchange* [2011] Lloyd's Rep IR 171 in which Christopher Clarke J commented that the English Court would have to determine the dividing line between those two cases.

(b) Consultation/co-operation in claims handling

5.14 Claims co-operation clauses impose an obligation upon the reinsured to co-operate with its reinsurer so as to put the reinsurer in a position where it can make a sensible judgement regarding any proposal to settle or compromise a claim. Consequently, the duty to co-operate will extend to matters concerning the determination of the nature, scope, and amount of any loss and whether it falls within the policy cover.

5.15 In *Gan Insurance Ltd v Tai Ping Insurance Co Ltd (No 2)*[23] the Court of Appeal held that the obligation to co-operate with reinsurers 'in the investigation and assessment of any loss and/or circumstances giving rise to a loss' did not require the reinsured to co-operate in any investigation the purpose of which was to demonstrate that the reinsured was in breach of the contract of reinsurance. However, the obligation to co-operate did cover investigation of whether the loss involved any breach by the underlying insured of any policy term or warranty. The obligation is likely to extend to investigation of possible non-disclosure/misrepresentation related to the circumstances later giving rise to the loss which might entitle the reinsured to avoid their policy with the underlying insured.[24] However, the duty to co-operate is unlikely to require the reinsured to investigate a potential breach of warranty or misrepresentation unrelated to the particular loss since it is that loss which triggers the duty.

5.16 In *Lexington Insurance Co v Multinacional De Seguros Sa*[25] there was a question whether or not the reinsurers' denial of liability meant that, as a matter of construction, there could be no '[cooperation] with the reinsurers in the adjustment and settlement of the claim' in accordance with a condition precedent. Christopher Clarke J held that this was dependent on the nature of the denial and the stance actually taken by reinsurers. A reinsurer who denies liability and thereafter refuses to have anything to do with the claim on that account precludes co-operation by his very refusal. However a reinsurer can maintain a contention that he has already been discharged from liability whilst actively co-operating with the adjustment and settlement of the claim without prejudice to that contention. That stance would not prevent the reinsured complying with its obligation to co-operate. On the facts of this case the reinsured was in breach of the claims co-operation clause as it had expressly waived the time bar of the claim. Its renunciation of the time bar was a plain breach of the obligation to co-operate with the reinsurers in the relevant settlement.

(c) Control of negotiations and settlement

5.17 A claims control clause gives a reinsurer even more influence in the handling of the original claim by the underlying insured. A typical clause would provide that

---

[23] [2001] Lloyd's Rep IR 667.
[24] *Gan Insurance Co Ltd v Tai Ping Insurance Co Ltd (No 3)* [2002] Lloyd's Rep IR 612.
[25] [2009] Lloyd's Rep IR 1.

the reinsurer shall have the right to control all negotiations, adjustments, and settlements in connection with the relevant loss or losses. Such clauses are used, for example, for fronted or captive risks where the reinsured has minimal or nil retention.

The right to control negotiations and settlements does not necessarily involve the **5.18** reinsurers themselves negotiating or settling the underlying insured's claim but it does entitle the reinsurer to control any negotiation or settlement that takes place.[26] Consequently, the reinsured will need to inform its reinsurer when negotiations begin so that the reinsurer can say (if it chooses) what form the negotiations should take and what offers should be made. Similarly, if the reinsured proposes to settle a claim, the reinsurer should be informed and its consent obtained. Strictly, there is no obligation on the reinsured under such a clause to inform reinsurers of any negotiations or settlement; however, if reinsurers do not control negotiations or settlement then (subject to waiver or estoppel) the reinsured will not be able to rely on any 'follow the settlements' provision and if the clause is a condition precedent the reinsurer will not be liable.[27]

Where the clause provides for control over 'negotiations and settlement' it is not **5.19** enough for a settlement to be controlled by the reinsurers, if the negotiations were not also controlled by them. In this regard, the word 'and' in a clause referring to control of 'negotiations and settlement' will be read as being disjunctive. This is important as if, for example, settlement is impossible because of poorly conducted negotiations and the reinsured was sued to judgment, the effect of the clause is that if the reinsurers were not given the opportunity to control the negotiations they would, if the clause is a condition precedent to liability, be able to rely on their rights under the clause as a defence to any claim by the reinsured.[28] As stated above, even if the clause is not a condition precedent, breach will preclude the reinsured relying on any follow the settlements provision and it will have to prove its liability to its underlying insured in order to recover from its reinsurer.[29]

In *Gan Insurance Ltd v Tai Ping Insurance Ltd (No 2)* the Court of Appeal held that **5.20** the following claims co-operation clause is to be construed disjunctively:

> No settlement and/or compromise shall be made and liability admitted without the prior approval of Reinsurers.

Consequently, under this form of clause the reinsurer's approval is required for all settlements whether they include an admission of liability or not.[30]

---

[26] *Eagle Star Insurance Co Limited v Cresswell* [2004] LRLR 537, 543.
[27] *Eagle Star Insurance Co Limited v Cresswell* [2004] LRLR 537, 544–545.
[28] *Eagle Star Insurance Co Limited v Cresswell* [2004] LRLR 537, 550. See also *Gan Insurance Co Ltd v Tai Ping Insurance Co Ltd (No 2)* [2001] Lloyd's Rep IR 667.
[29] *Insurance Co of Africa v Scor (UK) Reinsurance Co Ltd* [1985] 1 Lloyd's Rep 312. The effect on a follow the settlements clause of a claims co-operation clause is considered at para 4.42.
[30] *Gan Insurance Ltd v Tai Ping Insurance Co Ltd (No 2)* [2001] Lloyd's Rep IR 667, 687.

(2)   Costs of Litigation where the Reinsurer has Withheld its Approval[31]

5.21   Where a reinsurer refuses to give its approval to a proposed settlement the reinsured will, if the claims co-operation clause is a condition precedent, have to incur
the expense of litigation with its underlying insured if it wishes to recover under its
contract of reinsurance. Unless expressly provided for in the contract of insurance,
the reinsured cannot recover the costs of the litigation with its underlying insured
from the reinsurer even if the litigation results in a judgment on less favourable
terms than those in the proposed settlement.[32]

5.22   The irrecoverable nature of the costs incurred in investigating, settling or defending claims by an underlying insured extends also to proportional reinsurance.[33]
In *Baker v Black Sea and Baltic General Insurance Co Ltd*[34] the reinsured argued
that there was an implied term in a contract of proportional reinsurance that the
reinsurer would be liable for its share of the costs. In this regard, the reinsured said
that the essential characteristic of proportional reinsurance is that there is a sharing
of the same underwriting fortunes, both as to risk and premium. Consequently, it
was contended that such a term should be implied to give the contract business efficacy, or because it is what the parties to the contract must, as reasonable men, have
intended. Alternatively, it was argued that the term was to be implied by reason of
a trade practice or usage in the insurance market in London.

5.23   In relation to business efficacy, Lord Lloyd, with whom the rest of the House
of Lords agreed, said that the argument would be a strong one if proportional
reinsurance were in the nature of a partnership but it is not. Further, he noted that
the profits on the business ceded were not shared equally between reinsured and
reinsurer. The reinsured was entitled to 20% commission on profits before any
distribution. Even in a year when no profits were being made the reinsured was
entitled to 5% overriding commission. He said that it may well be that the parties
intended the cost of defending claims to come out of the 20% commission, or the
5% overrider, or both. Consequently, he said the test of necessity had not been satisfied in that case.[35]

5.24   As regards trade practice and usage, Potter J and the Court of Appeal had held
that there was no evidence of a universal and acknowledged practice of the market
for reinsurers to pay a proportion of the legal costs incurred by the reinsured. The
House of Lords, however, said that there had been some evidence below of such
a practice. That evidence, though, was not sufficient for their Lordships to imply
the term. Given its importance the House of Lords decided to remit the issue of

---

[31]   This is also discussed at paras 3.67 et seq.
[32]   *Insurance Co of Africa v Scor (UK) Reinsurance Co Ltd* [1985] 1 Lloyd's Rep 312, 333.
[33]   *Baker v Black Sea and Baltic General Insurance Co Ltd* [1998] 2 All ER 833; *Scottish Metropolitan
Assurance Co Ltd v Groom* (1924) 20 Ll L Rep 44.
[34]   [1998] 2 All ER 833.
[35]   [1998] 2 All ER 833, 838.

whether a term could be implied by reason of trade practice to the Commercial Court for determination following the hearing of further argument and after hearing any fresh evidence which the parties might wish to introduce. Unfortunately, before the remitted hearing could take place the reinsurers went into provisional liquidation and subsequently an insolvent scheme of arrangement. Consequently the remitted issue was not heard or determined.

(3) Claims Co-operation Clause: A Condition Precedent?

The effect of a breach of the obligation to co-operate will depend upon whether the clause is a condition precedent[36] to the reinsurer's liability to indemnify the reinsured under the contract of reinsurance. If the clause is a condition precedent to the reinsurer's liability, breach will preclude the reinsured from recovering under the reinsurance even if it can show in fact and in law that it was liable to its underlying insured.[37] **5.25**

In a series of cases the Court of Appeal has considered whether particular claims co-operation clauses were a condition precedent to the reinsurer's liability to indemnify. In *Insurance Co of Africa v Scor (UK) Reinsurance Ltd*[38] the clause provided that: **5.26**

> It is a condition precedent to liability under this Insurance that all claims be notified immediately to the Underwriters subscribing to this Policy and the Reassured hereby undertake that in arriving at the settlement of any claim, that they will co-operate with the Reassured Underwriters and that no settlement shall be made without the approval of the Underwriters subscribing to this Policy.

It was held that, properly construed, the clause was in two parts and that the obligations in the claims co-operation clause to co-operate with reinsurers and not to settle without underwriter's approval were not conditions precedent. Following this decision, the reinsurers redrafted the clause dividing up the obligations into separate sub-clauses so as to make clear that each was a condition precedent to the reinsurer's liability.[39] **5.27**

The redrafted clause provided, inter alia, that it was a condition precedent to the reinsurer's liability that the reinsured 'co-operate with reinsurers . . . in the investigation and assessment of any loss and/or circumstances giving rise to a loss'. In *Gan Insurance Co Ltd v Tai Ping Insurance Co Ltd (No 2)*[40] the reinsured sought to argue that this obligation was 'too vague to qualify as a condition precedent'. This argument was rejected by the Court of Appeal. The fact that the clause might require a degree of judgement to decide whether there had been a failure to 'co-operate' **5.28**

---

[36] For condition precedent see paras 6.58 et seq.
[37] *Gan Insurance Co Ltd v Tai Ping Insurance Co Ltd (No 2)* [2001] Lloyd's Rep IR 667, 687–688.
[38] [1985] 1 Lloyd's Rep 312.
[39] This amended clause was examined by the Court of Appeal in *Gan Insurance Co Ltd v Tai Ping Insurance Co Ltd (No 2)* [2001] Lloyd's Rep IR 667.
[40] *Gan Insurance Co Ltd v Tai Ping Insurance Co Ltd (No 2)* [2001] Lloyd's Rep IR 667.

could not preclude a conclusion that the clause was a condition precedent. Mance LJ noted that it can often occur that the continued operation of contractual obligations depends upon a careful evaluation and judgement of the significance of complex factual circumstances (for example, when deciding whether there has been a repudiatory breach). Mance LJ, however, stated that there was potentially a separate issue whether the clause refers to any or only significant or serious failures to co-operate.[41]

5.29 In *Eagle Star Insurance Co Limited v JN Cresswell*[42] the right to control negotiations and settlements under the following clause was considered to be a condition precedent to the reinsurer's liability:

> The Underwriters hereon shall control the negotiations and settlements of any claims under this Policy. In this event the Underwriters hereon will not be liable to pay any claim not controlled as set out above.

5.30 The effect of the words 'in this event' and 'any claim not controlled as set out above' was held to be that it was a condition precedent to the reinsurers' liability that the opportunity to control negotiations or settlements should be afforded to them. Rix LJ noted that these 'are strong words, if not the language of condition precedent, at any rate the language of exclusion'.[43] Consequently, even if the reinsured were able to prove it was liable to its underlying insured, the reinsurer would still have a defence that it was never given the opportunity to control negotiations or the settlement and thus cannot be liable. The court in *Eagle Star* rejected the argument that the words 'will not be liable to pay' relate not to the reinsurers' ultimate liability to indemnify, but only to their liability under the 'follow the settlements' clause. As the court noted, the clause does not say that there will be no liability to follow or pay a *settlement* which has not been negotiated and agreed under the reinsurers' control, but that the reinsurers will not be liable to pay 'any claim not controlled as set out above'.[44]

5.31 Whilst such clauses can operate harshly on a reinsured, the solutions are in a reinsured's own hands. It can take care to ensure that its reinsurers are kept in the picture of any negotiations or settlement activities. Moreover, if reinsurers simply refuse to exercise control, there remains the argument of waiver.

(4) Consequences of Breach of a Claims Co-operation/Control Clause which is not a Condition Precedent

5.32 Even if compliance with the obligations under a claims co-operation/control clause are not expressed to be a condition precedent, a failure to comply with

---

[41] *Gan Insurance Co Ltd v Tai Ping Insurance Co Ltd (No 2)* [2001] Lloyd's Rep IR 667, 687.
[42] [2004] Lloyd's Rep IR 537.
[43] [2004] Lloyd's Rep IR 537, 548.
[44] [2004] Lloyd's Rep IR 537, 549.

such obligations may prevent reliance on any 'follow the settlements' provision, although it will normally still be open to the reinsured to recover its loss by proving its liability for the settled claim.[45] Where, as in *Insurance Co of Africa v Scor*, the clause requires the consent of the reinsurers to any settlement, a 'follow the settlements' clause will be emasculated in that it will only apply to settlements made with the consent of the reinsurers.

An issue that has not expressly been decided in the reinsurance context, in England, is whether, in the absence of a requirement for the reinsurers' consent to a settlement, a breach of other requirements of a claims co-operation/control clause[46] would also have the effect of preventing a reinsured from relying on a follow the settlements clause. It is not clear whether, for example, breach of an obligation merely to notify within a specified time or to provide information would necessarily have the effect of precluding reliance on a follow the settlements provision or whether it would simply give rise to a remedy for breach of contract. The answer probably is that if the reinsured's obligation or set of obligations is directed at the involvement of the reinsurer in any settlement process, a breach of any such obligation is likely to prevent a reinsured from relying on a follow the settlements clause. **5.33**

Apart from any impact on the reinsured's entitlement to rely on a follow the settlements clause, the reinsurers' primary remedy for breach by the reinsured of a claims co-operation/control clause which is not a condition precedent will be damages. There has been controversy in the Court of Appeal as to whether a particularly serious breach of one of the requirements will entitle the reinsurer to refuse to indemnify its reinsured in relation to the particular claim (even if it could prove its liability to its underlying insured). **5.34**

The judgment which set the hare running was that of Waller LJ in *Alfred McAlpine Plc v BAI (Run-Off) Ltd*.[47] In that case the trial judge held that a breach of an obligation to notify in an insurance policy, which was not a condition precedent, would simply give rise to a claim for damages, ie if the insurer could prove that the breach had caused them quantifiable loss they would be entitled to damages to that extent which they could set off against their liability under the policy. **5.35**

In the Court of Appeal, however, Waller LJ (with whom the other two members of the Court agreed) said[48] that once a condition such as the condition to notify is construed as something less than a condition precedent, it will still be important to ascertain precisely what its contractual effect is intended to be and what the effect of a breach of that term will be. He said that a breach of such a condition might in some circumstances be so serious as to give rise to a right to reject the claim albeit it **5.36**

---

[45] *Insurance Co of Africa v Scor (UK) Reinsurance Co Ltd* [1985] 1 Lloyd's Rep 312, 330–331 and 334.
[46] Which is not a condition precedent.
[47] [2000] 1 Lloyd's Rep 437.
[48] [2000] 1 Lloyd's Rep 437, para 26.

was not repudiatory in the sense of enabling the insurer to accept a repudiation of the whole contract. The court was dealing with an obligation to notify and noted that the very fact that the obligation to notify is aimed at imposing obligations in relation to individual claims which the insurer might be obliged to pay ought logically to allow for the possibility of a 'repudiatory' breach leading to an entitlement to reject a claim. In this regard Waller LJ said:[49]

> It seems to me that the payment of individual claims are severable obligations and that where an insured is bound to carry out one obligation in order to receive the benefit of the insurer's obligation by implication the insured is accepting that if he fails in a serious way to carry out his part of that bargain he will not receive what he has bargained for.

5.37   In reaching this conclusion Waller LJ relied on an Australian reinsurance case, *Trans-Pacific Insurance Co (Australia) Ltd v Grand Union Insurance Co Ltd*.[50] In that case the reinsured had refused to provide its reinsurer with further information pending acknowledgement of liability by the reinsurer; as a result the reinsurer purported to avoid liability in relation to the particular claim. Giles J held that the claims co-operation clause, in that case, was an innominate term the consequences of any breach of which on any particular claim must depend on the nature and gravity of the relevant breach or breaches. He noted that there could be major or minor failures to co-operate, disagreement on what did or did not amount to co-operation, or breaches which could be readily rectified without any prejudice to the reinsurer. On the facts of that case, Giles J did not 'think that by the breach of the claims co-operation obligation Trans-Pacific evinced an intention no longer to be bound by the reinsurance contract relating' to the particular claim and therefore the reinsurer was not entitled to reject the particular claim.

5.38   In *McAlpine* the decision on the facts was that the insured's failure to notify did not have serious consequences and so there was no cause to apply the principle formulated by Waller LJ and what he said was, strictly, obiter.

5.39   The principle formulated by Waller LJ was rejected by Mance LJ in *Friends Provident Life & Pensions v Sirius International Insurance*.[51] In that case the trial judge had applied *McAlpine* to find that a repudiatory breach arising from the failure to give notice for some years permitted insurers to deny liability for the particular claim to which the failure related. The majority of the Court of Appeal (Waller LJ dissenting) held that a claims notification clause is an ancillary provision and may be an innominate term, but that breach was only capable of sounding in damages. The *McAlpine* approach was rejected on the grounds that the notification provision could not be construed so that insurers would be free of liability in the event of a serious breach or a breach with serious consequences. Neither were there grounds

---

[49] [2000] 1 Lloyd's Rep 437, para 32.
[50] (1989) 18 NSWLR 675.
[51] [2006] Lloyd's Rep IR 45.

for implying such a term because reasonableness was not the test for implying a term.[52] Mance LJ said that there was no basis for creating a new rule of law which would impose such a provision on parties to an insurance contract because 'parties to such contracts should be capable of looking after themselves'.[53]

Waller LJ, in a robust dissent, maintained that *McAlpine* was not heretical and **5.40** prayed in aid that textbooks and authorities had referred to the principle without adverse comment.[54] He said:

> What I was suggesting in relation to the contract of insurance in BAI was that a clause which provides that notice of a claim must be given 'as soon as possible' may not be a condition precedent, but may, if it is breached in a way which seriously prejudices the insurer, give a right to reject a claim rather than leave the insurer simply with a claim for damages.
>
> That the law should recognise that possibility seems to me to accord with what the parties would have contemplated where the insured has agreed to provide details 'as soon as possible' and where an inexcusable delay in so doing has caused serious prejudice. It also incidentally in my view accords with justice.

Waller LJ maintained that conceptually there was no difficulty in construing a notice provision as being an innominate term which provides the insurer with a right to reject the claim if there is a breach of sufficient gravity—a breach which has seriously prejudiced the insurer.

Where the courts are examining a reinsurance contract between two commer- **5.41** cial parties in which they have the opportunity to insert conditions precedent but choose not to, there is even more to commend the approach of Mance LJ and it has been applied in the reinsurance context in *Limit No 2 Ltd v Axa Versicherung AG*.[55] Therefore there would appear to be two potential consequences of a breach by the reinsured of the various requirements of a claims co-operation/control clause which is not a condition precedent. A breach might (a) preclude the reinsured from relying on a follow the settlements clause and so require it to prove its liability

---

[52] Sir William Aldous agreeing said that 'the principle suggested in the *Alfred McAlpine* case has no basis in the law of contract unless an appropriate term can be implied into the contract...there is no need to imply such a term and in any case it did not appear possible to set out with sufficient precision the term' (para 35).

[53] Para 33. Mance LJ found that that Longmore LJ was speaking obiter when he said in *K/S Merc-Skandia XXXXII v Certain Lloyd's Underwriters, The Mercandian Continent* [2001] 2 Lloyd's Rep 563 that 'this court decided that, at any rate in insurance cases, there was a further category of term in addition to the three categories identified above, namely a term a breach of which was so serious for underwriters that it would give them a right to reject the claim without having to accept the breach of contract as being a repudiation of the contract as a whole'.

[54] [2006] Lloyd's Rep IR 45, paras 50–51. He pointed out that *McAlpine* had been followed at appellate level in *K/S Merc-Skandia v Certain Lloyd's Underwriters* [2001] 2 Lloyd's Rep 563 and *The Beursgracht* [2002] Lloyd's Rep IR 335 as well as by Buckley J in *Bankers Insurance Company v South* [2004] Lloyd's Rep IR 1.

[55] [2008] Lloyd's Rep IR 330 affirmed in part on other grounds: [2009] Lloyd's Rep IR 369.

for the settled claim; or (b) simply entitle the reinsurer to recover or set off such damages as it has been caused by the breach.

(5) Qualification of the Reinsurer's Rights under a Claims Co-operation Clause

5.42 The courts will not imply a term or requirement that a reinsurer must have reasonable grounds for withholding approval of any settlement under a claims co-operation clause which requires such approval.[56] Consequently, where the clause provides that no settlement shall be made without the prior approval of reinsurers there is no requirement that the reinsurer, before withholding approval, must be able to establish positively that there are reasonable prospects of defeating a claim or bettering the proposed settlement. The reinsurer has a right to take the view that a particular claim is one that should be strictly proved by the underlying insured or to take a view as to an appropriate level of settlement prior to it being so proved. Such decisions are often 'difficult matters of judgment or feel, on which different people may well hold different views. A reinsurer is entitled . . . to impose his own judgment and policy on such matters.'[57] The court cannot substitute its own view of the reasonableness of a reinsurer's decision to withhold approval. However, it would interfere in circumstances which were so extreme that no reasonable reinsurer in its position could possibly withhold approval.[58]

5.43 The majority[59] of the court in *Gan Insurance Co Ltd v Tai Ping Insurance Co Ltd (No 2)* were prepared to accept as a general qualification upon the reinsured's rights under a claims co-operation clause that 'any withholding of approval by reinsurers should take place in good faith after consideration of and on the basis of the facts giving rise to the particular claim and not with reference to considerations wholly extraneous to the subject matter of the particular reinsurance'.[60] Consequently, the reinsurer should make the decision whether to approve a proposed settlement, so far as possible, objectively without regard to its narrower sectional exposure as reinsurer.

5.44 Mance LJ in *Gan Insurance Co Ltd v Tai Ping Insurance Co Ltd (No 2)*[61] said that he could, in the context of the right to withhold approval of any settlement, envisage

---

[56] See also paras 3.64–3.65.

[57] *Gan Insurance Co Ltd v Tai Ping Insurance Co Ltd (No 2)* [2001] Lloyd's Rep IR 667, 699–700 per Mance LJ (with whom Latham LJ agreed).

[58] *Gan Insurance Co Ltd v Tai Ping Insurance Co Ltd (No 2)* [2001] Lloyd's Rep IR 667, 699–700.

[59] Staughton LJ agreed that the reinsurer was not required to have reasonable grounds for withholding its approval but pointedly declined to express a view on whether any other limitation could be implied, at 702. Rix LJ in *Eagle Star Insurance Co v JN Cresswell* [2004] Lloyd's Rep IR 537 said this protection may, in any event, be inherent as a matter of law in the very essence of the reinsurers' mutual obligation of good faith (at para 54).

[60] [2001] Lloyd's Rep IR 667, 697.

[61] [2001] Lloyd's Rep IR 667, 695–696.

breaches of, inter alia, an implied mutual duty to co-operate by a reinsurer which were so serious or perhaps of such a kind as to deprive reinsurers of the right to expect their approval to be sought. However, he left open the question whether such breaches would always have to be repudiatory for such a result to follow.

C. Inspection of Reinsured's Records

Some reinsurance contracts contain an express term giving the reinsurer a right to inspect the reinsured's records. This right can be very valuable to a reinsurer to allow it to uncover a potential defence. As Hoffmann LJ said in *Société Anonyme d'Intermediaries Luxembourgeois v Farex Gie*:[62]   **5.45**

> Reinsurers are free to stipulate for whatever rights of inspection they please. This is a matter of commercial negotiation between the parties. If they are not entitled to inspection as a matter of contractual right and a dispute arises, English law gives them no procedural means of inspection unless they are first able to raise a triable issue on the material otherwise available to them. This may mean that reinsurers are unable to uncover defences which greater rights of inspection would have revealed. But this is a commercial risk which they accept at the time when the contract is made. I do not think that the court should be astute to give reinsurers the opportunity to delay payment of claims by raising speculative defences.

However, even in the absence of an express term the courts have shown a willingness to imply such a term. In *Phoenix General Insurance Co of Greece v Halvanon Insurance Co Ltd*[63] the implied term accepted by Hobhouse J[64] (at least in the context of a facultative obligatory contract of reinsurance) included the obligations on the part of the reinsured to: **5.46**

- keep full and proper records and accounts of all risks accepted or premiums received and receivable and all claims made or notified;
- keep full and proper accurate accounts showing at all times the amounts due and payable by the reinsured to the reinsurer and by the reinsurer to the reinsured under the contract;
- obtain, file or otherwise keep in a proper manner all accounting claims and other documents and records and make these reasonably available to the defendants.

---

[62] [1995] LRLR 116, 151. The reinsurer tried to defend a summary judgment application on the speculative basis that if it were given a chance to inspect the reinsured's records, evidence of non-disclosure might emerge. Other examples of the use of inspection to try to deflect summary judgment can be found in *Trinity Insurance Co Ltd v Overseas Union Insurance Ltd* [1996] LRLR 156 and *Aetna Reinsurance Co (UK) Ltd v Central Reinsurance Corporation Ltd* [1996] LRLR 165.
[63] [1985] 2 Lloyd's Rep 599, 613–614.
[64] On the basis of agreed expert evidence.

Hobhouse J stated that the terms had to be implied so that the reinsurer may be able to find out what his rights and obligations are.[65]

5.47 Webster J in *Charman v Guardian Royal Exchange Assurance Plc*,[66] in considering the reinsurer's obligation to follow the reinsured's settlements, was prepared to imply a term that the reinsured would provide the reinsurers with information and documents showing the claim that was made and how the claim was dealt with, including provision of any reports from loss adjusters.[67]

5.48 In *Charman* Webster J also considered to what extent a reinsurer can rely on a breach of the implied term to provide information as a defence to a reinsured's claim for summary judgment.[68] He noted that were it to be arguable that such an implied term had been broken, that would not lead to the conclusion that there was in relation to the claim 'an issue or question in dispute which ought to be tried',[69] since breach of such a term would not constitute a defence to a claim although it might give rise to a cross-claim for damages or some other relief. But if such a breach were arguable, it might constitute 'some other reason' for which there should be a trial of the claim, or at least part of it.[70]

5.49 The reinsurer in *Pacific & General Insurance Co Ltd v Baltica Insurance Co (UK) Ltd*[71] successfully relied on its right to inspection to resist an application for summary judgment. The clause in that case provided:

> All loss settlements made by the Reinsured, including compromise settlements, shall be unconditionally binding upon Reinsurers provided such settlements are within the conditions of the original policies and/or contracts and within the terms of this reinsurance, and amounts falling to the share of Reinsurers shall be payable by them upon reasonable evidence of the amount paid being given by the Reinsured. In the event of a claim arising hereunder notice shall be given to the Reinsurers... as soon as practicable, and all papers in connection therewith shall be at the command of the Reinsurers on this reinsurance or parties designated by them for inspection.

5.50 Rix J said that a court, when faced by a reinsured's claim under a follow the settlements clause and a reinsurer's concern about paying out under such a clause before it

---

[65] Note the implication of such terms has come under some scrunity. The Court of Appeal in *Bonner v Cox* [2006] Lloyd's Rep IR 385 held that non-proportional reinsurance was not subject to such implied terms and the existence of a duty of care might appear inconsistent with the approach in *Sphere Drake v EIU* [2003] 1 Lloyd's Rep IR 525. However Tuckey J followed the *Phoenix v Halvanon* approach in the unreported case *Economic v Le Assicurazioni d'Italia* (unreported, 27 November 1996).

[66] [1992] 2 Lloyd's Rep 607.

[67] [1992] 2 Lloyd's Rep 607, 614.

[68] [1992] 2 Lloyd's Rep 607, 616.

[69] The words of RSC Ord 14, r 3(1).

[70] See also *Baker v Black Sea and Baltic General Insurance Co Ltd* [1995] LRLR 261, 283–285 where Potter J emphasized that compliance with the implied term was not a condition precedent to recovery in an action.

[71] [1996] LRLR 8.

has been given inspection of relevant documents, has to look at three considerations. The first is whether the reinsured has given or refused to the reinsurer the latter's contractual rights of inspection. The second relevant consideration is the circumstances in which the claim to inspect comes forward. If a reinsurer does not invoke his right to inspect until the very last moment when he is 'under the lash' of a claim for summary judgment pursuant to a follow the settlements clause, the court will be reluctant to refuse summary judgment on the basis that if inspection belatedly takes place something may turn up. Where, however, there have been timely requests for inspection, the matter may well be different. The third consideration is whether some substantial reason has been put forward as to why inspection is requested or required and as to what a reinsurer hopes to find upon such inspection. If the point, if made good by the inspection, is one which could arguably give rise to a defence, then that is something that may be relevant to the court's decision.[72]

Rix J went on to say that the structure of the clause is that whilst the reinsurer must **5.51** pay a loss settlement upon provision of reasonable evidence of payment, nevertheless the notice and inspection provisions of the second paragraph of the clause are given to the reinsurer as his protection against what could otherwise be a unilateral assertion on the part of the reinsured as to the former's obligation to indemnify. It follows, he said, that where no notice of a claim has ever been given to the reinsurer and therefore it has never had the opportunity to request inspection in respect of that claim and thus to make any investigation for itself about it, a court should be cautious about giving summary judgment before an inspection has been allowed to take place.[73]

The right of a reinsurer to insist on its right of inspection has been considered in **5.52** the context of winding-up proceedings. In *In Re A Company Nos 008725/91, ex p Pritchard*[74] the contract of reinsurance provided that the reinsured's books:

> ... shall be open to the inspection of an authorized representative of the reinsurers at any reasonable time during the continuance of this reinsurance or any liability hereunder.

When the reinsurer's agents sought to exercise the right of inspection for the pur- **5.53** pose of run-off, the reinsured wrote back saying that there were claims unpaid and that no inspection would be allowed until payment was received. The reinsurer, however, refused to pay until it had been given the opportunity to inspect. The reinsured subsequently sought to enforce their claims by issuing a winding-up petition. The reinsurer applied to strike out the petition. Hoffmann J in allowing the application said:

> I accept that in the ordinary case, it is not enough for the company to say that an investigation yet to be undertaken may produce some grounds upon which

---

[72] [1996] LRLR 8, 11.
[73] [1996] LRLR 8, 12.
[74] [1992] LRLR 288.

the debt can be disputed. But the terms of the reinsurance treaty make this a far from ordinary case. The reinsured can in the first instance make a claim based on nothing but its own assertion that it has suffered a loss within the terms of the treaty. No more particulars need to be given and none have. But for the protection of the reinsurer, it has a contractual right to inspect the syndicates' books and papers. It is only by exercising that right that the reinsurer can satisfy itself that the claim is properly due. It does not seem to me that the syndicates are entitled, as they have done, to deny the right to inspect until all existing liabilities have been paid.[75]

5.54   The following inspection clause was considered in *Yasuda Fire & Marine Insurance Co of Europe Ltd v Orion Marine Insurance Underwriting Agency Ltd:*[76]

> a. ORION will maintain or arrange to be maintained all necessary books accounts records and other usual documentation appertaining to the marine insurance business transacted by it under the terms hereof. All such books accounts records and other usual documentation shall be the property of ORION and the duly authorized representatives of YASUDA (EUROPE) including its accountants shall be entitled to inspect the same at any reasonable time following a written request so to do and to make extracts and copies of any entries therein relating to the underwriting conducted hereunder on behalf of YASUDA (EUROPE).

5.55   Colman J held that on its proper construction the clause clearly includes inspection of all computer material. One of Orion's objections to inspection was that the computer records had been kept on a composite basis, including information not only about Yasuda's transactions but also unrelated business and therefore disclosure of the computer records would involve disclosure of irrelevant and to some extent confidential information. Colman J said that this was a problem created by Orion's record keeping and that it was not open to them to rely on the inseparability of irrelevant material as a basis for declining to permit inspection, extraction, and copying of relevant material.[77]

5.56   A reinsurer should be alive to the possibility of a waiver or affirmation argument if it relies on its contractual right to inspect when entitled to avoid the reinsurance on the grounds of non-disclosure or misrepresentation. An attempt to confirm suspicions by an inspection (without an express reservation of rights) can affirm the contract.[78] It has been suggested that exercise of an ancillary provision in a contract

---

[75] [1992] LRLR 288, 290. Hoffmann J noted that if there was evidence that the proposed inspection was excessive in scope or otherwise in bad faith, he would have taken a different view of the application.

[76] [1995] 1 Lloyd's Rep 525.

[77] [1995] 1 Lloyd's Rep 525, 534.

[78] *Iron Trades Mutual Insurance Co Ltd and Others v Companhia de Seguros Imperio* [1991] 1 Re LR 213. Hobhouse J said 'The insurer is under no obligation to elect to treat the contract as at an end within any particular length of time and accordingly mere delay, without more, does not deprive him of his right to do so. However if he does some act in affirmation of the contract, that is to say, some act which is only consistent with an intention not to treat the contract as at an end, he will

does not serve to affirm the primary obligations under the same contract,[79] but there will always be a danger of a finding of affirmation of the whole contract (primary and ancillary provisions taken together).

D. Declaratory Relief

A reinsurer is entitled to claim a declaration as to the invalidity of a contract of **5.57** reinsurance it has entered into with its reinsured. Similarly a reinsurer can issue proceedings to obtain a declaration that it is not liable to indemnify its reinsured in respect of a claim paid by the reinsured.

A reinsurer is not, however, entitled to obtain a declaration against an underlying **5.58** insured as to the liability of its reinsured to the underlying insured or as to the validity of the underlying contract of insurance between the reinsured and the underlying insured.[80] The court's jurisdiction to grant a declaration is limited to declaring contested legal rights subsisting or future of the parties in the litigation before it. Whilst a reinsurer will often have a direct interest in the validity of the underlying insured's claim against its reinsured, the relevant rights in issue are those of the underlying insured and the reinsured not the reinsurer albeit that the latter's legal rights may be dependent on the outcome of the dispute.

E. Subrogation

The doctrine of subrogation applies to contracts of reinsurance. Consequently, **5.59** the reinsurer is entitled to be subrogated to its reinsured's rights to the extent to which the reinsured has diminished or is able to diminish its loss. In *Assicurazioni Generali de Trieste v Empress Assurance Corp Limited*[81] the reinsurer was held to be entitled to recover from the reinsured monies it had paid to the reinsured in

---

thereafter have lost his right to do so provided he had actual knowledge of the facts which gave rise to the right'.

[79] Colman J in *Strive Shipping Corp & Another v Hellenic Mutual War Risks Association (Bermuda) Ltd (The Grecia Express)* [2002] Lloyd's Rep IR 669 said the request for further information, documents, and access to witnesses was advanced under a provision of the policy which is of an ancillary nature and not in the nature of a substantive or primary provision, such as the obligation to pay premium. Thus it has been held that, like arbitration clauses, such investigatory provisions are separate from the contract to which they are ancillary to the effect that they survive avoidance of the contract for repudiatory breach: see *Yasuda Fire & Marine Insurance Co of Europe v Orion Marine Insurance Underwriting Agency Ltd* [1995] QB 174.

[80] *Meadows Indemnity Co Ltd v Insurance Corp of Ireland Plc and International Commercial Bank Plc* [1989] 2 Lloyd's Rep 298.

[81] [1907] 2 KB 814.

circumstances where the reinsured subsequently[82] recovered damages from its underlying insured as a result of the discovery of fraudulent misrepresentations made by the underlying insured. The existence of the reinsurer's rights of subrogation, arising upon payment of a claim under the contract of reinsurance, was more recently recognized by Goff LJ in *Insurance Co of Africa v Scor*.[83]

5.60 The reinsurer's rights of subrogation do not extend to monies received by the reinsured in respect of risks not covered by the contract of reinsurance. In *Young v Merchant's Marine Insurance Co Ltd*[84] the reinsured had written a policy of marine insurance on a vessel against total loss and also against third party liabilities. It reinsured its liability for total loss only with the plaintiff reinsurers. Following a collision at sea the vessel became a total loss and the reinsurer indemnified the reinsured. The reinsured subsequently received a credit in respect of third party liabilities arising out of the collision. The reinsurer's claim to be subrogated to the benefit of the credit was rejected as the third party liability was not covered by the contract of reinsurance which was concerned only with the reinsurance of the amount of the total loss. Greer LJ stated:

> The substance of the matter is, in my judgment, accurately stated by MacKinnon J. towards the end of his judgment: 'The truth is that the shipowner has not received any sum in diminution of his total loss, and therefore the liability of the defendants [reinsured] to the shipowner to pay him a full total loss has not in any way diminished; and as the liability of the defendants to pay the shipowner in full his claim for a total loss has not in any way been diminished, so in my judgment the liability of the plaintiff [reinsurer] to pay the defendants in full has not been diminished in any way.' It follows that the defendants have not been overpaid by the plaintiff, and the plaintiff is not entitled to recover anything from the defendants.

---

[82] The effect of monies already received by the reinsured, from a third party, on the reinsurer's obligation to indemnify its reinsured was considered in *Merrett v Capitol Indemnity Corp* [1992] LRLR 46. This is discussed at paras 4.50–4.51.

[83] [1985] 1 Lloyd's Rep 312, 330.

[84] [1932] 2 KB 705.

6

DENYING LIABILITY

A. Non-disclosure and Misrepresentation

A reinsurer will expect to be given placing information by the reinsured or its bro- **6.01**
ker in order to inform itself about the risk and assess the value of the business. It is
vital that this information is accurate and complete: if inaccurate it may lead to the
defence of misrepresentation being raised and, if incomplete, it may lead to reliance on the defence of non-disclosure. It is not uncommon for a risk to turn out to
be something quite different from that which the reinsurer intended to reinsure.
Reinsurers are quick in those circumstances to look at what was and what was not
said about the risk prior to the scratching of the reinsurance contract, to explore
the possible defence of non-disclosure or misrepresentation. The defences, if established, will entitle the reinsurer to avoid the contract.

(1) The Duty of Utmost Good Faith

6.02 Before any reinsurance contract is concluded, the reinsured is under a duty to disclose to the reinsurer every circumstance which is material to the risk in the sense that it would influence the judgement of a prudent reinsurer in fixing the premium or determining whether he will take the risk. He is also under a duty not to misrepresent any material facts.[1] This is because a contract of reinsurance, in common with insurance, is a contract based upon utmost good faith between the parties.

6.03 The modern restatement and reformulation of the duty is found in the reinsurance case of *Pan Atlantic Insurance Co v Pine Top Insurance Co* in which the claimants were reinsured under excess of loss treaties. The reinsurers sought to avoid on the basis of the non-disclosure of the full loss record by the broker and misrepresentation by the presentation of an inaccurate loss record in one year, which failed to include a substantial amount of losses. The judge found on the facts that the full loss record had been available to the reinsurers, even though the risk was broked in a way which concentrated their mind on the short form of record. This, he found, was a fair presentation and the reinsurers ought to have studied the full record. However, he found that the inaccuracy was material and entitled the reinsurers to avoid. It was only in the House of Lords that the right to avoid was rejected, albeit on the grounds of lack of inducement.[2]

6.04 The basis for the extra-contractual[3] duty of good faith is that one party is in a much stronger position than the other to know or to discover the material facts and the other is at the equivalent disadvantage.[4] Whether the misrepresentation or concealment was the result of ignorance, mistake or was intentional, the outcome is the same[5] as the duty is not dependent on some unlawful conduct such as a deliberate, fraudulent or negligent failure to disclose. The duty is there to redress

---

[1] The ambit of this duty is defined in ss 17–20 of the Marine Insurance Act 1906 which codified the pre-existing common law and is generally as applicable to general reinsurance as to marine insurance: *PCW Syndicates v PCW Reinsurers* [1996] 1 WLR 1136, 1140; also see the judgment of Steyn J in *Highlands Insurance Co v Continental Insurance Co* [1987] 1 Lloyd's Rep 109, QBD; *Pan Atlantic Insurance Co v Pine Top Insurance Co* [1995] AC 501; *Société Anonyme D'Intermédiaires Luxembourgeois v Farex* [1995] LRLR 116 and *Manifest Shipping Co v Uni Polaris Insurance Co* [2001] Lloyd's Rep IR 247 which also emphasizes that this duty is a pre-contractual duty and does not have any application to material facts which arise after the formation of the contract of insurance or reinsurance (see para 6.08).

[2] See para 6.25.

[3] *La Banque Financière de la Cité v Westgate Insurance Co* [1989] 2 All ER 952 held that the duty did not arise from an implied term of the contract, thus there could be no claim for damages.

[4] A reinsured is generally in a better position to ascertain the truth than the reinsurer due to its proximity to the underlying insured. Thus a reinsured can be liable for a material misrepresentation by passing on false information from the insured to its reinsurer: *Highland Insurance v Continental Insurance* [1987] 1 Lloyd's Rep 109, even if the accuracy of such information was not within their direct knowledge: *Sirius International Insurance Corp v Oriental Assurance Corp* [1999] Lloyd's Rep IR 343; see para 2.20.

[5] *Greenhill v Federal Insurance* [1927] 1 KB 65.

the balance in what would otherwise be an unequal bargain. It is arguable whether this justification is applicable in certain classes of reinsurance business. There are some types of broker-led business where reinsurance terms have already been negotiated before potential reinsureds are approached. In such cases the reinsurers and the brokers may have a greater knowledge of the risks and circumstances than the reinsureds themselves. Lord Hobhouse questioned in the film finance cases whether it was appropriate for the duty of good faith to place such a burden on the reinsured.[6] However, in many classes of reinsurance where contracts are made with minimal formality, on the basis of abbreviated slips and summaries of information, the duty of utmost good faith is vital for ensuring that efficient and reliable business transactions can be made. Reinsurers can quickly sign up to enormous potential liabilities on the slimmest of documentation sure in the knowledge that the duty to give proper disclosure of the material necessary to make a good business decision is firmly on the reinsured and its brokers. A prudent reinsurer will ask questions to ensure that it has a good knowledge of the risk, but the principal duty of ensuring a fair presentation of the risk remains with the reinsured.

(2) Discharging the Duty of Utmost Good Faith

In general, a reinsurer will be heavily reliant on the reinsured and its broker for **6.05** information about the risk and the circumstances of the underlying insured. In such a situation there is not simply the usual duty to refrain from material misstatements,[7] but a positive duty to disclose all known material facts. As Lord Mustill pointed out in *Pan Atlantic Insurance Co v Pine Top Insurance Co*,[8] 'in practice the line between misrepresentation and non-disclosure is often imperceptible'. The line can be blurred even further as in some situations silence, where there is a duty to speak, may amount to misrepresentation.[9] Usually the distinction will make little practical difference, except that a misrepresentation may also give rise to a claim for damages under the Misrepresentation Act 1967 or a claim for negligent misstatement.[10]

Reinsurance slips usually include information that is subject to the duty of **6.06** good faith.[11] The 'information' section on the slip may contain various items of

---

[6] *HIH Casualty and General Insurance Ltd v Chase Manhattan Bank* [2003] Lloyd's Rep IR 230, 254.

[7] s 20 of the Marine Insurance Act 1906 deals with misrepresentations.

[8] [1995] 1 AC 501, 549.

[9] *HIH Casualty and General Insurance Ltd v Chase Manhattan Bank* [2003] Lloyd's Rep IR 230. See also *Brownlie v Campbell* (1880) 5 App Cas 925, 950, per Lord Blackburn; *Banque Keyser Ullmann SA v Skandia (UK) Insurance Co Ltd* [1990] 1 QB 665, 773–774 and 782–783, per Slade LJ.

[10] The claim for damages is unattractive compared with the opportunity to avoid: see paras 6.47 et seq.

[11] See paras 2.19 et seq, *WISE (Underwriting Agency) Ltd v Grupo Nacional Provincial* [2004] Lloyd's Rep IR 764, per Longmore LJ at para 114.

information about the original risk, which will constitute representations of fact (not just belief) by the reinsured to the reinsurer,[12] but are not usually warranties.[13] Any information that a broker thinks is important to include on a slip is likely to be material to the risk, since its inclusion tends to suggest it was considered relevant to the underwriter's decision. Other sections of a slip or draft slip may be looked at more critically if it is submitted that they contain or constitute representations of fact. A 50% retention clause in a draft reinsurance treaty was held not to be a representation of the present intention of the reinsured but was simply a condition or obligation of the contract.[14]

6.07   In order to comply with the duty of utmost good faith, the underlying insured must disclose to its insurer, the reinsured, every material circumstance known to it. In turn, the reinsured must pass on that information and all other material circumstances within its knowledge to the reinsurer. The reinsured is deemed to know every circumstance which, in the ordinary course of business, ought to be known to him and this will certainly include all the information in the underlying insured's proposal form and attached information. Material circumstances are those which would influence the judgement of a prudent reinsurer in fixing the premium, or determining whether he will take the risk. However, there is no duty to disclose any circumstance which diminishes the risk or any circumstance which is known or presumed to be known to the reinsurer. The reinsurer is presumed to know matters which it ought to know in the ordinary course of its business and also knows matters which are common knowledge.

(3) Post-contractual Duty of Utmost Good Faith

6.08   Although there is no express restriction of the duty of utmost good faith in s 17 of the Marine Insurance Act 1906 to pre-contractual disclosures, it is clear that the duty of disclosure does not continue in full force after conclusion of the contract of reinsurance.[15] The duty will be revived by an amendment or variation to the reinsurance contract as the parties are entering into a partially new bargain, but the new duty of disclosure only applies with regard to any matters which are material to the variation. Although it is possible to incorporate an express continuing obligation of disclosure it is difficult if not impossible to imply one. There is a clear distinction between the pre-contractual duty of disclosure and any continuing duty,

---

[12] *Highlands v Continental* [1987] 1 Lloyd's Rep 108.

[13] *Sirius International Insurance Corp v Oriental Assurance Corp* [1999] Lloyd's Rep IR 343.

[14] *Kingscroft Insurance Co Ltd v Nissan Fire & Marine Insurance Co Ltd (No 2)* [1999] Lloyd's Rep IR 603; *Showa Oil Tanker Co of Japan Ltd v Maravan SA of Caracas (The Larrisa)* [1983] 2 Lloyd's Rep 325, Hobhouse J: by offering a contract on certain terms a person is offering to be bound by those terms, but is not impliedly representing that he is willing and able to perform the contract in accordance with those terms.

[15] *Manifest Shipping Co v Uni Polaris Insurance Co (The Star Sea)* [2001] Lloyd's Rep IR 247 overruling *Black King Shipping v Massie (The Litsion Pride)* [1985] 1 Lloyd's Rep 437.

the main difference being that it would be inequitable to allow a reinsurer to avoid a contract ab initio for a breach of good faith which might occur long afterwards.[16] Where a false statement is made to a reinsurer after it has scratched the reinsurance slip, that reinsurer cannot avoid the policy as the false information was not relevant to its decision to accept the risk.[17]

The Court of Appeal in *Bonner v Cox*[18] noted with apparent approval that Morison J 'was clearly inclined to feel' that the scratch on the slip ought to be the moment in time up to which the duty of disclosure should run. The Court considered that Morison J probably had in mind a passage in the judgment of Lord Hobhouse in *The Star Sea*[19] to the effect that an underwriter cannot depart from the terms thus agreed in the slip 'without a breach of faith' so that there is no duty to disclose information which 'would expose him to a temptation to break his contract...he [the insured] is not bound to lead his neighbour into temptation'.[20] This accords with the approach of the Marine Insurance Act 1906 under which the obligation to disclose is before the contract is concluded in circumstances where s 21 provides that a contract is 'deemed to be concluded when the proposal of the assured is accepted by the insurer, whether the policy be then issued or not; and, for the purpose of showing when the proposal was accepted, reference may be made to the slip...'. In *Bonner* the experts (and therefore the parties) agreed that disclosure should continue until the reinsured accepts the offer by becoming a party to the cover as at that moment the contract is made and the pre-contractual duty of disclosure comes to an end.[21] **6.09**

Whatever post-contractual duty of good faith exists, it probably adds little to the reinsurer's armoury of defences as it will be co-extensive with its contractual rights to terminate for a repudiatory breach, such as fraud in the making of a claim under the policy.[22] Once the contract has been made and the claims process has begun, the inequality of bargaining and information which existed pre-contract is no longer relevant.[23] The reinsurer is able to, and often will, send its loss adjuster or other agent to investigate independently before paying a claim. **6.10**

---

[16] *K/S Merc-Scandia XXXXII v Lloyd's Underwriters (The Mercandian Continent)* [2001] Lloyd's Rep IR 802.

[17] *Sirius International Insurance Corp v Oriental Assurance Corp* [1999] Lloyd's Rep IR 345. NB *Limit No 2 Ltd v Axa Versicherung AG* [2008] Lloyd's Rep IR 330 in which between provision of renewal information for a facultative obligatory treaty covering oil rigs and the reinsurer deciding to renew the loss position deteriorated. The judge said that if the deterioration was '... sufficiently serious to alter the balance of the presentation' (ie more than would normally be expected) it should be disclosed.

[18] [2006] Lloyd's Rep IR 385.

[19] [2003] 1 AC 469, 496.

[20] *Cory v Patton* (1872) LR 7 QB 304, 308–309 per Blackburn J.

[21] *Bonner v Cox* [2006] Lloyd's Rep IR 385, paras 10–15.

[22] *K/S Merc-Scandia XXXXII v Lloyd's Underwriters (The Mercandian Continent)* [2001] Lloyd's Rep IR 802; *Orakpo v Barclays Insurance Services* [1995] LRLR 443.

[23] It is certainly clear that once litigation begins between the parties the duty of disclosure ceases to have any relevance and is replaced by the Civil Procedure Rules.

6.11   Continuous contracts of reinsurance will contain provisions permitting cancellation at each anniversary date. Reinsurers will often either write or stamp on the slip with the letters 'NCAD' meaning 'Notice of Cancellation at Anniversary Date' (the effect of which will be that a notice of cancellation is treated as having been served at each anniversary date) or serve a provisional notice of cancellation. In the latter case the notice is 'provisional' (rather than definite) in that the reinsurer is indicating a willingness to consider continuing with the contract. The existence of a right to serve a notice of cancellation does not give rise to a duty on the reinsured to give material disclosure of matters that might cause it to exercise that right.[24] In *Iron Trades Mutual v Companhia de Seguros Imperio*,[25] Hobhouse J held that a duty of disclosure did not arise by virtue of the service of a notice of cancellation either, on the grounds that the reinsured might be indifferent as to whether the reinsurer remained on risk. The reinsured's only duty would be not to misrepresent any material facts. In *Kingscroft Insurance Co v Nissan Fire & Marine Insurance Co (No 2)*[26] Moore-Bick J suggested that what Hobhouse J had said in the *Iron Trades* case only applied where the reinsured simply waited for the reinsurer to approach him with a request to withdraw the cancellation but it would be surprising if the existence of a duty of disclosure depended on who approached whom first. In the *Kingscroft* case, the reinsurer purported to withdraw its notice of cancellation. The issue for Moore-Bick J to decide was whether the reinsurer could rely on any misrepresentation or non-disclosure prior to inception of the contract in relation to the contract as continued after withdrawal of the notice of cancellation. He held that it could:[27]

> Giving provisional notice of cancellation meant that the contract would automatically terminate in the absence of some further agreement between the parties. By providing statistics for Nissan's consideration Weavers were, in effect, inviting it to continue on the same terms. It was not a case of a simple variation, but equally it was not a case of presenting a completely new risk. In my judgment the parties continued to owe each other a duty of the utmost good faith, but it was one which was conditioned by the existing relationship between them. Any misrepresentation or failure to make proper disclosure at the time when the treaties were originally offered to Nissan could still be presumed to have its effect on the mind of the underwriter, unless it had been overtaken by subsequent events.[28]

6.12   As has been explained in Chapter 2,[29] it is common for a series of reinsurance contracts to be made over a period of time as various reinsurers scratch a slip that

---

[24] *New Hampshire v MGN Ltd* [1997] IRLR 24.
[25] [1991] 1 Re LR 213.
[26] [1999] Lloyd's Rep IR 603, 637.
[27] [1999] Lloyd's Rep IR 603, 637.
[28] Moore-Bick J at 637. He sought to distinguish Hobhouse J's opposing view in *Iron Trades Mutual v Companhia de Seguros Imperio* [1991] 1 Re LR 213 by suggesting that it only applies where the reinsured simply waits for the reinsurer to approach him with a request to withdraw the cancellation. It might be thought surprising that Moore-Bick J thought that the duty of utmost good faith depended on who approached whom first.
[29] See paras 2.13 et seq.

is passed around the market. If information comes to light during the course of this process it can place a reinsured in a difficult position whereby the information has not been disclosed to the first reinsurer to scratch, but must be disclosed to all potential following reinsurers. The usual duty of utmost good faith has expired in relation to the earlier reinsurer and so there is no duty to go back and make disclosure, but it still survives in relation to the following reinsurers who may well insist on a different premium or different terms when the disclosure is made. The reinsured may as a result end up with different terms and conditions applying to one reinsurance slip. The earlier reinsurer should protect itself against such a situation by the inclusion of a term that it will be entitled to the benefit of any more advantageous terms or conditions imposed by the following market. It must be remembered that each reinsurer on the slip is treated as a separate party and a non-disclosure to one is not necessarily a non-disclosure to all and in particular each must show actual inducement.[30] However, the fact that a non-disclosure has been made to a leading underwriter whom other reinsurers are following and relied upon might itself be a material fact that needs to be disclosed to that following market.[31]

B. Elements of the Duty of Utmost Good Faith

Using the analysis derived from the leading case of *Pan Atlantic Insurance Co v Pine* **6.13**
Top Insurance Co,[32] there is a duty to disclose and not to misrepresent facts:

(a) that are material to risk;
(b) which induce the reinsurer;
(c) which are within knowledge of the reinsured;
(d) which are not within knowledge of the reinsurer.

(1) Materiality

Both a misrepresentation and a non-disclosure must be of a material fact. Whether **6.14**
any particular circumstance is material or not is, in each case, a question of fact.
The starting point for the objective test is the definition taken from s 18(2) of the
Marine Insurance Act 1906:

> Every circumstance is material which would influence the judgment of a prudent insurer in fixing the premium, or determining whether he will take the risk.

---

[30] *Sirius International Insurance Corp v Oriental Assurance Corp* [1999] Lloyd's Rep IR 345.
[31] *Aneco Reinsurance Underwriting v Johnson & Higgins* [1998] 1 Lloyd's Rep 565; however, note that the decision was appealed on other grounds: [2000] Lloyd's Rep IR 12, [2002] Lloyd's Rep IR 91 and the notion that the general fact of previous non-disclosures by a broker could itself be material was disapproved at first instance in *Container Transport International v Oceanus Mutual Underwriting* [1982] 2 Lloyd's Rep 178 but not mentioned on appeal.
[32] [1995] 1 AC 501, which applies to reinsurance contracts: *Assicurazioni Generali SpA v Arab Insurance Group* [2003] Lloyd's Rep IR 131.

6.15 The Court of Appeal[33] approved this test for use in general insurance and held that the presentation of the risk must be fair and substantially accurate. Kerr LJ said:[34]

> The question is simply to ask oneself having regard to all the circumstances known or deemed to be known to the insured and to his broker and ignoring those which are expressly excepted from the duty of disclosure, was the presentation in summary form to the underwriter a fair and substantially accurate presentation of the risk proposed for insurance so that the prudent insurer could form a proper judgment either on the presentation alone or by asking questions if he was sufficiently put on inquiry and wanted to know further details whether or not to accept the proposal and, if so, on what terms.

6.16 A prudent reinsurer may want to be aware of facts that influence considerations other than merely premium and risk, although these two would seem to cover most situations in practice.[35] It is an objective test which judges materiality against what the hypothetical reasonably prudent insurer would have wanted to be aware of in the circumstances.[36] The *CTI* test goes further than the 'Decisive Influence' test (that the fact must be capable of having a decisive influence on the mind of a prudent insurer) which was rejected by the House of Lords in *Pan Atlantic Insurance Co v Pine Top Insurance Co* as the judgement of the insurer is his decision and evaluation process, not only his decision. The *CTI* test also goes further than the 'Increased Risk' theory that the fact must be one which a prudent insurer would have regarded as increasing the risk.[37] A full and detailed presentation of facts is not required in all circumstances. Provided that the presentation of the material facts in summarized form is done fairly, there is no need for more: it is fair presentation on which the London market practice as well as the law is based.[38]

6.17 In reinsurance most material facts will revolve around those circumstances which affect the subject of the cover, the 'Physical Hazard' such as the previous claims history of the reinsured or the particular class of reinsurance contract that is being offered. The nature of the risks underwritten by the reinsured is likely to be material.[39]

---

[33] *Container Transport International v Oceanus Mutual Underwriting* [1984] 1 Lloyd's Rep 476 that was approved obiter by the majority of the House of Lords in *Pan Atlantic Insurance Co v Pine Top Insurance Co* [1995] 1 AC 501.

[34] *Container Transport International v Oceanus Mutual Underwriting* [1984] 1 Lloyd's Rep 476, 496.

[35] *Tate v Hyslop* (1883) 15 QBD 368 shows that the wide words of s 18(2) go beyond matters which are material to the risk in the sense of the likelihood and extent of the loss: *SAIL v Farex Gie* [1995] LRLR 116, 150, per Hoffmann LJ.

[36] An assessment which often calls for expert underwriting evidence as to what the market would deem to be material: *Commonwealth Insurance Co of Vancouver v Groupe Sprinks SA* [1983] 1 Lloyd's Rep 67.

[37] *St Paul Fire & Marine Co (UK) v McConnell Dowell Constructors* [1995] 2 Lloyd's Rep 116.

[38] Kerr LJ in *Container Transport International v Oceanus Mutual Underwriting* [1984] 1 Lloyd's Rep 476, 496.

[39] In *Toomey v Banco Vitalicio de Espana SA de Seguros y Reaseguros* [2004] Lloyd's Rep IR 354 affirmed on other grounds [2004] Lloyd's Rep IR 354 there was a material misrepresentation in the draft reinsurance slip as to the nature of the original policy. It was a valued policy and not an indemnity policy and so a larger loss was possible making the matter material. See also *GMA v Storebrand and Kansa* [1995] LRLR 333 in which Rix J found that the contents of a portfolio of reinsurances were material.

Even a relatively minor inaccuracy in the loss history of the reinsured may be a matter that would affect the mind of a prudent reinsurer, so key can it be to the reinsurer's decision making process.[40] However if insurance is written in the normal course of the business and that is what reinsurers were agreeing to cover, then no question of non-disclosure could arise. Also if a reinsurer fronts a risk (taking out 100% retrocession) it may have no interest in the nature of the business being written.[41]

Also of interest to a reinsurer may be the 'Moral Hazard' of the underlying **6.18** insured,[42] but there will also be many circumstances, particularly in relation to treaty reinsurance, in which there is a duty to disclose facts relating to the business of the reinsured itself. Of particular interest may well be the amount of the reinsured's retention,[43] and the absence of a significant retention on the part of the reinsured may be a material matter, but this is usually something that the reinsurer would be expected to ask about.[44] A treaty reinsurer may also want to know about the underwriting policy and history of the reinsured and about the classes of business that the reinsured usually writes.[45] All these matters are likely to be material, but expert evidence should be called to substantiate materiality in most cases.

A fact that diminishes the risk is not disclosable and neither is a fact that is relevant **6.19** to the reinsurer's own reinsurance (or retrocession) arrangements rather than the reinsurance between reinsured and reinsurer. The fact that a reinsured knows that

---

[40] Although note *Commonwealth Insurance Co of Vancouver v Groupe Sprinks SA* [1983] 1 Lloyd's Rep 67 in which a mistake in the gross loss ratio on a reinsurance account was held not to be substantial and therefore was immaterial.

[41] *Bonner v Cox* [2005] Lloyd's Rep IR 569, [2006] 2 Lloyd's Rep 152. In *WISE (Underwriting Agency) v Grupo Nacional Provincial SA* [2004] Lloyd's Rep IR 764 an insured shipment of clocks was in fact Rolex watches and so the judge found that there was a material non-disclosure (even though it was found on appeal that the reinsurer had affirmed the contract).

[42] eg, the fact that the underlying insured drove in races was disclosed to the reinsured but not the reinsurer and resulted in a successful avoidance in the Scottish case of *Equitable Life Assurance Society v General Accident Insurance Corp* (1904) 12 SLT 348. See also *Brotherton v Aseguradora Colseguros SA* [2003] Lloyd's Rep IR 746 where allegations of dishonesty against the insured bank were known to the reinsured, but not disclosed to reinsurers. See also *Sphere Drake v EIU* [2003] Lloyd's Rep IR 525 on the moral hazard of knowledge of a breach of fiduciary duty on the part of the reinsurer's own agent.

[43] Particularly in quota share reinsurance, but perhaps less so in non-proportional reinsurance such as excess of loss cover: *Kingscroft Insurance Co v Nissan Fire & Marine Insurance Co (No 2)* [1999] Lloyd's Rep IR 603, QBD.

[44] *Société Anonyme D'Intermédiaires Luxembourgeois (SAIL) v Farex Gie* [1995] LRLR 116, at first instance and unchallenged on appeal. Gatehouse J decided that this was a matter about which a reinsurer must either make inquiry or be taken to have waived disclosure of the information. There is no implied obligation on a reinsured to keep a retention and a prudent reinsurer will require a warranty as to the level of retention: *Phoenix General Insurance Co of Greece SA v Halvanon Insurance* [1985] 2 Lloyd's Rep 599, aff'd [1986] 2 Lloyd's Rep 552. On retention warranties see para 6.73. See also *Iron Trades Mutual Insurance Co Ltd v Companhia de Seguros Imperio* [1991] 1 Re LR 213 in which it was held that a misrepresentation of 50% retention instead of the actual 40% retention was found to be not material. See also para 3.63.

[45] See, eg, *GMA v Storebrand and Kansa* [1995] LRLR 333 where the presence of unusual reinsurance arrangements within a portfolio was held, obiter, to be a material matter.

its reinsurer's retrocession agreement is ineffective is not a material circumstance in relation to the reinsurance contract. A reinsurer's own arrangements for reinsuring a risk are not matters which would influence the judgement of a prudent insurer in fixing the premium of the underlying reinsurance, or determining whether he will take the risk. There is no obligation to disclose matters relevant only to a different contract to which the reinsured is not a party as the whole basis of the duty of disclosure is to reveal matters within the peculiar knowledge of the reinsured.[46]

6.20 Only facts need to be disclosed and not mere opinion, so the reinsured does not have to disclose matters that he has inferred from disclosed facts, unless the risk is so unusual that the reinsurer cannot be fairly expected to make his own inferences.

6.21 It is not consistent with s 20(5) of the Marine Insurance Act 1906 for a representation of expectation or belief to be subject to an implied representation that there are reasonable grounds for that belief.[47] As the statute deems an honest representation as to a matter of expectation or belief to be true, there is no scope for inquiry as to whether there were objectively reasonable grounds for that belief. However what may appear to be a representation merely of expectation or belief could in reality be an assertion of a specific fact governed by subss (3) and (4) rather than subs (5) of s 20.[48] There must be some basis for a representation of expectation or belief before it can be said to be made in good faith.[49]

(2) Inducement

6.22 *Pan Atlantic Insurance Co v Pine Top Insurance Co*[50] brought the law of insurance and reinsurance contracts into line with general contractual principles by adding another limb to the materiality test. The reinsurer must have been induced to enter into the contract by the reinsured's non-disclosure.[51] Therefore once the objective test has been fulfilled the reinsurer must yet show the subjective element to avoid the reinsurance contract. The question of the extent to which the reinsurer needs to be induced is not expressly dealt with in *Pan Atlantic Insurance Co v Pine Top Insurance Co*. Reinsurance law can draw upon general contract law and the test for misrepresentation. In such cases the representation need not be the sole inducement, but must have been a real and substantial cause affecting the decision of the representee to enter into the contract, or to do so on the terms agreed.[52] Clarke LJ

---

[46] *SAIL v Farex Gie* [1995] LRLR 116, 149 citing *Carter v Boehm* (1966) 3 Burr 1905.
[47] *Economides v Commercial Union Assurance Co* [1998] Lloyd's Rep IR 9, 16 and 21.
[48] *Economides v Commercial Union Assurance Co* [1998] Lloyd's Rep IR 9, 16 col 2 and see, eg, *Limit No 2 Ltd v Axa Versicherung AG* [2009] Lloyd's Rep IR 369, 402.
[49] *Economides v Commercial Union Assurance Co* [1998] Lloyd's Rep IR 9 cited and applied by Cresswell J in *Rendall v Combined Insurance Company of America* [2006] Lloyd's Rep IR 732, 748.
[50] [1995] 1 AC 501.
[51] *Marc Rich & Co AG v Portman* [1996] 1 Lloyd's Rep 430, aff'd [1997] 1 Lloyd's Rep 225; *Sirius International Insurance Corp v Oriental Assurance Corp* [1999] Lloyd's Rep IR 343, 351.
[52] *JEB Fasteners Ltd v Marks, Bloom & Co* [1983] 1 All ER 583 and *Edgington v Fitzmaurice* (1885) 29 Ch D 459.

adopted this approach in *Assicurazioni Generali SpA v Arab Insurance Group*[53] in which he said:[54]

> It seems to me that the true position is that the misrepresentation must be an effective cause of the particular insurer or reinsurer entering into the contract but need not of course be the sole cause. If the insurer would have entered into the contract on the same terms in any event, the representation or non-disclosure will not, however material, be an effective cause of the making of the contract and the insurer or reinsurer will not be entitled to avoid the contract.

No qualification to the inducement is made in that case, which may imply that any inducement to enter into the policy will be sufficient. The position is clear in cases where the reinsurer will say in evidence that he would not have agreed to reinsure had he known of the undisclosed facts. This position in practice is uncommon, as when a factor affecting the risk is known it often results in a change in the terms; by additional subjectivities, exclusions or simply an increase in the premium. However, a contract with additional exclusion clauses or at a higher premium is not the same contract that the reinsurer was induced into entering, and thus there should be sufficient inducement to avoid the contract.

6.23

Reinsurers can rely on the presumption of inducement which is of particular significance in cases where the underwriter cannot be called because he has died or has lost contact with his former employers.[55] It is not applicable where the underwriter gives evidence and that evidence is inconclusive on the question of actual inducement.[56] In *St Paul Fire & Marine Co (UK) v McConnell Dowell Constructors*[57] one of the insurers failed to give evidence of inducement and was held to be able to rely on this presumption which had to be rebutted by the assured.[58] The presumption arises once materiality is proved. Inducement cannot be inferred in law simply from the presence of a material non-disclosure or misrepresentation, but there may be cases where the materiality is so obvious as to justify an inference of fact that the representee was actually induced. In such exceptional cases, the inference is only a prima facie one and may be rebutted by counter-evidence.[59] The

6.24

---

[53] [2003] Lloyd's Rep IR 131.

[54] [2003] Lloyd's Rep IR 131, 148. Sir Christopher Staughton agreed at 170 saying that the appropriate test was not a 'but-for' test and Ward LJ agreed at 175 with the qualification that he was not entirely sure that it is necessary to require the misrepresentation to be an *effective* cause of a party's entering into the contract on the terms on which he did, unless that merely meant that it did actually play upon his mind and influence his decision.

[55] *Marc Rich & Co AG v Portman* [1996] 1 Lloyd's Rep 430.

[56] *Glencore International v Portman* [1997] 1 Lloyd's Rep 225.

[57] [1995] 2 Lloyd's Rep 116.

[58] See also the readiness of Rix J to apply the presumption in *GMA v Storebrand and Kansa* [1995] LRLR 333.

[59] *Assicurazioni Generali SpA v Arab Insurance Group* [2003] Lloyd's Rep IR 131 citing *Smith v Chadwick* (1884) 9 App Cas 187. In the *Assicurazioni Generali* case the reinsurer alleged that it had entered into the contract induced by a misrepresentation as to the participation of Munich Re as a co-reinsurer. The court held that even if the reinsurer had known the truth about Munich Re's involvement, it would still have written the risk.

presumption simply operates where the evidence before the court is enough to lead to the inference that the reinsurer was, as a matter of fact, induced to enter into the contract.[60]

(3) Knowledge of the Reinsured

6.25 The duty on the reinsured is essentially to make a fair presentation of the risk to the reinsurer of all material facts within its knowledge. It affords no defence to the reinsured that he mistakenly or forgetfully failed to disclose, as there is an absolute duty to disclose all facts known to a reinsured or, often, his broker. The duty, however, is limited to circumstances which are known or ought to be known to the reinsured. The reinsured is not under a duty to make inquiries or investigations as to facts outside his knowledge[61] although there is a duty to disclose matters which are within its constructive knowledge to which it has turned a blind eye. If the reinsured, suspicious of a material circumstance which ought to be disclosed, turns a blind eye and refrains from inquiry, he is to be regarded as knowing whatever such inquiry would have revealed.[62] However, the test of the reinsured's constructive knowledge is not an objective test of what ought to be known by a reasonable, prudent reinsured carrying on a business of the kind in question, but a test of what ought to be known by the actual reinsured in the ordinary course of carrying on his business in the manner in which he carries on that business. A failure to disclose a matter that would and should have been revealed by the reinsured's ordinary and reasonable inquiries is likely to be a non-disclosure.[63] However, in the ordinary course of business a reinsured is not taken to know that it is being defrauded.[64]

---

[60] *Toomey v Banco Vitalicio de Espana SA de Seguros y Reaseguros* [2004] Lloyd's Rep IR 354 aff'd on other grounds [2004] Lloyd's Rep IR 354 found that it should be inferred that an insurer who did not give evidence would not have underwritten the risk if he had been told that the underlying insurance was a valued policy and that the agreed value might well prove higher than the Spanish football club's actual loss. See also the first instance judgment in *Talbot Underwriting Ltd v Nausch Hogan & Murray* [2006] 2 Lloyd's Rep 195 on inferences as to inducement.

[61] In *Australia & New Zealand Bank v Colonial & Eagle Wharves Ltd* [1960] 2 Lloyd's Rep 241, 252 the judge rejected the submission that the insured ought to have known the material facts because they would have known them if they had made such inquiries as to their system as a reasonable, prudent board of such company in the ordinary course of business would have made. 'To impose such an obligation upon the proposer is tantamount to holding that insurers only insure persons who conduct their business prudently, whereas it is a commonplace that one of the purposes of insurance is to cover yourself against your own negligence or the negligence of your servants.' The same principle applies to reinsureds (*Simner v New India Assurance* [1995] 1 LRLR 240).

[62] *Simner v New India Assurance* [1995] 1 LRLR 240, 254, and see the insurance example of *Manifest Shipping Co v Uni Polaris Insurance Co* [2001] Lloyd's Rep IR 247.

[63] Contrast the approach to a consumer insurance contract where a person was not acting in the course of business: *Economides v Commercial Union Assurance Co* [1998] Lloyd's Rep IR 9.

[64] In *Group Josi Re v Walbrook Insurance Co* [1996] 1 Lloyd's Rep 345, the dishonesty of broker and agents was not within the knowledge of the very reinsureds who were being defrauded; see also *PCW Syndicates v PCW Reinsurers* [1996] 1 Lloyd's Rep 241.

The reinsured will also be deemed to know certain circumstances. In *London*   **6.26**
General Insurance Co Ltd v General Marine Underwriters' Association Ltd[65] it was
held that a reinsured was deemed to have knowledge of a casualty slip received by
the underwriters employed by them. The underwriters had in fact done nothing to
make use of the information contained in the slips. In contrast, in *Simner v New*
India Assurance[66] the reinsured and its broker were unaware of large scale losses
when they signed up to a binder and then placed stop loss reinsurance, telling the
reinsurers that there were no claims figures. The original broker who placed the
binder knew about the claims, but had told only the leader and not the reinsured,
and had no duty to forward new information on to the reinsured once he had
signed up to the insurance.

The judge in *Simner v New India Assurance* summarized the law stating that the   **6.27**
knowledge of an agent of the reinsured will be deemed to be within the knowledge
of the reinsured in three situations.

The first is where the agent is relied on by a reinsured for information concerning   **6.28**
the subject matter of the proposed reinsurance.[67] The reinsured is deemed to know
circumstances which such agents ought to have communicated to the reinsured in
the ordinary course of business.

Secondly, there is deemed knowledge where the agent is in such a predominant   **6.29**
position in relation to the reinsured that his knowledge can be regarded as the
knowledge of the reinsured. Agents who have or appear to have full authority of the
principal in all respects should pass on all their knowledge to the reinsurer.[68] This
will be common where an agent has binding authority.

The third situation where the reinsured will be deemed to know circumstances   **6.30**
which lie within the knowledge of his agent is where the agent has effected the
relevant reinsurance.[69]

---

[65] [1921] 1 KB 104, (1920) 4 Ll L Rep 382.

[66] [1995] LRLR 240.

[67] 'The insurer is entitled to assume that the insured will take the necessary measures, by the
employment of competent and honest agents, to obtain, through the ordinary channels of intelli-
gence in use in the mercantile world, all due information as to the subject matter of the insurance.
This condition is not complied with where, by the fraud or negligence of the agent, the party proposing the insurance is kept in ignorance of a material fact, which ought to have been made known
to the underwriter, and through such ignorance fails to disclose it': Cockburn CJ in *Proudfoot v
Montefiore* (1867) LR 2 QB 511, 521.

[68] *Blackburn Low v Vigors* (1887) 12 App Cas 531, 537–538.

[69] '…where an insurance is effected through the medium of an agent, the ordinary rule of law
applies, and non-disclosure of material facts, known to the agent only, will affect his principal, and
give the insurer good ground for avoiding contract', *Blackburn Low v Vigors* (1887) 12 App Cas 531,
539 per Lord Watson; see also *Blackburn v Haslam* (1888) 21 QBD 144. See also s 19 of the Marine
Insurance Act 1906 which also provides that an agent to insure is deemed to know every circumstance which ought to be known by, or ought to have been communicated to, him.

6.31 Agents are very commonly used in reinsurance business and so the first of the *Simner* examples is often of real importance. Reinsureds have to place a great deal of reliance on their brokers in order to avoid a non-disclosure about a matter of which they have imputed knowledge. However, not all knowledge that a reinsured's broker has will be imputed to the reinsured, it will depend on the capacity in which the broker was acting when it received the information. The *SAIL* case[70] held that the knowledge of a broker is not imputed to his reinsured, where that knowledge was gleaned in the course of the broker's business for the reinsurer.[71] Therefore it would appear that the relevant knowledge of brokers is restricted to that knowledge that comes to the broker in his capacity as agent for the reinsured, and does not include any coincidental knowledge that the broker may have obtained from another source. However, it is doubtful whether the same principle can be applied to all agents, as opposed to brokers who will often act for more than one party in a transaction.

6.32 A broker or other agent who effects the reinsurance owes an independent duty of good faith to the reinsurer to make disclosure. Such an agent is deemed to know every circumstance which in the ordinary course of business ought to be known by, or to have been communicated to, him.[72] Even if the knowledge cannot be imputed to the reinsured, the undisclosed knowledge of material facts by the broker may allow the reinsurer to avoid the policy. The *SAIL* case approved the view that the broker's duty of disclosure is derived from s 19 of the Marine Insurance Act 1906,[73] which it was conceded was of general application to all insurance and therefore to reinsurance.

(4) Facts Within Knowledge of Reinsurer

6.33 The last element in the duty of utmost good faith may seem to be stating the obvious: there is no duty to disclose material facts already known to the reinsurer. If there is some undisclosed material fact that is within the actual knowledge of the reinsurer, even if the information was withheld by the reinsured or its broker, there can be no avoidance on the ground of non-disclosure as the reinsurer entered into

---

[70] *Société Anonyme D'Intermédiaires Luxembourgeois v Farex Gie* [1995] LRLR 116.
[71] Hoffmann LJ at 150 approves the analysis of Lord Macnaghten in *Blackburn Low & Co v Vigors* (1887) 12 App Cas 531, 542: 'But that is not because the knowledge of the agent is to be imputed to the principal but because the agent of the reinsured is bound as the principal is bound to communicate to the underwriters all material facts within his knowledge'.
[72] *HIH Casualty and General Insurance Ltd v Chase Manhattan Bank* [2003] Lloyd's Rep IR 230; *Blackburn, Low & Co v Vigors* (1887) 12 App Cas 531, 542–543 per Lord Macnaghten.
[73] s 19 provides: 'Subject to the provisions of the preceding section as to circumstances which need not be disclosed, where an insurance is effected for the reinsured by an agent, the agent must disclose to the reinsured—(a) Every material circumstance which is known to himself, and an agent to insure is deemed to know every circumstance which in the ordinary course of business ought to be known by, or to have been communicated to, him; and (b) Every material circumstance which the reinsured is bound to disclose, unless it come to his knowledge too late to communicate it to the agent.'

the contract that he thought that he was entering into.[74] The reinsurer is taken to know those facts which are contained in information within its possession, even if the reinsured does not specifically mention the fact or highlight it. If the material fact is reasonably clear from the disclosed information, the reinsurer cannot avoid.[75] The likely area of dispute is over facts which the reinsurer once knew but had forgotten, or information that the reinsurer ought to have known at the time the risk was entered into. If the reinsurer has genuinely forgotten old information and cannot reasonably be expected to have remembered it, then the material facts must be disclosed and if they are not, the reinsurer can still avoid. The test is in part subjective, looking at the actual knowledge of the reinsurer at the time it scratched the slip and in part objective, looking at whether it turned a blind eye, Nelson-like, to the old information or whether it could not reasonably have been expected to have had the information at its fingertips.

The more thorny issue surrounds the constructive knowledge of the reinsurer: those matters which it ought to know and of which it is deemed to have knowledge. These fall into three general categories. **6.34**

(a) Where the reinsurer is put on inquiry

If the reinsurer is reasonably put on inquiry as to the existence of the material fact and has the means of reasonably discovering that fact, there is no non-disclosure. The reinsurer will be put on inquiry by the disclosure of facts which would raise in the mind of a reasonable reinsurer at least a suspicion that there were other circumstances which would or might vitiate the presentation made to him.[76] The reinsured must make a fair presentation of this information to the reinsurer, else it will not put him on inquiry.[77] This means that reinsureds do not necessarily have to ensure that they disclose the details of each material fact as long as they call the reinsurer's attention to the existence of such facts, so that the reinsurer knows that he ought to ask if further information is required and so long as the overall presentation is a fair presentation. **6.35**

(b) Ordinary incidents and attributes of risk

The reinsurer is presumed to have business expertise in the particular area he insures.[78] He should know the custom and practice of the trade or area he reinsures, **6.36**

---

[74] *Société Anonyme D'Intermédiaires Luxembourgeois v Farex Gie* [1995] LRLR 116 per Saville LJ at 156 applying s 18(3)(b) of the Marine Insurance Act 1906 in holding that a reinsurer ought to know the state of its own retrocession; *London General Insurance Co v General Marine Underwriters' Association* [1921] 1 KB 104, (1920) 4 Ll L Rep 382; *Pimm v Lewis* (1862) 2 F & F 778.

[75] See the analogous insurance case of *St Margarets Trust v Navigators and General Insurance Co* (1949) 82 Ll LR 752.

[76] *Container Transport International v Oceanus Mutual Underwriting* [1984] 1 Lloyd's Rep 476, 511, per Parker LJ.

[77] *Newbury International v Reliance National Insurance Co* [1994] 1 Lloyd's Rep 83.

[78] In *North British Fishing Boat Insurance Co Ltd v Starr* (1922) 13 Ll L Rep 206 Rowlatt J said of a marine reinsurer at 210: 'I must look at the underwriter in this case as a person doing the business

including the usual terms and conditions appropriate for that area of business, such as whether it is usual for a reinsured to take out excess of loss cover.[79] The reinsurer is also taken to know those matters which someone with knowledge of the particular area could naturally infer from the general description of the risk. It is only, for example, when the underlying insured is carrying out an activity which is unusual for his area of business or concern that the particular risk must be disclosed. A reserving policy which is said to be unusual or imprudent will only be material if it is unknown to current market practice.[80]

(c) Common public knowledge

6.37 All reinsurers are presumed to know matters of common public knowledge and thus cannot avoid the reinsurance contract for matters which a reasonably well-informed person might be expected to know.[81] Matters of public notoriety such as wars can often affect reinsurance policies, but the reinsured has no duty to disclose common knowledge.[82]

(5) Waiver

6.38 The duty of disclosure can be circumscribed by the reinsurer. Any information which is waived by the reinsurer falls outside the duty of disclosure. A reinsurer can waive disclosure of any material and otherwise disclosable circumstances expressly or by implication. As Rix LJ said:[83]

> In truth it is not possible to determine whether a presentation is unfair or not without taking into account, where the issue is raised, the other side of the section 18 coin. It will be recalled that the setting of section 18 is that 'the utmost good faith' is to be observed by both parties (section 17). It is a mutual duty: *Banque Keyser Ullmann SA v Skandia (UK) Insurance Co Ltd* [1990] 1 QB 665, [1991] 2 AC 249...the doctrine of waiver is ultimately founded on the concept of fairness. It would not in my judgment be fair to castigate a presentation as unfair and thus put an assured in peril of the draconian remedy of avoidance where an insurer

---

of insuring ships and as necessarily conversant with the course of losses affecting particular classes of ships. What he is not bound to know in the ordinary course of his business are particular circumstances specially affecting ships or lines of ships, and specially affecting some limited number of ships.'

[79] *Trinity Insurance Co v Singapore Aviation & General Insurance* (1993) 2 Re LR 111, QBD.

[80] *Assicurazioni Generali SpA v Arab Insurance Group* [2003] Lloyd's Rep IR 131.

[81] *Kingscroft Insurance Co v Nissan Fire & Marine Insurance Co (No 2)* [1999] Lloyd's Rep IR 603, QBD citing *Bates v Hewitt* (1867) LR 2 QB 595 which concerned the insurance of a vessel *Georgia* which had been a Confederate cruiser, a fact which the insured had omitted to disclose to the insurer.

[82] *Brotherton v Aseguradora Colseguros SA* [2003] Lloyd's Rep IR 746, in which allegations of misconduct by the president of a Colombian state-owned bank were made in the Colombian media prior to the writing of the reinsurance and were found not to be common knowledge within the London reinsurance market.

[83] *WISE (Underwriting Agency) Ltd v Grupo Nacional Provincial* [2004] Lloyd's Rep IR 764, 775. See also *Rendall v Combined Insurance Company Of America* [2006] Lloyd's Rep IR 732.

had waived the relevant information. The mutuality of the doctrine of good faith underlines this proposition.

The easiest cases are where an insurer or reinsurer expressly waives disclosure, but these are uncommon in reinsurance. An express waiver is unlikely to be found in a reinsurance policy (which by its nature will most often post-date the duty to disclose) and the pre-contractual proposal form that is common in insurance is rare in reinsurance. **6.39**

Most cases of waiver will be by implication. If the reinsurer is given information that should put the reasonably prudent reinsurer on inquiry and the reinsurer fails to make that simple inquiry, he can be said to have waived the information such inquiry would have revealed. The reinsurer might be put on inquiry by obviously incomplete answers from the broker or contained in the information on or attached to the slip. **6.40**

The reinsurer may by his words or conduct to the reinsured waive the need for disclosure by showing indifference towards particular material matters or by giving the impression that disclosure is not required in full or in part. An insurer may ask its insured questions about material matters in the proposal form which have a limited scope and thus waive facts which fall outside the scope of the question.[84] This is because if questions are asked about one aspect of a material matter, those questions can by implication waive disclosure as to other aspects or details about that material matter. If the reinsurer decides to offer reinsurance on the basis of the same proposal form without further inquiry, it is likely that it will have waived further information about the underlying insured. **6.41**

Section 18(3) of the Marine Insurance Act 1906 provides the starting point. It provides that any circumstance as to which information is waived by the insurer need not be disclosed, nor should any circumstance which it is superfluous to disclose by reason of any express or implied warranty. It follows that where the doctrine of waiver applies, there is no need for disclosure, and a reinsurer cannot avoid on grounds of non-disclosure no matter how material the matter may be.[85] **6.42**

As is expressed in the passage from the judgment of Rix LJ cited at para 6.38, the concepts of waiver or what the reinsurer already knows are essential elements of whether a presentation is unfair or not. The duty of utmost good faith is a mutual duty[86] and the doctrine of waiver is ultimately founded on the concept of fairness between the two parties.[87] **6.43**

---

[84] *Roberts v Plaisted* [1989] 2 Lloyd's Rep 341; *Hair v Prudential Assurance Co* [1983] 2 Lloyd's Rep 667.

[85] *WISE (Underwriting Agency) Ltd v Grupo Nacional Provincial* [2004] Lloyd's Rep IR 764.

[86] *Banque Keyser Ullmann SA v Skandia (UK) Insurance Co Ltd* [1990] 1 QB 665, [1991] 2 AC 249.

[87] In *Iron Trades Mutual Insurance Co Ltd v Companhia de Seguros Imperio* [1991] 1 Re LR 213, 224 Hobhouse J said: 'If a proposer has made a fair presentation of the risk, he has discharged his duty; if he has not, then a failure by an insurer to inquire will not relieve the proposer of his duty to make proper disclosure'.

6.44   The doctrine of waiver cannot be applied to undisclosed facts which are unusual or special, so that their non-disclosure distorts the presentation of the risk. In such cases the underwriter is not put on inquiry about the existence of any such facts[88] and waiver must not be used to whittle away the duty of disclosure.[89] Waiver by implication is unlikely to provide an effective answer to extreme cases of non-disclosure unless the circumstances are particularly clear.

6.45   In order to establish waiver by implication from non-inquiry the reinsurer must be put on inquiry by the disclosure of facts which would raise in the mind of a reasonable reinsurer at least a suspicion that there were other circumstances which would or might vitiate the presentation made to him. Certainly it is not enough for the reinsured to demonstrate that a reinsurer was aware of a mere possibility of the existence of other material facts. Sufficient disclosure must be made so that the reinsurer is fairly put on inquiry about them and chooses to ignore them.[90] A distinction should be drawn between complex commercial reinsurance and domestic insurance where the insurer can waive merely by asking limited questions in a proposal form. However, a reinsurer cannot expect to be told every minute detail and the limits of waiver will still apply where the reinsurer shuts his eyes to obvious incompleteness.

6.46   Finally on waiver, the 'waiver of rights' clause analysed in *HIH Casualty & General Insurance Ltd v New Hampshire Insurance Co*[91] should be noted. The exclusion in the insurance policy provided that the insurer agreed that it would not be entitled to avoid or rescind the policy or reject any claim or seek any remedy on the grounds of non-disclosure or misrepresentation. The clause was held to be a term of the reinsurance contract which had an 'as original' wording but only in an unmanipulated form (so as to preclude the reinsurers from taking against the reinsured a defence based on the assertion that the reinsured could have avoided the insurance). This extraordinarily wide purported exclusion of all the insurer's (and therefore reinsurer's) rights was held not to apply to a defence based on breach of warranty or the lack of contractual cover, although it did effectively exclude defences of non-disclosure and misrepresentation based on the extra-contractual duty of utmost good faith.[92]

---

[88] *Container Transport International v Oceanus Mutual Underwriting* [1984] 1 Lloyd's Rep 476.
[89] *Greenhill v Federal Insurance Co Ltd* [1927] 1 KB 65, (1926) 24 Ll L Rep 383 in which the assured failed to disclose to cargo insurers that the cargo had already suffered injury during an earlier leg of the carriage.
[90] See *New Hampshire Insurance Co v Oil Refineries Ltd* [2003] Lloyd's Rep IR 386 in which a five-year claims history given by the insured omitted the very large claim that just pre-dated it. Silence by the insurer in the face of a five-year claims history was not waiver of any claims outside that period, indeed such limited disclosure came with an implication that there was nothing else material that had not been included.
[91] [2001] Lloyd's Rep IR 596.
[92] Such exclusion did not fall foul of the *Canada Steamship Lines v The King* [1952] AC 192 principle that liability for one's own negligence can only be excluded by the clearest words as the defence of non-disclosure or misrepresentation does not depend on any negligence but solely on a breach of the duty of utmost good faith: *HIH Casualty & General Insurance Ltd v New Hampshire Insurance Co* [2001] Lloyd's Rep IR 596, 627.

C. Breach of the Duty of Utmost Good Faith

(1) Avoidance

The attraction of the defence founded upon the duty of utmost good faith is that **6.47** if the duty is not observed by the reinsured, by a material misrepresentation or non-disclosure, then the reinsurance contract may be avoided by the reinsurer.[93] If there is non-disclosure of a material fact, the reinsurance is voidable because it was offered on a different basis from that actually existing.[94] The duty applies equally to both parties and the reinsured can avoid if the reinsurer is in breach of duty, but for obvious reasons the remedy of avoidance ab initio will rarely be an attractive remedy for a reinsured.[95] As previously noted the duty of utmost good faith on its own does not give rise to a claim in damages.[96]

Although the original information about the risk will invariably come from the **6.48** underlying insured, the duty of good faith to the reinsurer is owed by the reinsured. The reinsured must ensure that the reinsurer has sight of all information received from the underlying insured as, where it fails to pass on material information about the risk, the reinsurer can avoid the reinsurance contract. If the reinsurer is not told about a material fact which was revealed by the underlying insured to the reinsured, then the reinsured will have granted an indemnity (the duty to it having been discharged) whilst being without any reinsurance cover itself (the duty having been breached and the reinsurance being voidable).[97] The reinsurer might also seek to rely upon a breach of the duty by the underlying insured itself, in failing to disclose material facts to the reinsured.[98] If the reinsured misses the point or pays the claim despite the non-disclosure, then the reinsurer can argue that there is nothing

---

[93] Albeit at the cost of returning the premium.

[94] Lord Mansfield made the classic statement of the doctrine in *Carter v Boehm* (1766) 3 Burr 1905, 1909: 'Insurance is a contract of speculation. The special facts upon which the contingent chance is to be computed lie most commonly in the knowledge of the assured only; the underwriter trusts to his representation, and proceeds upon confidence that he does not keep back any circumstance in his knowledge to mislead the underwriter into a belief that the circumstance does not exist…Although the suppression should happen through mistake, without any fraudulent intention, yet still the underwriter is deceived and the policy is void; because the risque run is really different from the risque understood and intended to be run at the time of the agreement.'

[95] *Banque Financière de la Cité SA (formerly Banque Keyser Ullmann SA) v Westgate Insurance Co Ltd (formerly Hodge General & Mercantile Co Ltd)* [1991] 2 AC 249.

[96] *Banque Financière de la Cité SA (formerly Banque Keyser Ullmann SA) v Westgate Insurance Co Ltd (formerly Hodge General & Mercantile Co Ltd)* [1991] 2 AC 249; *HIH Casualty and General Insurance Ltd v Chase Manhattan Bank* [2003] Lloyd's Rep IR 230, 254.

[97] *Equitable Life Assurance Society v General Accident Insurance Corp* (1904) 12 SLT 348.

[98] Or for making material misrepresentations, see eg *Australian Widows Fund Life Assurance Society v National Mutual Life Association of Australasia* [1914] AC 634 in which the reinsurer avoided the contract of reinsurance where the misrepresentations in the underlying proposal form were made the basis of the reinsurance contract.

to indemnify as the reinsured made an ex gratia payment rather than a payment under the contract of insurance which it was legally liable to pay.[99]

6.49 If the reinsured passes to the reinsurer, without qualification, information provided by the reinsured, it will be guilty of misrepresentation if the information is false. In *Sirius International Insurance Corp v Oriental Assurance Corp*[100] Longmore J rejected the submission that it was uncommercial to expect a reinsured to verify every piece of information he passes on to the reinsurer or be at risk of losing his reinsurance protection by reason of mistakes made by the original insured leading to mistaken information passed on in good faith. He held that:

> ...the traditional and effective way in which the reinsured gets his protection is that he himself receives his information from the assured; if that information is material but wrong the reinsurer can avoid against the reinsured and the reinsured can avoid against the original assured. In that way, parity is secured up and down the line.[101]

6.50 Reinsurance is often complicated by the number of parties offering reinsurance: either by a following market scratching the slip which is led by a leading underwriter or by different reinsurers offering cover to different layers of the risk. The question arises whether a breach of the duty of utmost good faith as regards the leader or first layer reinsurer entitles other reinsurers to avoid their contracts. If the failure is one of non-disclosure, then each reinsurer will be able to avoid so long as it can show its own inducement (and so long as the disclosure is material to its layer or participation). However, the position may be different as regards misrepresentation. Here the leading reinsurer may have heard and relied on the false statement, but if the following market was given no similar representation themselves, it is questionable how they can show that they relied on it and were induced by it when entering into their separate contracts.[102] One answer may be that the following market relied on the risk having been properly presented by the reinsured or its broker to the leader.[103] Certainly there may be evidence that the following market viewed it as material that the leader had written the risk and so implicitly relied on a fair presentation to the leader, although this may vary from case to case depending on the facts and the prevailing market practice.[104]

(2) Affirmation

6.51 Affirmation in the present context means that the reinsurer elects to affirm the policy after he has acquired full knowledge of the material facts which would entitle

---

[99] Except, possibly, under a widely worded follow the settlements clause.
[100] [1999] Lloyd's Rep IR 345.
[101] [1999] Lloyd's Rep IR 345, 350.
[102] [1999] Lloyd's Rep IR 345, 350.
[103] *Aneco Reinsurance Underwriting Ltd v Johnson & Higgins* [1998] 1 Lloyd's Rep 565.
[104] *Brotherton v Aseguradora Colseguros (No 3)* [2003] Lloyd's Rep IR 762.

him to avoid it.[105] Having the means of knowledge, or having been put on inquiry is not enough.[106] He must affirm either expressly by deciding to continue providing cover under the reinsurance contract or by implication by acting in a way that is only consistent with an intention not to treat the contract as at an end. Clear and unequivocal conduct can lead to such affirmation and it must be communicated to the other party.[107] Such conduct could be the sending of a message confirming that a claim will be paid[108] or a demand for premium.[109] Silence, on the other hand, is likely to be found to be equivocal,[110] at least if it does not extend for an unreasonably long time.

It will normally be appropriate and prudent for a reinsurer specifically to reserve **6.52** his rights if he intends taking any step which might reasonably be regarded by the reinsured as an affirmation of the contract unless accompanied by such reservation.[111] Before repudiating it may be appropriate to seek an explanation, but it will also usually be appropriate to reserve rights in the meantime. A reservation of rights could expressly use that expression or could be evidenced by marking correspondence 'without prejudice'.[112]

A reinsurer does not have to make its election immediately and a reasonable delay **6.53** will not, without more, lead to an affirmation.[113] Invoking or asserting a contractual right such as the right to inspect the reinsured's records is an example of electing not to treat the contract as at an end.[114] Requesting inspection is likely to be an unequivocal indication sufficient for affirmation. Similarly, an extension of or endorsement to the contract will provide clear evidence that the contract is not at

---

[105] *Container Transport International v Oceanus Mutual Underwriting* [1984] 1 Lloyd's Rep 476; see generally on the different types of waiver and affirmation: *Kammins Ballrooms Co Ltd v Zenith Investments (Torquay) Ltd* [1971] AC 850, 882–883; *Peyman v Lanjani* [1985] 1 Ch 457. See also *HIH Casualty & General Insurance Ltd v Axa Corporate Solutions* [2003] Lloyd's Rep IR 1 on waiver by estoppel and estoppel by convention.

[106] *McCormick v National Motor & Accident Insurance Union Ltd* (1934) 49 Ll L Rep 361, in particular per Scrutton LJ at 365. Although it may be enough if the reinsurer's legal advisers have the knowledge and not the reinsurer personally: *Moore Large & Co Ltd v Hermes Credit & Guarantee plc* [2003] 1 Lloyd's Rep 163; *ICCI v Royal Hotel* [1998] Lloyd's Rep IR 151.

[107] *China National Foreign Trade Transportation Corp v Evlogia Shipping Co SA of Panama (The Mihalios Xilas)* [1979] 2 Lloyd's Rep 303, 307, per Lord Diplock.

[108] *Irish National Insurance Co Ltd v Oman Insurance Co Ltd* [1983] 2 Lloyd's Rep 453.

[109] *Compagnia Tirrena Di Assicurazioni SpA v Grand Union Insurance Co Ltd* [1991] 2 Lloyd's Rep 243.

[110] *Callaghan and Hedges v Thompson* [2000] Lloyd's Rep IR 125.

[111] *Barber v Imperio Reinsurance Co (UK) Ltd* (CA, 15 July 1993) cited in *Svenska Handelsbanken v Sun Alliance & London Insurance Plc* [1996] 1 Lloyd's Rep 519.

[112] *Callaghan and Hedges v Thompson* [2000] Lloyd's Rep IR 125, 133.

[113] *Iron Trades Mutual Insurance Co Ltd v Companhia de Seguros Imperio* [1991] 1 Re LR 213 cited by Waller J in *Pan Atlantic Insurance Co v Pine Top Insurance Co* [1992] 1 Lloyd's Rep 101, 106. However, if the election is not made within a reasonable time the reinsurer may be taken to have affirmed by default; see *Svenska Handelsbanken v Sun Alliance & London Insurance Plc* [1996] 1 Lloyd's Rep 519 and by way of analogy, the charter-party case of *The Laconia* [1977] AC 850.

[114] *Pan Atlantic Insurance Co v Pine Top Insurance Co* [1992] 1 Lloyd's Rep 101, 106 per Waller J.

an end.[115] It has been said that an insurer or reinsurer must also be aware that the law confers a right to avoid before it can affirm,[116] but a commercial reinsurer will normally be acutely aware of its right to avoid so long as it knows that there has been a material and inducing non-disclosure or misrepresentation. Affirmation is the abandonment of a right which arises by virtue of a party making an election. In such circumstances, unless the election is made, the right to choose is lost.[117] Therefore where, with knowledge of the relevant non-disclosure, the reinsurer has acted in a manner which is consistent only with continuing the contract and not avoiding it, it is held to have made the election accordingly.

D. Conditions and Warranties

6.54   The reinsurance contract will probably contain various conditions and warranties. In the standard MRC[118] slip format these should be set out expressly under defined headings, so that any reinsurer scratching the slip should be able to see immediately what conditions and warranties are contained in the contract. However, the label placed upon such terms of the contract is not determinative of their status. The term itself must always be examined to ensure that it is apt to be a condition or condition precedent, a warranty or an 'innominate term'.

6.55   Conditions and warranties are vital tools for reinsurers who rely upon them to try to achieve certainty about the risk and its limits. Conditions precedent are of great significance as the breach or non-fulfilment of a condition precedent may discharge the reinsurer from liability under the reinsurance contract either generally or for a particular claim. Warranties bear the same particular meaning as they do in the context of insurance law. Under general contract law, a breach of warranty by one party entitles the innocent party to damages but does not entitle him to treat himself as discharged from any further obligations under the contract. In the context of insurance and reinsurance, the position is reversed. A breach of warranty by the warrantor will not entitle the innocent party (ie the reinsurer) to damages (not even at its option), but instead will discharge the reinsurer from any liability under the reinsurance. The consequences of a breach of a simple condition (not a condition precedent) will depend on the severity of the breach. A reinsurance condition is likely to be construed as an innominate term[119] of the contract. If the

---

[115] *Simner v New India Assurance* [1995] LRLR 240; *Kingscroft Insurance Co Ltd v Nissan Fire & Marine Insurance Co Ltd (No 2)* [1999] Lloyd's Rep IR 603, per Moore-Bick J at 637: 'By expressly agreeing to accept an increased line on the primary layer treaty for the 1977/78 year Nissan affirmed the contract and waived any right to complain of misrepresentation or non-disclosure relating to retention'.

[116] *ICCI v Royal Hotel* [1998] Lloyd's Rep IR 151.

[117] *The Kanchenjunga* [1990] 1 Lloyd's Rep 391, 397, per Lord Goff.

[118] Market Reform Contract replacing the London Market Principles: see para 2.13.

[119] *Hong Kong Fir Shipping Co Ltd v Kawasaki Kisen Kaisha Ltd* [1962] 2 QB 26.

breach of such a condition is important and results in serious prejudice to the innocent party then the reinsurer may be entitled to treat the breach as repudiatory and
terminate the contract. However, a minor breach of a simple condition will result
in a claim for damages alone. It has been argued that serious breaches of claims
conditions may allow reinsurers to reject the claim to which the breach related,
but without entitling the reinsurers to terminate the contract as a whole.[120] The
Court of Appeal in *Friends Provident Life & Pensions v Sirius International Ins*[121]
has however rejected this approach.[122] The measure of certainty achieved by the use
of conditions precedent and warranties will be immediately apparent. Reinsurers
are discharged from liability for any breach whatsoever and are not required to go
into the difficult exercise of characterizing the breach as serious and going to the
root of the contract.

A breach of a 'condition' in a reinsurance contract may therefore have one of several   **6.56**
effects:

(a) it may allow a reinsurer to treat a reinsurance contract as never having come
     into effect;
(b) it may allow the reinsurer to treat the contract as coming to an end with
     effect from the date of the breach;
(c) the reinsurer may repudiate liability under the policy in respect of a particu-
     lar claim (and leaving the reinsurance otherwise intact); or
(d) it may only entitle the reinsurer to damages for breach of contract.

Which remedy is available will depend on the precise nature of the condition in
question and the circumstances of the breach.

(1) General Conditions

General or simple conditions regulate the contract of reinsurance. Such ordinary   **6.57**
conditions may cover aspects of the reinsurance where there is no express obligation placed upon the reinsured, such as exclusions. Certain conditions may, however, pertain to the conduct of the reinsured throughout the period of reinsurance,
or in the course of making or following the making of a claim, such as permitting
the reinsurer to inspect its records on demand. The breach of a simple condition by
a reinsured gives the ordinary contractual remedy of a claim for damages. This is a
remedy that is often unattractive to reinsurers because it can be difficult or impossible to quantify the measure of damages sustained by a reinsurer. In many cases a
breach of an ordinary condition by a reinsured is of little consequence.

---

[120] *K/S Merc-Scandia XXXXII v Lloyd's Underwriters (The Mercandian Continent)* [2001] Lloyd's
Rep IR 802, 811.
[121] [2006] Lloyd's Rep IR 45
[122] See para 6.62 et seq.

(2) Conditions Precedent

6.58   Certain conditions may be described as being 'conditions precedent'. These may, depending upon their precise wording, be conditions precedent to the existence of a binding contract, or conditions precedent to the liability of the reinsurers.

6.59   The effect of a 'condition precedent to the contract' is that a breach of the condition by the reinsured will have the effect of the contract of reinsurance being treated as if it had never been made. This is on the ground that because the condition was never fulfilled by the reinsured, cover never attached, and reinsurers never came on risk.

6.60   By the use of a 'condition precedent to liability', reinsurers can make it a condition precedent to any liability on their part that the reinsured must have complied with some requirement or obligation. For example, reinsurers may make notification of the claim a condition precedent to liability. Provided the condition, on a true and proper construction, can be shown in fact to be a condition precedent to liability, then reinsurers will be entitled to repudiate liability for any claim in respect of which the reinsured has failed to notify in accordance with the condition. The reinsurance contract generally will continue in force; it is simply in respect of the particular claim that reinsurers will be able to repudiate liability.

6.61   A reinsurance condition precedent may stipulate that the reinsured shall supply certain information or be required to have the subject matter of the underlying insurance inspected and a reinsured may be obliged to comply with any recommendations from the inspection.[123] An extension to cover may be subject to a condition precedent to an extension of the cover provided under the insuring clause.[124] If a condition precedent is not complied with and is a condition precedent to the conclusion of the reinsurance contract, the effect is not dissimilar to breach of warranty since the reinsurer never becomes on risk.

6.62   Whether a condition is a condition precedent or not depends to a substantial extent, but not solely, on whether that label or a similar one is given to it.[125] The label is not determinative, and although some conditions may be described as 'precedent' in the slip or policy wording, it will always be a matter of construction as to whether the condition is as described, or whether it is instead a simple condition.[126] It is not uncommon in insurance contracts for conditions relating to obligations

---

[123]   In *M J Harrington Syndicate 2000 and Others v Axa Oyak Sigorta AS* [2007] Lloyd's Rep IR 60 a reinsurance policy was made subject to the receipt of confirmation that all survey recommendations had been carried out. If the confirmation was not received, reinsurers never came on risk.

[124]   *HLB Kidsons v Lloyd's Underwriters* [2009] 1 Lloyd's Rep 8.

[125]   *Eagle Star v Cresswell* [2004] Lloyd's Rep IR 537 per Longmore LJ: 'it is not essential that the very words "condition precedent" be used to achieve the result that reinsurers will not be liable unless a certain event happens. Other words can be used, if they are clear.' Breach of the claims control condition precedent entitled the reinsurer to decline an indemnity notwithstanding the presence of a follow the fortunes clause.

[126]   *Bradley v Essex & Suffolk Accident Indemnity Society* [1912] 1 KB 415; see also *Eagle Star Insurance Co Ltd v JN Cresswell* [2004] Lloyd's Rep IR 537 and para 4.44.

of the insured to be made conditions precedent by a 'due observance' clause which provides that the due observance and fulfilment of the terms of the policy shall be conditions precedent to any liability.[127]

In reinsurance contracts terms that are often argued to be conditions precedent are those relating to claims control and/or co-operation. **6.63**

In that context, the use of the words 'condition precedent' was held in *Gan v Tai Ping*[128] to introduce 'emphatically' a condition precedent. However, the Court still recognized that the presence of the label was not the end of the matter and it was still necessary to examine the three conditions to which those words referred to see if each was capable of being a condition precedent. **6.64**

A condition will be construed carefully and strictly and loose wording is unlikely to find favour as a condition precedent due to the draconian remedy that it affords to a reinsurer.[129] A reinsurer who wishes a number of terms to all be condition precedent to liability under the reinsurance contract should make it explicit that the condition precedent label applies to each term. **6.65**

If a claims co-operation clause is not expressed to be or construed to be a condition precedent it will be regarded as an innominate term.[130] Breach of such a term only gives rise to a right to treat the contract as terminated if the consequences of the breach are such as substantially to deprive the innocent party of the whole benefit of the contract. **6.66**

In *Friends Provident Life & Pensions v Sirius International Ins*[131] it was suggested, relying on the reasoning of Waller LJ in *BAI v McAlpine*,[132] that a repudiatory breach arising from the failure to give notice for some years may mean that insurers could deny liability for the particular claim to which the failure related. Mance LJ in the majority held that a claims notification clause is an ancillary provision and breach is only capable of sounding in damages. He rejected the submission that either by way of construction or implication the insurers could evade liability in the event of a serious breach.[133] Waller LJ dissented and maintained that his analysis in **6.67**

---

[127] *Pioneer Concrete (UK) Ltd v National Employers Mutual General Insurance Association Ltd* [1985] 1 Lloyd's Rep 274.

[128] [2001] Lloyd's Rep IR 667. See para 5.28. On claims co-operation clauses generally, see paras 5.07 et seq.

[129] *Insurance Co of Africa v Scor (UK) Reinsurance Co Ltd* [1983] 1 Lloyd's Rep 541 aff'd [1985] 1 Lloyd's Rep 312.

[130] *Alfred McAlpine Plc v BAI (Run-Off) Ltd* [2000] 1 Lloyd's Rep 437, 443 per Waller LJ: 'once a condition...is construed as something less than a condition precedent, it will still be important to ascertain precisely what its contractual effect is intended to be and what the effect of a breach of that term will be'.

[131] [2006] Lloyd's Rep IR 45.

[132] [2000] 1 Lloyd's Rep 437

[133] Sir William Aldous agreed: 'the principle suggested in the *Alfred McAlpine* case has no basis in the law of contract unless an appropriate term can be implied into the contract...there is no need

BAI v McAlpine (in which he had given the leading judgment) was good law and had been followed without adverse comment but his view has been treated as having been authoritatively rejected in the reinsurance case of *Limit No 2 Ltd v Axa Versicherungs AG*.[134] A reinsurer ought to ensure that any claims co-operation or notification clause in its policy is expressed to be a condition precedent in order to avoid liability else it will simply have an unquantifiable claim for damages.

(3) Warranties

6.68 By an express contractual warranty a reinsurer can add to the protection afforded by the extra contractual duty of good faith.[135] It is possible and indeed common for a reinsurer to stipulate for an additional contractual duty of disclosure in relation to certain matters. A warranty can be used to procure from the reinsured a contractual guarantee of the truth and the accuracy of specified information or a promise that a certain condition or obligation shall be fulfilled.[136] This may be a warranty of information given to the reinsurer or pre-contractual statements made by the reinsured or its broker, either relating to an existing state of affairs or a statement of future intention.[137] Though less common in reinsurance, an insured may often give warranties in relation to the obligation to take certain precautions or conduct itself in a particular way throughout the duration of the insurance.

6.69 A warranty does not need to be in any particular form so long as it is incorporated into the contract, is in writing, and the intention to warrant is clear from the words of the contract.[138] The use of the words 'warranted' or indeed 'warranty' itself in a clause of the contract are not conclusive as those words have been used in some cases in conditions which were actually found to be exclusion clauses and not warranties properly so understood.[139] There needs to be a disclosure of information or a positive obligation on the reinsured or a fact or state of affairs which is warranted so that breach will discharge the reinsurer from further liability under the reinsurance

---

to imply such a term and in any case it did not appear possible to set out with sufficient precision the term' (para 35).

[134] [2008] Lloyd's Rep IR 330; the dissenting view of Waller LJ in the *Friends Provident* case is at paras 50–51.

[135] Non-marine warranties must always be expressly created, although the Marine Insurance Act 1906, ss 36–41 provides for warranties to be implied into certain contracts of marine insurance.

[136] Marine Insurance Act 1906, s 33(1) defines a promissory warranty as 'a warranty by which the assured undertakes that some particular thing shall or shall not be done, or that some condition shall be fulfilled, or whereby he affirms or negatives the existence of a particular state of facts'.

[137] See the categorization of warranties in *Transthene Packaging Ltd v Royal Insurance (UK) Ltd* [1996] LRLR 32.

[138] Marine Insurance Act 1906, s 35.

[139] *CTN Cash & Carry Ltd v General Accident Fire & Life Assurance Corp plc* [1989] 1 Lloyd's Rep 299; *Roberts v Anglo Saxon Insurance* (1927) 27 Ll LR 313 in which a motor insurance policy 'warranted' that a vehicle was to be used only for commercial travel. This was construed in favour of the insured so that it operated as an exclusion of liability while the vehicle was not travelling commercially, but reinstated the cover for all commercial trips.

contract. Normally in modern contracts of reinsurance, where the word 'warranty' is used in relation to such an obligation there will be a fair presumption that the parties intended to create a warranty, even if it is not conclusive.[140] The question can only be resolved by proper construction of the wording of the obligation in its context, carefully and critically examining the words used and giving them their ordinary and natural meaning. The policy as a whole may be considered to discern whether the intention of the parties was that a breach of the 'warranty' should result in discharge from all liability under the contract or merely suspending or excluding cover.[141] If damages would be an inadequate or unsatisfactory remedy for a breach of the obligation by the reinsured, then this may provide weight for construing the obligation as a warranty.[142]

Rix LJ summarized the position nicely in *HIH Casualty and General Insurance Ltd*   **6.70**
v New Hampshire Insurance Co when he said:

> It is a question of construction, and the presence or absence of the word 'warranty' or 'warranted' is not conclusive. One test is whether it is a term which goes to the root of the transaction; a second, whether it is descriptive of or bears materially on the risk of loss; a third, whether damages would be an unsatisfactory or inadequate remedy. Lord Justice Bowen said in *Barnard v Faber* [1893] QB 340 at p 344: 'A term as regards the risk must be a condition.' Otherwise the insurer is merely left to a cross-claim in a matter which goes to the risk itself, which is unbusinesslike . . .[143]

The exercise of construing provisions said to amount to warranties will need to be   **6.71**
careful and even strict as the consequences of their breach are draconian. The words will be construed to determine the intention of the parties, but ambiguity is likely to be resolved in favour of the reinsured and against the reinsurer who seeks to rely on them. Reinsurers who desire comfort about a continuing state of affairs in relation to a risk will have to look with care at the terms of any warranty proffered by the reinsured's broker as it is unlikely to extend expressly into the future.[144] Indeed the usual jargon and abbreviation contained in reinsurance slips may make it entirely ambiguous as to the temporal application of a warranty. There is no principle of

---

[140] *HIH Casualty & General Insurance Ltd v New Hampshire Insurance Co* [2001] Lloyd's Rep IR 596.

[141] See the analysis in *De Maurier (Jewels) Ltd v Bastion Insurance Co Ltd* [1967] 2 Lloyd's Rep 550 in which the distinction was made between a warranty and a clause which limits or describes the risk.

[142] *HIH Casualty & General Insurance Ltd v New Hampshire Insurance Co* [2001] Lloyd's Rep IR 596, 622 per Rix LJ. He also pointed to terms that go to the root of the transaction or matters that bear materially on the risk of loss as indicators of warranties in holding that a term of the insurance that six films would be made was a warranty of the reinsurance contract.

[143] [2001] 2 Lloyd's Rep 161, para 101.

[144] Note the insurance case of *Hussain v Brown* [1996] 1 Lloyd's Rep 627 in which a warranty that premises were fitted with an intruder alarm was held to relate only to the state of affairs in existence at the time when the warranty was given.

insurance law requiring warranties to be read as importing promises as to the future. As Saville LJ noted:

> Whether or not they do depends upon ordinary rules of construction, namely consideration of the words the parties have used in the light of the context in which they have used them and (where the words admit of more than one meaning) selection of that meaning which seems most closely to correspond with the presumed intention of the parties.[145]

6.72 The description of the underlying insurance can be a warranty in a reinsurance contract as it goes to the root of the transaction and has a material bearing on the risk: the terms of the underlying insurance are so fundamental to reinsurance that the fact that a breach of warranty discharges the contract is an appropriate and not a draconian remedy.[146] Where underwriters had entered into a reinsurance without sight of the underlying policy, the term as to the description of that policy went to the root of the transaction and bore materially on the risk. The reinsurers' obligation was to provide proportional reinsurance of the risk insured under the underlying policy by the insured. They were therefore entitled to treat the description of the underlying policy as a warranty, as it provided the description of the risk they had agreed to reinsure. The fact that a breach discharges the entire reinsurance may not be a draconian remedy where the terms of the underlying contract are important to what the reinsurers think that they are reinsuring.[147]

6.73 One aspect where a reinsurer may wish to protect its position with warranties is in respect of the reinsured's retention. The object of requiring a retention is to ensure that the reinsured has a financial interest in the 'quality' of the primary contracts and in their proper administration by the investigation of claims.[148] There is no implied obligation in reinsurance that a reinsured will maintain a retention, so the matter must be dealt with expressly.[149] The warranty should be clearly worded as in *Assicurazioni Generali SpA v Arab Insurance Group*[150] it was held that the incorporation of the level of retention in the slip conditions was not sufficient to be a continuing warranty, but did no more than assert a statement of fact as to the reinsured's present retention. Had there been a mutual intention that this should amount to a continuing warranty then clearer words would have been required. The reinsured was allowed to alter the level of its retention during the currency of the policy. A retention warranty in a quota share treaty will preclude the reinsured

---

145 *Hussain v Brown* [1996] 1 Lloyd's Rep 627, 629.
146 *Toomey v Banco Vitalicio de España SA de Seguros y Reaseguros* [2005] Lloyd's Rep IR 423.
147 *Toomey v Banco Vitalicio de España SA de Seguros y Reaseguros* [2005] Lloyd's Rep IR 423, para 46.
148 *Phoenix General Insurance Co of Greece SA v Administratia Asigurarilor De Stat* [1986] 2 Lloyd's Rep 552, 573 in which the amount of the retention had been left blank on the slip and so any warranty was ineffective.
149 *Phoenix General Insurance Co of Greece SA v Halvanon Insurance* [1985] 2 Lloyd's Rep 599, aff'd [1986] 2 Lloyd's Rep 552.
150 [2002] Lloyd's Rep IR 633, aff'd on other grounds [2003] Lloyd's Rep IR 131.

from ceding to other quota share reinsurers any part of the risks he had undertaken to retain; however, it does not, without clear wording, prevent a reinsured from taking out excess of loss cover.[151]

(4) Breach of Warranty

Strictly speaking, reinsurers who successfully rely on a breach of warranty by the reinsured do not 'avoid' the reinsurance, but are rather automatically discharged from any liability under the reinsurance.[152] This is because the rationale of warranties is that the reinsurer only accepts the risk provided that the warranty is fulfilled. It follows that the immediate effect of a breach of a warranty is to discharge the reinsurer from liability as from the date of the breach.[153] Consequently a breach of a warranty (unlike a breach of warranty in other areas of contract law) does not entitle the innocent party to any recovery of damages.

6.74

A loose use of language leads many people to talk of an insurer or reinsurer avoiding for a breach of warranty, perhaps because the remedy is often coupled with avoiding for a material non-disclosure. There is, however, an important distinction. Avoidance for breach of the duty of utmost good faith takes its effect from the very start of the contract or ab initio. The insurer never properly entered into the contract of reinsurance if it did so induced by a material non-disclosure. However, a breach of warranty only provides relief as from the date of the breach. In some circumstances, when the warranty relates to a pre-contractual matter, the effect will be the same. However, a warranty of a continuing state of affairs or something relating to the conduct of the reinsured's business, such as the level of its retention, may be breached only later in time. The reinsurer is on risk until the breach and is discharged from liability as from the date of the breach.

6.75

The other major distinction between a breach of warranty and a breach of the duty of utmost good faith is that a warranted statement need not be material.[154] If there is a warranty it is part of the contract that the matter is such as it is represented to be. Therefore the materiality or immateriality of the representation is irrelevant. The only question is whether the facts warranted are true or not[155] and it does not matter that the inaccurate statement may have been made innocently by the reinsured.[156]

6.76

---

[151] *Kingscroft Insurance Co Ltd v Nissan Fire & Marine Insurance Co Ltd (No 2)* [1999] Lloyd's Rep IR 603, 621 et seq.

[152] *Bank of Nova Scotia v Hellenic (The Good Luck)* [1992] 1 AC 233, certainly so far as marine policies are concerned and probably non-marine policies also (certainly it was the view of May LJ ([1989] 2 Lloyd's Rep 238, 259, CA) that s 33(3) of the Marine Insurance Act 1906 reflected the common law as it related to non-marine insurance policies).

[153] Marine Insurance Act 1906, s 33(3).

[154] Marine Insurance Act 1906, s 33(3): 'A warranty . . . is a condition which must be exactly complied with whether it be material to the risk or not'.

[155] *Newcastle Fire Insurance Co v Macmorran & Co* (1815) 3 Dow 255, 262, per Eldon C.

[156] *MacDonald v Law Union Insurance Co* (1874) QB 328.

A warranty may be limited to only material facts and matters by express words in the terms of the warranty itself.[157]

(5) Waiver by Election or Estoppel

6.77 There are two forms of waiver which may be relevant to a breach of condition precedent or warranty: waiver by election and waiver by estoppel. Election is the exercise of a right to choose between inconsistent remedies. It generally requires knowledge of the facts giving rise to the choice on the part of the party electing, and knowledge of the choice having been made on the part of the other party. Estoppel, however, is a promise supported not by consideration but by reliance. It is a promise not to rely on a defence or a right. It requires a representation in words or conduct, which must be unequivocal and must have been relied on in circumstances where it would be inequitable for the promise to be withdrawn.[158]

6.78 In *Lexington Insurance Co v Multinacional De Seguros Sa*[159] the claims co-operation clause was expressed to be a condition precedent. The clause required the reinsured to 'cooperate with the reinsurers in the adjustment and settlement of the claim'. The reinsurers denied liability for breach of the condition, but continued to negotiate with the reinsured. The question for the Court was whether the reinsured was subsequently in breach of the condition by waiving a time bar defence against the underlying assured. It was argued that the stance taken by reinsurers that they were discharged from any liability because of an alleged earlier breach of the clause meant that there was no room for its continued operation or that they had waived any right to rely on the clause. Christopher Clarke J held that the doctrine of waiver by election was not engaged as the reinsurers were not presented with a choice between two mutually inconsistent rights. If they were right to contend that the reinsured was in breach of a condition precedent, then they were automatically discharged from liability. If they were wrong, they were not, but there was no choice for the reinsurer to make. Furthermore, the reinsured's obligation to co-operate continued to apply as long as the reinsurers' stance was that, without prejudice to their denial of liability, they were still prepared to engage with the reinsured in relation to the claim.

6.79 In any event, Christopher Clarke J thought that invocation of the doctrine of election was problematic for the reinsured for another reason. Waiver by election arises in a situation where a person is entitled to alternative rights inconsistent with one

---

[157] *Dawsons Ltd v Bonnin* (1922) 2 AC 413.

[158] See the summary in *Lexington Insurance Co v Multinacional De Seguros Sa* [2009] Lloyd's Rep IR 1 drawing on *Kosmar Villa Holidays plc v Trustees of Syndicate 1243* [2008] Lloyd's Rep IR 489 which cited the classic statements as to the difference between waiver by election and waiver by estoppel of Lord Diplock in *Kammins Ballrooms Co Ltd v Zenith Investments(Torquay) Ltd* [1971] AC 850 and by Lord Goff of Chieveley in *Motor Oils Hellas (Corinth) Refineries SA v Shipping Corporation of India (The Kanchenjunga)* [1990] 1 Lloyd's Rep 391.

[159] [2009] Lloyd's Rep IR 1.

another. If he has knowledge of the facts which give rise in law to these alternative rights and acts in a manner which is consistent only with his having chosen to rely on one of them, the law holds him to his choice. However the doctrine is premised upon the existence of facts which give rise in law to alternative rights, but such facts were not proved, indeed were vigorously denied, by the reinsured in this case. It could not argue for an election having taken place when it denied the facts that gave rise to the election.

E. Notification

A reinsurer may wish to defend a claim under the reinsurance contract if it was **6.80** not given proper notice that a loss had occurred. Notification clauses appear in reinsurance contracts either where unusually there is an express clause in a facultative or treaty wording or where there is a notification clause in the incorporated underlying wording and it is apt to incorporate such a clause into the reinsurance contract. Where an express clause does appear it will often be a part of a wider claims co-operation clause.[160] The rationale for notification between reinsured and reinsurer may often be different from that between underlying insured and insurer and so care should be taken in applying insurance notification principles to the reinsurance context.

Notification has to be considered objectively. The question is what the notifica- **6.81** tion by the reinsured reasonably conveys to its intended recipients, not what the reinsured intended to notify.[161] Some reinsurance policies require the notification to be made 'immediately' or 'forthwith' even if that causes real practical difficulties for the reinsured.[162] A more flexible wording requires notification 'as soon as is reasonably practicable' and a court will take into account all the circumstances in deciding when it was reasonably feasible for a notice to be sent.

A reinsured will often have to notify a claim, but some reinsurance policy word- **6.82** ings will require notification of a loss. Where a reinsured was required to notify within 72 hours of knowledge of a loss which might give rise to a claim, the Court of Appeal held that the relevant loss was that of the third party claimant seeking to recover from the insured.[163] A reinsured could not know about a loss until it settled the claim as before that it was only an alleged loss.[164] A reinsured may only have

---

[160] See para 5.09.
[161] *HLB Kidsons v Lloyd's Underwriters* [2009] Lloyd's Rep IR 178.
[162] *Re Williams and Thomas and The Lancashire and Yorkshire Insurance Co* (1902) 19 TLR 82.
[163] *Royal & Sun Alliance Insurance plc v Dornoch* [2005] Lloyd's Rep IR 544.
[164] The directors of a company insured under an E & O policy were alleged to have made false statements and the shareholders claimed that the value of the company shares had been inflated. Only when the loss was settled did it become a loss rather than an allegation of loss, so the notification clause was not triggered by the fall in the value of the shares. Contrast *AIG Europe (Ireland) Ltd v Faraday Capital Ltd* [2008] Lloyd's Rep IR 454 where the Court of Appeal distinguished *Dornoch*,

actual knowledge of a loss once it has been proved or admitted in court or arbitration proceedings or accepted as part of a settlement, but may get actual knowledge of an actual loss from a third party source in which case it will be fixed with knowledge of the loss from that moment.

(1) Facultative Proportional Reinsurance

6.83 A reinsurer who reinsures a proportion of a particular risk will often want to know about the loss as soon as the underlying insurer knows about it. In this situation a reinsurer may want to be involved in the investigation and adjusting of the loss, particularly where its participation is substantial. The notification clause will place an obligation to notify the reinsurer within a specified timescale. If the clause uses words such as 'immediate' or 'forthwith', the inevitable delay between notification to the underlying insurer and passing on information to the reinsurer would probably serve to dilute apparent strictness of the clause, in line with the approach to the requirement of 'immediate' notice that was adopted in the insurance case of *Aspen Insurance v Pectel*[165] of requiring notice 'with all reasonable speed considering the circumstances of the case'. More appropriate to the reinsurance setting may be wording such as notification 'as soon as is reasonably practicable' which only requires the reinsured to act reasonably after taking into account all the circumstances of the loss, the insurance, and the reinsurance.[166]

(2) Treaty Reinsurance

6.84 Where a reinsurer accepts a proportion of each risk that a reinsured undertakes in a specified class of business or under a particular book of insurance, it will often be following the fortunes and the settlements of the reinsured under one of the familiar clauses. There are often likely to be a large number of modest or moderate payments and the reinsurer will not be entitled (and it would not be commercial) for the reinsurer to investigate each loss for itself. In such contracts notification clauses relating to the loss are rare and there is no obligation on the reinsured to notify a claim when it is received from the underlying insured. More common is a clause whereby the reinsured notifies in arrears at the end of an annual or six-monthly cycle in a schedule called a bordereaux. This commonly contains figures showing:

(a) all of the reinsured's paid claims during the previous period;
(b) the amount of its outstanding claims; and

---

holding that the shareholders had suffered a loss as a result of a sharp fall in the company's share price. In *Stonebridge Underwriting Ltd v Ontario Municipal Insurance Exchange* [2011] Lloyd's Rep IR 171 Christopher Clarke J said that a court would have to determine the dividing line between those two cases.

[165] [2009] Lloyd's Rep IR 440.

[166] See the analogous insurance case of *Alfred McAlpine v BAI (Run-off) Ltd* [2002] Lloyd's Rep IR 352 which analyses the wording 'as soon as possible' and see also *HLB Kidsons v Lloyd's Underwriters* [2008] Lloyd's Rep IR 237, Gloster J.

(c) the estimate of the amount of claims which the reinsured believes have been incurred by the underlying insurance, but have not yet been notified to it or received by it (IBNR).

The protection of the reinsurer's position is usually achieved through its right to **6.85** inspect the reinsured's records on demand rather than through notification of losses. It can then avail itself, if it wishes, of an opportunity to look at the claims on a periodic basis rather than as and when they are notified to the reinsured. Although the reinsurer's liability to pay its proportion of the paid claims is only triggered by its receipt of the bordereaux or accounts, a failure by the reinsured to submit its accounts immediately or within a reasonable time is unlikely to extinguish the reinsurer's liability. Accounts which are rendered late, but within the appropriate limitation period, will still trigger the reinsurer's liability to pay unless the reinsurance contract expressly makes prompt submission of accounts a condition precedent to payment.

(3) Excess of Loss Reinsurance

An excess of loss reinsurer will often want prompt notification of a claim as it will **6.86** want to investigate liability and the likely arguments on quantum so that it can determine whether its excess layer will be breached or not. However, it may not be sufficient for a reinsurer simply to rely on the notification provisions in the underlying insurance. An immediate notice and claims control clause were found not apt for incorporation from the underlying liability insurance into an excess of loss reinsurance where the slips included the terms 'conditions as underlying'.[167] The combination of the two obligations was fatal to incorporation as when there were numerous layers of excess reinsurance, they could not all take over control of the claim. It was impossible for each reinsurer to be able to exercise rights. A notice provision alone may have found its way into the reinsurance as the answer to the judge's question, 'if incorporated, to whom should the insurer give notice?', would lead to the answer: to all those parties who reinsure that insurer.[168]

F. Limitation

Limitation can sometimes be very important in reinsurance claims and can pro- **6.87** vide an effective defence for reinsurers. In certain long-tail business such as asbestos or pollution claims, a number of years can pass while the underlying insured or primary insurer engage in lengthy legal proceedings. It may not be until years later that reinsurers and retrocessionaires are called upon to pay their share. The defence of limitation should always be examined, as the six-year time limit in the

---

[167] *Municipal Mutual Insurance Ltd v Sea Insurance Co Ltd* [1996] LRLR 265.
[168] *Municipal Mutual Insurance Ltd v Sea Insurance Co Ltd* [1996] LRLR 265, 275, per Waller J.

Limitation Act 1980 is not a jurisdictional matter but a defence that can be taken or not, at the defendant's option.

6.88 The time at which a reinsurer is in breach of an obligation to pay a ceding company requires careful consideration of the policy. Depending on the wording, the reinsurer's obligation could arise at different times. There are four alternatives that can be argued as being the accrual of a reinsurer's cause of action for limitation purposes. They are, in chronological order:

(a) *Time runs from original insured loss or event.* The time limit commences immediately upon the happening of the event against which the original assured obtained cover (so that reinsurance contracts are treated in the same way as property insurance contracts).

(b) *Time runs from ascertainment of the reinsured's liability.* Limitation starts to run from the date upon which the liability of the reinsured arising out of the underlying cover is quantified either by judgment, award or agreement (so that reinsurance contracts are treated in the same way as policies of liability insurance).

(c) *Time runs from payment by reinsured.* Time only starts to run for limitation purposes once the reinsured has paid out in respect of its liability to its underlying insured.

(d) *Time runs from rendering of accounts to the reinsurer.* The reinsurance treaty provides for regular accounts to be rendered by the reinsured setting out the premium payable against the amount of claims, and the reinsurer's liability only crystallizes once the amounts due (if any) are specified in the accounts.

6.89 The conventional analysis is that (b) is correct in the absence of clear words to the opposite effect, such as a treaty containing express terms for payment being conditional upon the rendering of an account. This is based on two factors: the first, a pragmatic approach so that reinsurance works in a businesslike way and the second, a conceptual approach, which draws a parallel between reinsurance and liability insurance. As it is the conventional analysis, (b) will be considered first.

(1) Time Runs from Ascertainment of the Reinsured's Liability[169]

6.90 This approach has been conventionally accepted as the correct one for a number of years. The authorities suggest that the limitation period begins to run against the reinsured upon the ascertainment of its underlying liability. Once its liability to its insured is established by a judgment, an award, a settlement or some other agreement, then it has six years[170] from that date to sue its reinsurer.

---

[169] See paras 4.85 et seq.
[170] Limitation Act 1980, s 5: the time limit for an action founded on simple contract is six years.

This was the clear conclusion of the Court of Appeal in the old case of *Daugava v* **6.91**
Henderson[171] in which Scrutton LJ commented that he could not see how a reinsurer
could be liable to pay an amount until that amount had been fixed between the
insurer and the insured. This was echoed more recently by the Court of Appeal in
Gan Insurance Co Ltd v Tai Ping Insurance Co Ltd (No 2):[172]

> The current state of authority in this court appears to me to indicate that ascer-
> tainment of liability is a pre-condition to the accrual of insurers' rights against
> reinsurers—in whichever of the alternative ways, identified by Lord Mustill,
> liability is relevant...A proposition that insurers' rights against reinsurers (or
> presumably reinsurers' rights against retrocessionaires under a retrocession) arise
> at the earlier stage of any original loss would also create very great potential dif-
> ficulties, in the operation of reinsurances and retrocessions and in matters of
> limitation.[173]

However, note that there could be room for argument here as the underlying word- **6.92**
ing in *Daugava v Henderson* was that the insurer must pay within one month of
agreement of the amount or ascertainment by legal decision. The reinsurance was
made on an 'as original' wording, so the express wording of the reinsurance pointed
to the necessity for ascertainment before limitation started to run.

The conventional approach was assumed to apply in the judgment in *Baker v Black* **6.93**
Sea and Baltic General Insurance Co Ltd:[174]

> A contract of reinsurance being a contract of indemnity for the losses of the rein-
> sured, the reinsurer's liability to indemnify the reinsured arises on the date on
> which the reinsured sustained a loss. In final submissions, it was common ground
> between the parties that the date on which a reinsured sustains a loss is the date on
> which his liability to his underlying assured is ascertained, whether by agreement,
> arbitration, award or judgment.

However, note that neither party appears to have contradicted the conventional
approach and neither suggested that conceptually a contract of reinsurance is not
an indemnity for the losses of the reinsured.

The contention that time runs later, from rendering of accounts, has been roundly **6.94**
dismissed.[175] The commencement of the limitation period is not normally deferred

---

[171] (1934) 49 Ll LR 252.
[172] [2001] Lloyd's Rep IR 667. See also *Hong Kong Borneo Services v Pilcher* [1992] 2 Lloyd's Rep 593.
[173] *Gan Insurance Co Ltd v Tai Ping Insurance Co Ltd (No 2)* [2001] Lloyd's Rep IR 677, 690 relying on *Versicherungs und Transport AG Daugava v Henderson* (1934) 49 Lloyd's Rep 252, 253–254,
per Scrutton and Maugham LJJ, a fire reinsurance case and *Charter Reinsurance Co Ltd v Fagan*
[1997] AC 313, 333 and 341–342.
[174] [1995] LRLR 261.
[175] *Halvanon Insurance Co Ltd v Companhia de Seguros do Estado de Sao Paulo* [1995] LRLR 303,
306 per Steyn LJ: 'In the absence of special clauses...the cause of action arises when the underlying
liability is ascertained by agreement, by award or by judgment. It is not postponed until the rendering of an account.'

past ascertainment of the reinsured's liability unless there is a 'special clause' to that effect in the reinsurance contract.

6.95 The start of the limitation period may be more uncertain where the reinsurance is an aggregate excess of loss cover. In such a case the question is whether the limitation period commences as soon as the reinsured has settled any claims with an aggregate value greater than the excess point or whether time would not start to run until the final outcome of the account is known.[176]

6.96 A reinsuring clause which provides that the reinsurer will indemnify the reinsured in respect of its liability for losses on policies issued during the period of the reinsurance focuses on the reinsured's liability rather than the underlying loss. In *North Atlantic Insurance Co Ltd v Bishopsgate Insurance Ltd*[177] the judge held that time started running once an aggregate figure in settlements had been reached, and there was no requirement in the contract to wait until the final accounting had been completed and the amount of the excess fully ascertained. Such a requirement would call for 'a clear and unequivocal contractual provision to that effect', particularly because the alternative construction argued for was commercially unrealistic: it could create uncertainty as to whether or not a particular claim was payable by the reinsurer at all.

6.97 This conventional approach to reinsurance limitation works well in both proportional and excess of loss reinsurance. In an aggregate excess of loss reinsurance it would be difficult to know which losses triggered the excess point until the amounts of such claims are ascertained. Ascertainment is essential to knowing whether the excess point is passed or not.

(2) Prior Wrong Results in Earlier Time Bar

6.98 A different limitation period could arise where the reinsurer commits an actionable wrong before the loss is ascertained. If the reinsurer, without justifiable grounds for doing so, avoids the reinsurance for an alleged non-disclosure and the reinsured accepted what would therefore be a repudiation, so as to bring the contract to an immediate end, limitation would begin running before ascertainment of the underlying loss.[178] If, as is invariably the case, the repudiation is ignored and the reinsured insists on performance of the contract, then the usual limitation period will apply.

(3) Time Runs from Original Insured Loss or Event

6.99 The view that the limitation period commences on the happening of the originally insured peril derives not from authorities on reinsurance limitation, which

[176] *North Atlantic Insurance Co Ltd v Bishopsgate Insurance Ltd* [1998] 1 Lloyd's Rep 459.
[177] *North Atlantic Insurance Co Ltd v Bishopsgate Insurance Ltd* [1998] 1 Lloyd's Rep 459.
[178] *Lefevre v White* [1990] 1 Lloyd's Rep 569.

all take the conventional approach outlined above, but on fundamental principles of reinsurance law. As Lord Hoffmann said in *Charter Reinsurance Co Ltd v
Fagan*:[179]

> Contracts of reinsurance are not an insurance of the primary insurer's potential
> liability or disbursement. It is an independent contract between reinsured and
> reinsurer in which the subject matter of the insurance is the same as that of the
> primary insurance, that is to say, the risk to the ship or goods or whatever might be
> insured. The difference lies in the nature of the insurable interest, which in the case
> of the primary insurer arises from his liability under the original policy.[180]

The House of Lords suggested that the normal reinsurance contract covered the   **6.100**
occurrence of a loss suffered by the underlying insured through the operation of
an insured peril.[181] This analysis was confirmed by the House of Lords in *Wasa
International v Lexington Insurance Co.*[182] A reinsurer could argue that if reinsurance is not an insurance of the reinsured's liability but an insurance of the underlying risk, then the limitation period ought not to start on the ascertainment of the
reinsured's liability, but on the happening of the original peril.

For the purposes of this argument the analysis of the application to limitation of   **6.101**
the nature of reinsurance is as follows:

(a) In normal circumstances, the original insurer is liable and the limitation
    period starts running as soon as the insured event or loss occurs.
(b) If the insurer has reinsured this loss or event, then the reinsurer is instantly
    liable.
(c) The insurer does not have to wait until it is found to be liable before claiming
    on the reinsurance: it can do so immediately.
(d) In which case, the reinsurance limitation period starts running immediately
    too and the law on limitation as stated in *Daugava*,[183] *Halvanon*[184] and *Gan v
    Tai Ping (No 2)*[185] is open to question.
(e) The more conservative analysis is that *Charter Re v Fagan* and *Wasa v
    Lexington*[186] were not considering limitation at all but simply the operation of

---

[179] [1997] AC 313.
[180] See Buckley LJ in *British Dominions General Insurance Co Ltd v Duder* [1915] 2 KB 394, 400.
[181] This approach was also taken by the Court of Appeal in *Toomey v Eagle Star* [1994] 1 Lloyd's
Rep 516, but again not expressly with reference to a limitation issue.
[182] [2009] Lloyd's Rep IR 675.
[183] *Versicherungs und Transport AG Daugava v Henderson* (1934) 49 Lloyd's Rep 252 which pro-
ceeded on the basis that '[a] policy of reinsurance is an agreement by way of complete or partial
indemnity of the insurer. That has long been settled and has been stated in more than one case'
per Maugham LJ and '[t]he liability of the [reinsurer] is only to indemnify the insurer, the reassured, in respect of a loss for which he is liable to the assured by reason of his insurance policy' per
Scrutton LJ, both at 254. This contrasts with the modern approach in *Charter Re v Fagan* [1997]
AC 313.
[184] *Halvanon Insurance Co Ltd v Companhia de Seguros do Estado de Sao Paulo* [1995] LRLR 303.
[185] [2001] Lloyd's Rep IR 667.
[186] [1997] AC 313 and [2009] Lloyd's Rep IR 675.

a particular form of ultimate net loss clause[187] and the approach to limitation is as set out by the Court of Appeal in *Gan v Tai Ping* where the pragmatic and commercial view was preferred.

6.102 On the application of limitation periods, the courts have been content to adopt a less than rigorous legal analysis and assume that a contract of reinsurance is indeed an insurance of the reinsurer's liability under the inward policy in order to achieve a workable system. If the *Charter Re v Fagan* analysis was used in practice in all reinsurance, then a limitation period could start running between reinsured and reinsurer well before the loss was known by either party or more importantly well before the quantification of the loss. Much time could and often does pass before the reinsured is ready and able to ascertain the reinsurer's proportion of the loss. In practice reinsureds may run up against limitation problems through no fault of their own, when they progressed the claim as fast as circumstances or the under-lying insurers would allow. It is suggested that this is why the theoretically impure approach has been adopted by the courts when addressing limitation. Nonetheless attention must be paid in each case to the wording of the reinsurance contract to ensure that some other commencement date for the obligation to indemnify has not been specified.

(4) Time Runs from Payment by Reinsured

6.103 The argument that time only starts to run once the reinsured has paid out in respect of its liability to its underlying insured is the least convincing of the options.[188] In order to succeed there would need to be a reinsurance wording which expressly or by necessary implication unambiguously defers the reinsurer's obligation to pay claims until the reinsured has itself paid. One problem of this argument is that if it were upheld a reinsurer would never be liable to an insolvent reinsured.[189]

6.104 It is clear that even apparently clear words will not be permitted to oust the nor-mal position as in *Charter Re v Fagan* even a fairly clear 'actually paid' clause was not construed literally and was held in the context not to refer to actual payment. Such a clause is, though, possible to draft in the insurance field[190] and so may still be possible in the reinsurance field.

---

[187] This was the approach adopted by Timothy Walker J in *North Atlantic Insurance Co Ltd v Bishopsgate Insurance Ltd* [1998] 1 Lloyd's Rep 459 who said at 462 that *Charter Re v Fagan* involved a 'different contract' and was a case in which 'the defendant reinsurers did not dispute that all the requirements of a valid claim against them by the plaintiff reinsured existed, save for the fact that the plaintiff reinsured had not actually paid the inwards claims against them. It was thus inherent in the whole decision that the relevant excess point had been reached, so that this issue was not addressed at all.'

[188] *Charter Re v Fagan* [1997] AC 313.

[189] *In Re Eddystone Marine Insurance* [1892] 2 Ch 423.

[190] *The Fanti* [1990] 2 Lloyd's Rep 191.

(5) Time Runs from Rendering of Accounts

In many reinsurance treaties a reinsurer may share the fortunes of the reinsured on **6.105** a very large number of claims and agree to reinsure a specified proportion of those claims. It would be uncommercial to pay a proportion on individual claims and so the reinsurer is only presented with an account showing all the claims falling within the reinsurance during a specified period.

Periodic accounts in some treaties can lead to payments being made in different **6.106** directions: to the reinsurer if it has been a profitable period with few losses and good premiums, or a payment to the reinsured if the reverse is true.

Generally such treaties will include an express obligation to make payment within **6.107** a specified period after the account is rendered or agreed. The account wording must be sufficiently clear to replace the general approach that the reinsurer is liable from the ascertainment of each loss in the account by the reinsured. Steyn LJ said in *Halvanon Insurance Co Ltd v Companhia de Seguros do Estado de Sao Paulo*[191] that:

> The new evidence is based on the proposition that a cause of action in this field arises when an account is rendered. In my judgment that proposition is contrary to well-established principles. In the absence of special clauses that is not the case. The cause of action arises when the underlying liability is ascertained by agreement, by an award or by judgment. It is not postponed until the rendering of an account. Here I pause to say that nobody has in this case suggested that there was any account stated in the classic sense.[192]

Plainly the conventional approach espoused by Steyn LJ that the cause of action **6.108** arises when the underlying liability is ascertained could lead to hardship and an unbusinesslike approach in a large reinsurance treaty as each small claim within a mass of claims listed in a six-monthly account will have a different ascertainment date. Finding out the dates that limitation periods started running would be nearly impossible.

This problem was addressed by Waller J in *Nissan Fire & Marine Insurance Co v* **6.109** *Malaysia British Assurance*.[193] He accepted that provisions for accounts in a quota share retrocession agreement could be 'special clauses'. Waller J noted that the accounts mechanism could result in a payment to either contracting party and so it was impossible to find a liability under the agreement before the account was rendered. The contention that this would allow a reinsured to postpone indefinitely the triggering of any entitlement under the contract by delaying submission of the accounts or agreement of the accounts was answered by the fact that the contract provided for a specific time period in which accounts must be confirmed. Even

---

[191] [1995] LRLR 303.
[192] [1995] LRLR 303, 306.
[193] QBD, Comm Ct, 8 July 1996.

with no express time limits the contract would necessarily imply that accounts must be rendered within a reasonable time and a reinsurer could bring a claim to compel submission of accounts.

6.110   He found that there was a sharing concept involved in such accounts with a reinsurer not able to claim small parts of premium at different dates and in the same way, a reinsured not being able to claim small parts of different losses. What was sauce for the goose was sauce for the gander. He held that the cause of action arose at the end of each quarter and not when each liability was ascertained in accordance with the general rule. He appeared to reach this conclusion on a pragmatic basis: that the contract would otherwise be unworkable.

6.111   Therefore each account in such a treaty which is not settled by the reinsurer in accordance with the contract will trigger a separate cause of action on a separate date. No time bar will operate until six years following the date upon which the reinsurer received the periodic accounts and had to pay them.

6.112   This decision can be contrasted with the decision in *Re Home and Colonial Insurance Co*[194] which also involved a reinsured rendering quarterly accounts in a quota share treaty and asking the reinsurer to confirm the accounts and pay up. The reinsurer did not confirm the accounts and it was held that this was not an 'account stated' because it had not been agreed.[195]

6.113   An 'account stated' is an account which includes items on both sides and which the parties have agreed to reflect a set-off, with only the balance payable.[196] The less pragmatic and legally strict approach is that a new cause of action only occurs when a true account stated comes into being by an agreement between the parties.

6.114   This result is sought to be forced upon reluctant reinsurers in the wording of some accounts clauses which provide that unless any queries are raised on the accounts, they are deemed to be confirmed. This type of clause will be strictly construed, and only if the words are very clear will they be upheld. However, in these circumstances it is at least highly arguable that an unchallenged account will lead to a new cause of action for the reinsured (which might well include a number of individual claims which would themselves have otherwise been time-barred).

(6) Standstill Agreements

6.115   Reinsurance claims are factually and legally complicated and suffer from terrible delays while underlying insurance disputes are resolved. Many claims are not

---

[194]   [1930] Ch 102.

[195]   The point was not even argued in *River Thames v Al Ahleia* [1973] 1 Lloyd's Rep 2 which involved a treaty account that had been initialled as agreed and therefore could have been an 'account stated'. Note that in *Halvanon Insurance Co Ltd v Companhia de Seguros do Estado de Sao Paulo* [1995] LRLR 303 there was no 'account stated in the classic sense' (see para 6.105).

[196]   *Laycock v Pickles* (1863) 4 B & S 497.

settled for years. The answer is to suspend limitation by agreement for a specified period. Such a standstill agreement[197] is valid because a defendant must elect to raise a limitation defence, and so he can waive or be estopped from asserting the right so to do by a standstill agreement.[198]

The standstill agreement should provide that the reinsurer agrees, in consider-   **6.116** ation of the reinsured abstaining from commencing legal proceedings against the reinsurer under the reinsurance contract, that for the purposes of the Limitation Act 1980 the time within which the reinsured must commence proceedings shall stop running. The agreement should also provide for a termination provision by the giving of written notice, so that both parties are clear about the date on which time recommences running.

---

[197] Also referred to as moratoria, standstills or tolling agreements.
[198] See *Orion Compañia Española de Seguros v Belfort Maatschappij voor Algemene Verzekgringeen* [1962] 2 Lloyd's Rep 257 which held that parties can alter statutory limitation periods by agreement so long as it is not contrary to public policy. Megaw J said 'Of course...the parties can by their contract...provide that certain incidents of law which would otherwise attach should not attach, such as the exclusion or alteration of the statutory period of limitation...or such like matters. There is no possible objection to that, so long as there is nothing contrary to public policy in the exclusion or alteration of the provisions which, in the absence of agreement, would attach.'

7

APPLICABLE LAW AND JURISDICTION

A. Applicable Law

(1) Rome Convention and Rome I Regulation on Conflicts of Laws

The identification of the proper law of the contract may be of very great import- **7.01**
ance because it is likely to have a crucial impact on the shape and possible outcome
of the case.[1] Section 2(1) of the Contracts (Applicable Law) Act 1990 provides for
the incorporation of the Rome Convention into the law of the United Kingdom.
Article 1(4) of the Convention expressly provides that reinsurance contracts,
unlike contracts of insurance, are subject to the rules of the Convention. Further,
there is nothing in the Convention which limits its scope to contracts made in or
between nationals of contracting states. However, the Convention does not have
retrospective effect and therefore only applies to contracts entered into after April
1991 when the Convention came into force.[2] For a contract concluded before that
date, the determination of its proper law depended and still depends on common
law principles.

---

[1] See the comments of Aikens J in *Dornoch Ltd v Mauritius Union Assurance Co Ltd* [2006]
Lloyd's Rep IR 127, para 72 (upheld [2006] 2 Lloyd's Rep 475).

[2] Rome Convention, reg 17 which provides that the Convention applies only to contracts entered
into after it comes into force with regard to a contracting state (1 April 1991 for the UK). The
Financial Services and Markets Act 2000 (Law Applicable to Contracts of Insurance) Regulations
2001 (SI 2001 No 2635) do not apply to reinsurance contracts under reg 3(1).

7.02 Reinsurance contracts concluded after 17 December 2009 are governed by the 'Rome I Regulation' under EC Regulation on the Law applicable to Contractual Obligations which consolidates the Rome Convention.[3] Article 7 of the Regulation does not apply to reinsurance contracts so, as under the Rome Convention, reinsurance is excluded from the mandatory choice of law provisions that apply to contracts of insurance.[4]

7.03 The general common law rule was that, in the absence of an express choice, an intention with regard to the law to govern the contract could be inferred from the terms and nature of the contract and from the general circumstances of the case. When the intention was not expressed and could not be inferred from the circumstances, the contract was governed by the system of law with which the contract had its closest and most real connection.[5]

7.04 The Rome Convention and Rome I Regulation are by and large consistent with the common law approach to determining the governing or applicable law. At common law, the starting point is to investigate whether the parties have expressly selected a body of law at the time of contracting or whether such selection can be implied from the express terms of the contract. If the court is unable to ascertain the governing law from the contract it will then look to determine with which system of law the contract has the closest connection.

(2) Express or Implied Choice of Law

7.05 Article 3(1) of the Convention under the heading 'Freedom of choice' provides:

> A contract shall be governed by the law chosen by the parties. The choice must be express or demonstrated with reasonable certainty by the terms of the contract or the circumstances of the case. By their choice the parties can select the law applicable to the whole or a part only of the contract.

7.06 Where a reinsurance contract contains an express choice of governing law and/or provision for jurisdiction or arbitration in a particular forum, the court or arbitrators are bound to apply that law and the conflicts rules of that law and that forum

---

[3] Regulation No 593/2008 of 17 June 2008.

[4] Under art 1(a) of the Reinsurance Directive (2005/68/EC) reinsurance is defined as the activity consisting in accepting risks ceded by an insurance undertaking or by another reinsurance undertaking.

[5] *Whitworth Street Estates (Manchester) Ltd v James Miller and Partners Ltd* [1970] AC 583; *Cie Tunisienne de Navigation SA v Cie d'Armement Maritime SA* [1971] AC 572; *Amin Rasheed Shipping Corpn v Kuwait Insurance Co* [1984] AC 50. See also Lord Collins at para 90 of *Wasa International Insurance Co v Lexington Insurance Co* [2010] 1 AC 180, [2009] 2 Lloyd's Rep 508. He cited *Dicey & Morris, Conflict of Laws*, 9th edn (1973), rule 159 which stated that 'if an intention to choose the proper law has not been expressed in the insurance policy and cannot be inferred from circumstances, and if there is nothing to show that the contract is more closely connected with another system of law, the contract is governed by the law of the country in which the insurer carries on his business, and, if he carries on his business in two or more countries, by the law of the country in which his head office is situated.'

when determining the dispute.[6] However there is frequently more complication as the reinsurance may not itself specify a choice of law and one needs to be implied or inferred.

An example given in the Giuiliano-Lagarde Report on the Rome Convention as a **7.07** circumstance which could demonstrate an inferred intention was a contract in a standard form which is known to be governed by a particular system of law even though there is no express statement to this effect, such as a Lloyd's policy of marine insurance. The report was cited on this point by Thomas LJ in *Gard Marine v Glacier Reinsurance*.[7] The report had in mind the old SG form annexed as a schedule to the Marine Insurance Act 1906,[8] but the same considerations applied to the Lloyd's J(A) form on which the contract of reinsurance was made. The use of that form, London market terminology, and London market clauses throughout the slip indicated the choice of English law.[9]

This approach was also applied in the reinsurance context in *Gan Insurance Co Ltd* **7.08** *v Tai Ping Insurance Co Ltd*[10] where the Court of Appeal held that the inclusion in the slip of various standard form clauses commonly found in reinsurance contracts placed on the London market pointed to an implied choice of English law. This implied choice was further demonstrated by the circumstances of the placing of the business in London using London brokers who presented the risk to reinsurers in the conventional way in concluding a contract of reinsurance governed by English law.

In this regard, Hobhouse J in *Forsikringsaktieselskapet Vesta v JNE Butcher*[11] noted **7.09** that:

> Where a contract such as the present provides that its terms and conditions are to be the same as those of another contract and where its clear commercial purpose is to provide corresponding cover to that provided by the other contract then unless some other powerful consideration is to intervene the conclusion must be that there is an intention that both contracts are to be governed by the same law. However, there remains something surprising and improbable about the conclusion that the Lloyd's slip and the Lloyd's policy are governed by anything other than English law.

---

[6] *CGU International Insurance v Astrazeneca Insurance Co* [2006] Lloyd's Rep IR 409. The MRC slip used in the London market will, if correctly completed, have the express choice of law specified under a mandatory and specific heading (see para 2.17).

[7] [2011] Lloyd's Rep IR 489.

[8] See Mance LJ in *American Motorists Insurance Co v Cellstar Corporation* [2003] Lloyd's Rep IR 295, para 43.

[9] See also *Aegis Electrical and Gas International Services Ltd v Continental Casualty Co* [2008] Lloyd's Rep IR 17, paras 39–41 and *Dornoch Ltd v Mauritius Union Assurance Co Ltd* [2006] Lloyd's Rep IR 786, para 43.

[10] [1999] Lloyd's Rep IR 472. See also *Assicurazioni Generali SpA v Ege Sigorta AS* [2002] 1 Lloyd's Rep 480 and *Lincoln National Life Insurance Co v Employers Reinsurance Corp* [2002] Lloyd's Rep IR 853, 858.

[11] [1986] 2 Lloyd's Rep 179, 193.

7.10 There is thus a 'very strong inference' that contracts of reinsurance placed on the London market and recorded in policies issued in London are, in the absence of strong contrary intentions, intended to be governed by English law.[12] This is also reflected in the following passage from the judgment of Bingham LJ in *EI Du Pont De Nemours & Co*:[13]

> I think it plain, almost beyond argument, that the proper law of that policy is English. It was a Lloyd's policy, negotiated by Lloyd's brokers and issued by the Lloyd's Policy Signing Office in London. Notice of potential claims was to be given to Lloyd's brokers. The policy was for world-wide cover. Unless displaced, the inference that English law was intended to govern is in my view overwhelming.

7.11 References in the slip to 'as original', 'following original' and 'as more fully described in the original policy wording' will not be sufficient to impute to the parties an intention that the reinsurance contract be governed by the same law as the original contract. Such words are intended to ensure that the risk undertaken by the reinsurer is identical as to period, geographical limits, and nature of the risk with the risk undertaken by the reinsured as direct insurer, ie they define the risk.[14]

7.12 The presence of an exclusive jurisdiction clause in a contract of reinsurance may be a relevant circumstance from which it is possible to infer the parties' intention as to the applicable law.[15] In *Norske Atlas Insurance Co Ltd v London General Insurance Co Ltd*[16] it was held that the parties' intention that the applicable law should be Norwegian law was clearly indicated by the presence of an arbitration clause which provided for arbitration in Norway by Norwegian or Danish arbitrators.

7.13 The significance or weight to be attached to an arbitration clause will depend on its precise terms, but it can be an indication of the applicable law whether or not it is mandatory for arbitrators to apply a particular law. The clause in *Norske* was a compulsory clause which provided that any disputes which arose under the reinsurance 'shall always be decided' by arbitration in Norway. In *King v Brandywine*[17] (in which there was a 'package' of policies in three sections—I, IIIA, and IIIB) the arbitration clauses in sections I and IIIA were not compulsory, but simply provided that if the parties agreed to refer any dispute to arbitration it would take place in New York (with the arbitrators applying New York law to the extent that they

---

[12] *King v Brandywine* [2005] 1 Lloyd's Rep 655 and its reference to *EI Du Pont v Agnew* [1987] 2 Lloyd's Rep 585. In *Stonebridge Underwriting Ltd v Ontario Municipal Insurance Exchange* [2011] Lloyd's Rep IR 171 it was held that English law was probably the applicable law of a reinsurance contract placed in London by London brokers with a London reinsurer and incorporating a number of standard London market clauses.

[13] [1987] 2 Lloyd's Rep 585, 592.

[14] *Gan Insurance Co Ltd v Tai Ping Insurance Co Ltd* [1999] Lloyd's Rep IR 47, 480. The problems which may arise where the original contract of insurance and the contract of reinsurance have, or are held to have, different governing laws are discussed at paras 3.53–3.57.

[15] *Royal Exchange Assurance Corp v Sjoforsakrings Aktiebolaget Vega* [1902] KB 384.

[16] (1927) 28 Ll L Rep 104.

[17] [2005] 1 Lloyd's Rep 655.

chose to follow any rules of law). The arbitration clause in section IIIB provided for compulsory arbitration in New York should either party request it. Although the arbitrators might abstain from strictly following the rules of law, they had to apply New York law if applying any law. In *Commercial Union Assurance Co Plc v NRG Victory Reinsurance Ltd*[18] Clarke J, considering the same contracts, had expressed the obiter view that the proper law of the contracts was New York law. At first instance in *King* Colman J suggested that where the arbitrators were given discretion not to apply strict rules of law, little weight could be attached to the arbitration clauses as indicia of the proper law.[19] The Court of Appeal disagreed.[20]

The Court of Appeal noted that the arbitration clauses in sections I and IIIA were **7.14** largely in the same form as the arbitration clause in section IIIB, except arbitration was not compulsory and there was express choice of New York law. They noted that if the arbitration and service of suit clauses were viewed as a whole they pointed strongly to an inferred choice of New York law. They then examined whether the circumstances of the placement in the London market displaced that inference, but held that the New York arbitration clause in section IIIB meant that it was difficult, if not impossible, to infer a choice of English law as the law to govern the contract.

It will be noted that the Court of Appeal also took the service of suit clause into **7.15** account as a relevant circumstance which assisted in determining the parties' intention.[21] One service of suit clause provided for the insurers to submit to the jurisdiction of any court of competent jurisdiction within the United States, not simply within the State of New York. The Court of Appeal held that as the dispute was between the laws of England and New York, this did not detract from the effect of the arbitration clause, which pointed to New York law. The service of suit clauses in the other two sections provided that the insurers would, at the request of the insured, 'submit to the jurisdiction of any court of competent jurisdiction within the State of New York', and that 'all matters arising hereunder shall be determined in accordance with the law and practice of such court'.[22] The fact that these clauses provided for submission to the jurisdiction of a New York court and for the provision for service of process on an officer specified by a New York statute were factors which pointed (when taken together with the wording of the arbitration clause) to New York law as the proper law.[23]

(3) Applicable Law where there is No Express or Implied Choice of Law

To the extent that the law applicable to the contract has not been chosen in accord- **7.16** ance with Article 3, the Convention and Rome I Regulation provide that the contract

---

[18] [1988] 1 Lloyd's Rep 80, reversed on other grounds at [1998] 2 Lloyd's Rep 600.
[19] [2004] Lloyd's Rep IR 554.
[20] [2005] 1 Lloyd's Rep 655, paras 35–49.
[21] [2005] 1 Lloyd's Rep 655, paras 42–47.
[22] There was further provision for service of process in New York.
[23] Distinguishing *El Du Pont v Agnew* [1987] 2 Lloyd's Rep 585 in which a Lloyd's policy, negotiated by Lloyd's brokers and issued in London was held to be governed by English Law

shall be governed by the law of the country with which it is most closely connected, subject to the qualification that a severable part of the contract which has a closer connection with another country may be governed by the law of that other country.[24]

7.17 Article 4(1) of the Rome I Regulation provides specific rules for specific types of contract, not including reinsurance contracts. It then points to the law of the country where the party required to effect the characteristic performance has his habitual residence unless it is clear from all the circumstances of the case that the contract is manifestly more closely connected with another country.[25] If the applicable law cannot be determined under Article 4(1) or (2) the contract shall be governed by the law of the country with which it is most closely connected.[26]

7.18 The Rome Convention presumed[27] that the contract is most closely connected with the country where the party who is to effect the performance which is characteristic of the contract has its principal place of business or, where under the terms of the contract the performance is to be effected through a place of business other than the principal place of business, the country in which that other place of business is situated. The characteristic performance of the contract of reinsurance is the provision of cover or the payment of a claim by the reinsurer.[28] Therefore, where the presumption applies, the applicable law is determined by reference to the country from which the reinsurer effects its performance.

7.19 However, this presumption does not apply if it appears from the circumstances as a whole that the contract is more closely connected with another country.[29] The authors of *Dicey and Morris on The Conflict of Laws*[30] state that in the context of reinsurance the presumption is more likely to be disregarded than applied because its operation ignores the important role of brokers in reinsurance. It is not uncommon for a broker to place reinsurance on the same slip, in respect of the same risk, with a number of reinsurers each of whom has their principal place of business in different jurisdictions. It would make little sense to hold that each of the reinsurer's obligations was governed by the law of a different country.[31] In such circumstances

---

notwithstanding a reference to New York in the service of suit clause on the grounds that it was not inconsistent with an English proper law: *Armadora Occidental SA v Horace Mann Insurance Co* [1977] 1 WLR 520. In *King* the Court of Appeal noted that there was no New York arbitration clause in the *El Du Pont* case.

[24] Rome Convention, Art 4(1).

[25] Rome I Regulation Art 4(2) and (3).

[26] Rome I Regulation Art 4(4)

[27] Rome Convention, Art 4(2).

[28] *Lincoln National Life Insurance Co v Employers Reinsurance Corp* [2002] Lloyd's Rep IR 853, 858. See also Aikens J in *Dornoch Ltd v Mauritius Union Assurance Co Ltd* [2006] Lloyd's Rep IR 127, para 72 (upheld [2006] 2 Lloyd's Rep 475). As the leading reinsurers were based in England, the characteristic performance of an excess reinsurance would be performed in England (see para 70).

[29] Rome Convention, Art 4(5) and Rome I Regulation Art 4(4).

[30] 14th edn (2006), 33–217–33–219.

[31] *Lincoln National Life Insurance Co v Employers Reinsurance Corp* [2002] Lloyd's Rep IR 853, 858.

it will be necessary to consider whether the contracts have a close connection with any one country whose law would then apply to govern all the obligations arising under them.

Some of the relevant factors in determining with which country the contract is **7.20** most closely connected are the manner in which the reinsurance was placed, the type of cover placed and the inclusion of any standard form clauses. This is demonstrated by the following passage from the judgment of Moore-Bick J in *Lincoln National Life Insurance v Employers Reinsurance Corp*:[32]

> …the contracts in this case were not made by reference to a standard English form, nor were they all made in the London market in the sense of being placed by London brokers direct with London underwriters in each case…However, all the contracts were negotiated through brokers in London, Bradstock, and were made in the usual manner of the London market, that is, by the signature of a slip which summarized the essential terms of the contract. Two other factors point strongly towards England as the country with which the contracts have their closest connection. The first is the nature of the cover itself, described in the slips as 'General Aviation Personal Accident Carve out Reinsurance'. The evidence shows that in 1995 aviation bodily injury carve out reinsurance was a relatively new and specialized form of reinsurance developed in the London market. The second that the slips incorporated by reference a number of standard London market Clauses. The fact that the limits of liability were expressed in US dollars seems to me to be of little significance by comparison since much of the business written in the London market is written in dollars.

(4) Floating Choice of Law Clause

In *Heath Lambert Ltd v Sociedad de Corretaje de Seguros*[33] the cover note pro- **7.21** vided that the reinsurance was 'Subject to Venezuelan Law and/or Venezuelan Jurisdiction if required'. This was held to be a floating choice of law clause which gave the option to demand Venezuelan law and/or jurisdiction. The court said that 'it by no means followed' from the inclusion of the floating choice of law clause that the parties intended the governing law to be Venezuelan rather than English law. The contract of reinsurance, which was placed in London, was held to be governed by English law with the option to select Venezuelan law.[34]

(5) The Effect of Different Governing Laws

An insurance contract and the reinsurance taken out in respect of the same risk may **7.22** be governed by different laws. The question whether the conflict can be resolved is not a question of conflicts of law, but a question of construction.

---

[32] *Lincoln National Life Insurance Co v Employers Reinsurance Corp* [2002] Lloyd's Rep IR 853, 858.
[33] [2004] 1 Lloyd's Rep 495.
[34] [2004] 1 Lloyd's Rep 495, 500.

7.23   In *St Paul Fire and Marine Insurance Co v Morice*[35] the life of a bull shipped from New York to Buenos Aires was insured by St Paul under 'the rules and customs of insurance in Boston or New York'. As it was infected with foot and mouth, it had to be slaughtered on arrival. The reinsured claimed on the reinsurance which was subject to the same terms '... as original policy' but was governed by English Law. The dispute arose because under the US law the reinsured was liable to pay the insured for the bull under the words 'all risks of mortality', but under English law it was argued that mortality meant accidental death and not intentional killing. In fact the case was resolved by the judge rejecting the expert evidence as to the effect of US law and finding that under both laws the words 'all risks of mortality' applied only to accidental and not intentional death.

7.24   In both *Forsikringaktieselskapet Vesta v Butcher*[36] and *Groupama Navigation v Catatumbo*[37] the insurance and reinsurance were written using the same or similar language, but were governed by different laws. The problem was that identical or similar wording had to be construed in different ways under the different laws. In both the reinsurers took the point that they were relieved from liability because the original insured (and not the reinsured) had been guilty of a breach of a warranty, which was a term of both the insurance and the reinsurance contracts and which breach was not causative of the loss. In each case the governing law of the insurance contract did not afford a defence to the reinsurer where the breach was non-causative.

7.25   In *Vesta* the insurance was for loss or damage to a fish farm in Norway. The reinsurance policy was put in place before the original insurance was written (as is common, both were broked in London as part of a package), using a local insurance company to obtain the business. The local insurer was told by the brokers that they would be able to reinsure 90% of the risk. The insurance contract was governed by Norwegian law, and the reinsurance contract was governed by English law. The insurance contract contained a warranty that a 24-hour watch be kept over the site and specified that failure to comply with a warranty rendered the policy null and void. The reinsurance slip annexed the original insurance terms, so that it was argued that the warranty in the insurance contract was also a term of the reinsurance.[38]

7.26   The express term that failure to comply with the warranties rendered the policy null and void was ineffective under Norwegian law if the breach was non-causative, whereas a similar term in the reinsurance would be valid under English law. The

---

[35] (1906) 11 Com Cas 153.
[36] [1989] AC 852.
[37] [2000] 2 Lloyd's Rep 350.
[38] Although Lord Griffiths doubted whether the effect of Form J.1—the standard form of reinsurance policy—did indeed incorporate the warranty in the reinsurance at p 896 and Lord Collins commented in *Wasa International Insurance Co v Lexington Insurance Co* [2010] 1 AC 180, [2009] 2 Lloyd's Rep 508, para 69 that this had 'considerable force'.

reinsurers failed because the reinsurance was held to have the same effect as the insurance as a matter of construction of the reinsurance contract. Lord Templeman concluded that:[39]

> The effect of a warranty in the reinsurance policy is governed by the effect of the warranty in the insurance policy because the reinsurance policy is a contract by the underwriters to indemnify Vesta against liability under the insurance policy.

Lord Lowry reached the same conclusion saying that the relevant words in the **7.27** reinsurance contract ('failure to comply') had the same meaning and effect as they had in the Norwegian insurance contract.

Catatumbo[40] concerned hull and machinery insurance for a fleet of vessels. There **7.28** was a warranty as to maintenance of existing class in the insurance contract and the reinsurance also 'warranted existing class maintained'. However the insurance policy was issued in Spanish by a Venezuelan insurance company to a Venezuelan insured providing for jurisdiction of a Venezuelan court if the parties did not agree to arbitration. It was therefore governed by Venezuelan law, whereas the reinsurance contract was governed by English law. In Venezuelan law a breach of warranty affected the insurance cover only if it were causative, while English law discharged an insurer from the date of the breach irrespective of causation or whether it had been remedied before the loss.[41]

It was held that the parties to the reinsurance contract must be taken to have **7.29** intended that the incorporation in the reinsurance contract of terms in the original insurance retained the same significance which they had in the original insurance. It was a question of construction, against the background that 'reinsurers conducting international business must be taken to have intended that the warranties in the two contracts will have the same effect'.[42]

Tuckey LJ held that reinsurers conducting international business must be taken **7.30** to have intended that warranties in insurance and reinsurance will have the same effect. The reinsurer is aware that some foreign laws give a restrictive effect to warranties compared to English law, but 'that is a risk they must be taken to have assumed by writing international business'. He held that the reinsurer is protected to the same extent as the insurer. Mance LJ took a similar approach, stating that the argument that the warranty incorporated by reference into the reinsurance retained a 'stubbornly domestic English significance' in the reinsurance, trumping the limited significance of the same warranty in the original from which it was incorporated, was both commercially and legally unattractive.

---

[39] [1989] AC 852, 892.
[40] [2000] 2 Lloyd's Rep 350.
[41] Marine Insurance Act 1906, ss 33(3), 34(2).
[42] [2000] 2 Lloyd's Rep 350, para 20, per Tuckey LJ. Mance LJ agreed saying at para 26 that the 'reinsurance is...a contract which in terms relates to and must be read in conjunction with the terms of the original insurance'.

7.31　In *Wasa International Insurance Co v Lexington Insurance Co*[43] Lord Collins said that neither *Vesta* nor *Catatumbo* applied as when the insurance and reinsurance were concluded, no identifiable system of law was applicable to the insurance contract which could have provided a basis for construing the contract of reinsurance in a manner different from its ordinary meaning in the London insurance market. Furthermore, at that time, the US courts had not yet developed the theory of joint and several liability for all damage, even that occurring outside the policy period.

B.　Jurisdiction

7.32　In general terms, the English courts will have jurisdiction to hear any dispute where service has been properly effected on the defendant (wherever they are domiciled) or when a defendant submits to the jurisdiction of the English court. There is a considerable amount of authority in relation to the service of proceedings out of the jurisdiction, on companies incorporated out of the jurisdiction but who have a presence within the jurisdiction, and on submission to the jurisdiction. The reader who wishes to obtain further information on those matters should consult the standard texts.[44] This chapter addresses issues that have arisen specifically in relation to reinsurance.

(1)　The Position of Defendants Domiciled in the European Union and the European Free Trade Association

7.33　The Civil Jurisdiction and Judgments Act 1982 incorporated into English law the Brussels Convention on Jurisdiction and the Enforcement of Judgments in Civil and Commercial Matters 1968 and the Lugano Convention on Jurisdiction and the Enforcement of Judgments in Civil and Commercial Matters 1988 (as inserted by s 1 of the Civil Jurisdiction and Judgments Act 1991). Since then jurisdiction provisions have been consolidated into the Brussels I Regulation[45] which applies to claims commenced after 1 March 2002. The Brussels I Regulation does not apply to reinsurance contracts with arbitration clauses.[46] The Regulation and conventions were concerned with harmonizing the rules as to the choice of jurisdiction between the contracting states. The relevant provisions of both conventions for the purposes of this chapter are identical but the Lugano Convention governed the

---

[43] [2010] 1 AC 180, [2009] 2 Lloyd's Rep 508.

[44] See *Civil Procedure—The White Book Service; Dicey and Morris on The Conflict of Laws* 14th edn (2006).

[45] Council Regulation (EC) No 44/2001 of 22 December 2000 on Jurisdiction and the Recognition and Enforcement of Judgments in Civil and Commercial Matters.

[46] Including court proceedings to support arbitral proceedings: *Marc Rich & Co v Società Italiana Impianti (The Atlantic Emperor)* [1992] 1 Lloyd's Rep 34 but cf *The Xing Su Hai* [1995] 2 Lloyd's Rep 15.

position in respect of members of the European Free Trade Association while the Brussels Convention governed the position in respect of the European Union.

The general approach under the Brussels I Regulation is the same as that under its **7.34** precedessor conventions and is that parties should be sued in the state in which they are domiciled. If proceedings in relation to the reinsurance dispute have already been started in another member state, no other court has jurisdiction until that other court decides it has no jurisdiction. If the reinsurer or reinsured has submitted to jurisdiction, then the court to which they have submitted will have jurisdiction to hear the dispute.[47] If there is a jurisdiction clause in the reinsurance contract then the Regulation will uphold the express jurisdiction clause as exclusive.[48]

There are exceptions to the general principle that the member state country in which **7.35** the defendant is domiciled will have jurisdiction to hear the dispute. As reinsurance contracts often include a number of parties domiciled in different countries, Article 6(1) is of particular significance. Under Article 6(1) a claimant may bring a claim against one defendant in the courts of any member state in which another defendant in the same proceedings is domiciled where the claims are so closely connected that it is expedient to hear and determine them together to avoid the risk of irreconcilable judgments resulting from separate proceedings.

The interplay between the defendant's domicile and article 6(1) of the Lugano **7.36** Convention in a reinsurance context was explored by the Court of Appeal in *Gard Marine v Glacier Reinsurance*.[49] Following hurricane damage, the insurer settled with the insured energy company and made a claim against its reinsurers. One of the reinsurers, Glacier, was Swiss and objected to the jurisdiction of the English court, on the basis that it had already commenced proceedings in Switzerland. When the Swiss Federal Court held that it had no jurisdiction over the reinsured because it was not domiciled in Switzerland, the stay of the English action was lifted. However the reinsurer continued to contest jurisdiction on the basis that it was domiciled in Switzerland. The reinsured argued that the English court had jurisdiction under article 6(1) of the Lugano Convention.

The Court of Appeal held that English law had, under article 3 of the Rome **7.37** Convention, been chosen with reasonable certainty by reference to the circumstances of the placement. The underlying policy was governed by English law and it would be usual for the excess of loss reinsurance to be governed by the same law as the underlying insurance, so that the provisions were interpreted consistently. The reinsurance was a London market placement, the form of reinsurance slip was that used in the London market, and its terms and language were from the London market terms. The Court commented that it would make no commercial sense for

---

[47] Art 24 of the Brussels I Regulation.
[48] Art 23.
[49] [2011] Lloyd's Rep IR 489.

one part of the reinsurance to be governed by one system of law and another to be governed by a different system. Although there was a presumption in favour of the reinsurer's place of business under article 4(2) of the Convention, in the light of all the other factors there was a strong case that the presumption ought to be disregarded under article 4(5). In all the circumstances, the excess of loss reinsurance was more closely connected with England. In the light of the participation of other reinsurers in the same excess of loss reinsurance, there would be a risk of irreconcilable judgments if different courts decided the issues.

7.38   A court should approach the matter in the light of the policy to produce predictable results but having regard to the principle that jurisdiction was generally based on the defendant's domicile. In deciding whether an exception to the general rule of jurisdiction by reference to the defendant's domicile existed in a given case, the court had to assess the connection between the claims to see whether there was a risk of irreconcilable judgments arising out separate proceedings such that there might be a divergence in the outcome where there was 'the same situation in law and fact'. In so doing, it is necessary for a national court to look at all the factors.

7.39   The Brussels I Regulation[50] provides that where one of the parties is domiciled in a member state and the parties have agreed in writing that the courts of a member state are to have jurisdiction in relation to disputes between them, then that court shall have jurisdiction.[51] In *AIG Group (UK) Ltd v. The Ethniki*[52] it was held that 'as original' language in the reinsurance slip policy did not amount to a jurisdiction agreement for the purposes of Article 23. Such language could only incorporate a jurisdiction clause from an original policy into a facultative reinsurance contract if the intention of the parties was absolutely clear.

7.40   Under Article 5 in matters relating to a contract, a claim can be brought in the courts of a member state other than that where the defendant is domiciled if they are the courts 'for the place of performance of the obligation in question'.[53] However, this exception is in turn overridden by a provision[54] that in 'matters relating to

---

[50] Art 23.

[51] Exclusive jurisdiction unless expressly agreed otherwise.

[52] [2000] Lloyd's Rep IR 343. The Court of Appeal also referred to European jurisprudence which requires 'clear and precise demonstration' in the reinsurance contract that the jurisdiction clause relied on was in fact the subject of a consensus between the parties.

[53] 'The place of the performance of the obligation in question.' Where there is more than one obligation in issue then the court will be required to identify the principal obligation—Case 266/85 *Shenavai v Kreischer* [1987] ECR 239; *Union Transport plc v Continental Lines SA* [1992] 1 Lloyd's Rep 229; *AIG Europe (UK) Ltd v Anonymous Greek Insurance Co of General Insurances (The Ethniki)* [2000] Lloyd's Rep IR 343. A further question arises when it is possible to identify two 'principal' obligations neither subordinate to the other and of equal rank. In those circumstances, each issue may have to be determined in a different jurisdiction—see Case C-420/97 *Leathertex Divisione Sintetici SpA v Bodetex BVBA* [1999] 2 All ER (Comm) 769. The ECJ held that although there might be disadvantages in such fragmentation, the claimant always had the option to bring his entire claim before the courts for the place where the defendant was domiciled.

[54] Section 3, Art 11.

insurance' an insurer may bring proceedings only in the courts of the contracting state in which the defendant is domiciled, whether he is the policyholder, the insured or a beneficiary.[55] The courts have therefore had to address the question of whether reinsurance is a 'matter relating to insurance' within the meaning of the conventions.

In *Agnew v Lansforsakringsbolagens AB*,[56] a case involving the Lugano Convention, **7.41** the claimants carried on reinsurance business in the London market. The defendant was an insurance company incorporated in Sweden and the claimants underwrote facultative reinsurance in relation to the defendant's exposure under original suppliers' and manufacturers' guarantee insurance. The claimants issued proceedings in London asserting that they were entitled to avoid the reinsurance contracts on the grounds that they had been induced to enter into them by material misrepresentations and non-disclosure during the negotiation and presentation of the risks in London. The defendant applied to have the proceedings set aside on the grounds that the English courts had no jurisdiction to hear the claim pursuant to the provisions in the Lugano Convention that the reinsured had to be sued in the state in which he was domiciled. The House of Lords held that 'matters relating to insurance' did not include reinsurance and that the court had prima facie jurisdiction to hear the claim. Lord Woolf justified the distinction in the approach to insurance and reinsurance contracts on the grounds that the purpose of the provisions in relation to insurance was to protect the consumer, who was to be regarded as the weaker party, and that it was not apt to extend that approach to disputes between reinsurers and their reinsured, where the latter cannot conventionally be regarded as the weaker party.[57] Lord Woolf also stated that the insurance provisions of the Convention were drafted with consumer protection (rather than disputes between insurance companies) in mind.

The House of Lords also held that as a matter of ordinary language and the policy **7.42** of the Convention, the place of the performance of the obligation in question in matters relating to a contract included pre-contractual obligations. Lord Woolf set out that the obligations in question were to make a fair presentation of the risk, not to misrepresent it and to disclose material facts, and that those obligations

---

[55] This does not affect the right to bring a counterclaim in the court in which the original claim is pending.

[56] [2001] 1 AC 223.

[57] [2001] 1 AC 223, 237H. Lord Woolf also had regard to a number of earlier authorities. In *Arkwright Mutual Insurance Co v Bryanston Insurance Co Ltd* [1990] 2 QB 649 it was common ground that reinsurance was not included in s 3 of the Lugano Convention. In *Trade Indemnity plc v Forsakringsaktiebolaget Njord* [1995] 1 All ER 796, Rix J concluded that the provision did not apply to reinsurance, although the point had not been argued before him. In *Jordan Grand Prix Ltd v Baltic Insurance Group* [1999] 2 AC 127, Lord Steyn indicated that the purpose of s 3 was to protect the insured who was more frequently faced with a predetermined contract and who was in a weaker position.

were to be performed in London. Accordingly the English courts were held to have jurisdiction to hear the claim.

7.43   A similar approach has been taken to the question of reinsurance by the European Court of Justice in relation to the Brussels Convention. In *Universal General Insurance Co (UCIC) v Group Josi Reinsurance Co SA*,[58] the defendant was a Belgian reinsurance company which had agreed to take a share in a contract of reinsurance effected by the claimant, a Canadian insurance company, but later refused to pay its share of the risk on the ground that it had been induced to enter into the agreement by misrepresentations. The claimant brought proceedings for the recovery of money in France, where the claimant's broker had its registered office. The defendant averred that it was domiciled in Belgium and could therefore only be sued in that country. The European Court of Justice held that the rules of special jurisdiction in the Convention in respect of 'matters relating to insurance' did not apply to disputes between reinsurers and reinsureds in the context of reinsurance contracts.[59] The European Court of Justice also held that as a general rule the place where the claimant is domiciled is not relevant for the purposes of applying the rules of jurisdiction under the Convention, even where the claimant was domiciled in a non-member country, because the application of those rules was dependent solely on the criterion of the defendant's domicile being in a contracting state.

7.44   Under the conventions, the greatest degree of certainty that reinsurer and reinsured can achieve in relation to the determination of the courts to be seised of any disputes that may arise between them will be accomplished by the reinsurer and reinsured agreeing a particular jurisdiction for the determination of such disputes.[60] To be fully effective, at least one of the parties to the agreement must be domiciled in a contracting state.

7.45   Because of its derogation from the fundamental principle enshrined in the conventions that defendants should be sued in the countries in which they live, a strict approach will be taken to the application of a jurisdiction clause. Not only will such a clause be interpreted strictly, but also, and pertinently in the reinsurance context, the court will look for a clear and precise demonstration that the jurisdiction clause relied upon is in fact the subject of a consensus between the

---

[58] [2001] QB 68.

[59] The ECJ held that although the rules of special jurisdiction in matters relating to insurance did not refer to disputes between a reinsured and his reinsurer in connection with a reinsurance contract, they were fully applicable where under the law of a contracting state, the policyholder, the insured or the beneficiary of an insurance contract has the option to approach directly any reinsurer of the insurer in order to assert his rights under that contract as against that reinsurer, eg in the case of the bankruptcy or liquidation of the insurer. In such a situation the claimant is in a weak position compared with the professional reinsurer so that the objective of the special protection inherent in the special provisions relating to insurance justified the application of the special protection which it applied.

[60] Note that the Brussels and Lugano conventions do not apply to arbitrations. Any exclusive arbitration clause will not, therefore, fall for consideration under the conventions.

parties.[61] In considering the nature of the agreement needed to satisfy that test, the court does not look to the presumed or actual intention of the parties as derived from extrinsic evidence, but to the form of the contract. Only a clear reference to the terms containing the jurisdiction clause will suffice, and it will also be necessary to be confident that the jurisdiction clause was effectively brought to the attention of the other contracting party so as to satisfy the need for genuine consensus.[62]

In *AIG Europe (UK) Ltd v The Ethniki*[63] the Court was concerned with the incorp-   **7.46**
oration into a contract of reinsurance of a jurisdiction clause in favour of the courts of Athens contained in the underlying contract of insurance. The underlying contract provided that the contracting parties agreed to submit any dispute arising out of the policy to the jurisdiction of the courts of Athens and waived the right to contest the jurisdiction of the courts of Athens for any reason. The reinsurance contract provided simply: 'Wording as original'. Colman J held that these general words in the contract of reinsurance were not apt to incorporate the jurisdiction clause in the underlying policy, finding that such clauses were ancillary and accordingly were not incorporated by general words of incorporation in the reinsurance contract.[64] The Court of Appeal, upholding the decision of Colman J, held that the right approach in any given case was to ask whether the parties to the contract in which the general words of incorporation appeared intended that their contract should include the particular term from the other contract referred to. Evans LJ stated that the jurisdiction clause in the underlying contract did nothing to define the risk and that, if regard were had to its terms, it was wholly inappropriate to disputes arising between insurers and reinsurers under a contract that was probably governed by English law. He held that the requisite 'clear and precise demonstration that the jurisdiction clause was the subject of a consensus between the parties', as required by European jurisprudence,[65] was not present.

In summary, where there is no express choice of jurisdiction in the reinsurance con-   **7.47**
tract wording, but it was said that the parties had agreed one by incorporating the wording of an underlying contract, the courts adopt a fairly strict approach.[66]

---

[61] Note that special requirements exist for exclusive jurisdiction agreements with parties domiciled in Luxembourg (Art 1 of the 1968 Protocol). See *Prifti v Musini Sociedad Anónima de Seguros y Reaseguros* [2004] Lloyd's Rep IR 528.

[62] See, eg, *AIG Europe SA v QBE International Insurance Ltd* [2002] Lloyd's Rep IR 22. In *AIG* Moore-Bick J stated that it did not follow that it was necessary to ignore the background to the agreement and the commercial context should be taken into account.

[63] [1999] Lloyd's Rep IR 221, upheld on appeal [2000] Lloyd's Rep IR 343.

[64] See also para 3.52 on exclusive jurisdiction.

[65] [2000] Lloyd's Rep IR 343, para 41.

[66] *AIG Europe (UK) Ltd v The Ethniki* [2000] Lloyd's Rep IR 343, [2000] 2 All ER 566; *AIG Europe v QBE International Insurance* [2001] 2 Lloyd's Rep 268; *Assicurazioni Generali SpA v Ege Sigorta AS* [2002] Lloyd's Rep IR 480.

7.48   In *Arig Insurance Co Ltd v Sasa Assicurazione Riassicurazione SpA*[67] the underlying
policy provided that the court of competent jurisdiction was exclusively that of the
place of the residence or office of the Italian insured. The policy also contained certain standard terms including that the court of competent jurisdiction, chosen by
the claimant, was exclusively that of the place of residence or the registered office of
the defendant, or that of the place where the agency to which the policy was assigned
had its office. Tuckey J held that the only question for the court was whether the
words 'policy wording as original' in the reinsurance contract amounted to a clear
demonstration that the jurisdiction clause in the underlying policy of insurance
was the subject of consensus between the parties. He held that it was not, relying in
part on the commercial background to the reinsurance contract.

7.49   In *AIG Europe SA v QBE International Insurance Ltd*[68] Moore-Bick J, having
reviewed the authorities cited at paras 7.46 to 7.48, identified the emphasis which
had been placed by the European Court of Justice[69] on the need to be confident that
the jurisdiction clause had been effectively brought to the attention of the other
contracting party so as to satisfy the need for genuine consensus. In *AIG* the underlying policy contained a clause that the French courts would have sole jurisdiction
in the event of a dispute between the underlying insured and the reinsured. The
reinsurance agreement provided 'All terms, Clauses and conditions as original and
to follow the original in all respects including settlements'. The commercial background, which Moore-Bick J stated it was permissible for the courts to consider,
supported rather than undermined the likelihood of consensus because QBE's
Paris office operated largely independently so that it could be said that both parties to the contract were in substance French, the reinsurance was placed through
Luxembourg brokers, and further it was likely that the proper law of the contract
was French law. However, despite the reference to '*all* terms, clauses and conditions
as original' in the reinsurance agreement, it was clear that some of the terms of the
original policy were not intended to apply to the contract of reinsurance and in the
absence of any other indication that the parties had addressed their minds to the
question, the word 'all' was not to be given a weight which it could not bear. A consensus had not been clearly and precisely demonstrated. Moore-Bick J stated that:

> …reinsurance jurisdiction Clauses, being ancillary in nature and having no bear-
> ing on the definition of the risk, are not germane to the substance either of the
> underlying policy or of the reinsurance contract. In those circumstances, general
> words of incorporation will not suffice to demonstrate with sufficient certainty to
> satisfy the requirements of Article 17[70] the existence of the necessary consensus.

---

[67]   10 February 1998, referred to by Moore-Bick J in *AIG Europe SA v QBE International Insurance Ltd* [2002] Lloyd's Rep IR 22.
[68]   [2002] Lloyd's Rep IR 22.
[69]   See Case 24/76 *Estasis Salotti di Colzani Aimo e Gianmario Colzani v RUWA Polstereimaschinen GmbH* [1976] ECR 1831.
[70]   The article concerned with an agreement as to jurisdiction.

Although the commercial background does not reinforce this conclusion (as it did in both *AIG Europe (UK) Ltd v The Ethniki* and *Arig v Sasa*),[71] it is not of sufficient weight to make good this deficiency in the language of the contract.

The court will also ensure that the particular dispute pending before it falls within **7.50** the ambit of the jurisdiction clause relied upon. If a party tries to sidestep the choice of court clause by asserting that the particular dispute falls outside the scope of the clause, the national court will determine whether the dispute is caught by the clause according to principles of national law. Once agreed, a party cannot circumvent the jurisdiction clause agreed merely by asserting that the contract containing the clause is void.[72]

Under the current rules of procedure in the English courts, proceedings can be **7.51** served on a defendant that is domiciled out of the jurisdiction but in a country that is subject to the Brussels I Regulation (formerly a signatory to the Brussels or Lugano Conventions) without the permission of the court if the claim is one which the court has power to determine under the Civil Jurisdiction and Judgments Act 1982 and there are no proceedings between the parties concerning the same claim in the courts of any other part of the United Kingdom or any other Convention territory.[73]

(2) The Position in Respect of Defendants Domiciled Outside the European Union and the European Free Trade Association

Where a defendant is not domiciled in a country that is is subject to the Brussels I **7.52** Regulation (or a signatory to the Brussels or Lugano Conventions) then permission of the court to serve out of the jurisdiction is required. The provisions relating to service out of the jurisdiction are set out at rule 6.20 of the Civil Procedure Rules. So far as contract claims are concerned, the court may give permission to serve out of the jurisdiction if the claim is made in respect of:

(a) a contract that was made within the jurisdiction;
(b) a contract that was made by or through an agent trading or residing within the jurisdiction;
(c) a contract that is governed by English law;
(d) a contract that contains a term to the effect that the court shall have jurisdiction to determine any claim in respect of the contract;
(e) a breach of contract committed within the jurisdiction;
(f) a declaration that no contract exists where, if the contract was found to exist, it would comply with the conditions set out in sub-paras (a)–(d) above.

---

[71] [2000] Lloyd's Rep IR 343 and *Arig Insurance Company Ltd v Sasa Assicurazione Riassicurazione Spa* (unreported, 10 February 1998).
[72] See *Benicasa v Dentalkit Srl* [1997] ECR I-3767.
[73] For further detail on the procedural position see *The White Book*.

7.53   The Rules further provide that the court will not grant permission to serve on a defendant out of the jurisdiction unless it is satisfied that England is the proper place in which to bring the claim. In this regard the courts in reinsurance cases will have regard to the principles set out by the House of Lords in *Spiliada Maritime Corp v Consulex Ltd*[74] (although that was a case in which a stay of proceedings was sought on the grounds that England was not the appropriate forum for the determination of the action),[75] which are as follows:

(a) the burden will be on the claimant to persuade the court that England is the appropriate forum for the trial of the dispute;

(b) the appropriate forum is that forum where the case may be most suitably tried in the interests of all of the parties and the ends of justice;

(c) the first consideration is what the natural forum of the dispute is—namely that with which the action has its most real and substantial connection. Connecting factors will include convenience and expense (such as the location of witnesses), the law governing the contract, and the places where the parties reside and carry on business;

(d) ordinary English procedural advantages such as the power to award interest are normally irrelevant, as are more generous English limitation periods where the claimant has failed to act prudently in respect of a shorter limitation period elsewhere;

(e) if the court concludes that there is another forum which apparently is as suitable or more suitable than England, it will normally refuse permission unless there are circumstances by reason of which justice requires that permission should nevertheless be granted. In this inquiry the court will consider all the circumstances of the case, including circumstances which go beyond those taken into account when considering connecting factors with other jurisdiction. One such factor can be the fact, if established by cogent objective evidence, that the claimant will not obtain justice in the foreign jurisdiction.

7.54   In practical terms, therefore, once the hurdle of bringing a claim within the ambit of CPR 6.20 has been satisfied, jurisdiction cases are determined on the basis of whether England is the appropriate forum, or *forum conveniens*, for the dispute.

7.55   The fact that a contract is governed by English law and that there are issues of English reinsurance law does not lead inevitably to the conclusion that England is the appropriate forum. The courts have also stated that in considering the question of whether the English court is the appropriate forum for the dispute to be tried,

---

[74] [1987] AC 460.

[75] See *Konkola Copper Mines Plc v Coromin Ltd* [2007] Lloyd's Rep IR 247 for an example of how a judge should exercise his discretion in relation to an application to stay a claim under a reinsurance contract on the grounds of jurisdiction. See also *Prifti v Musini Sociedad Anonima De Seguros Y Reaseguros (No 2)* [2006] Lloyd's Rep IR 221 and *Amlin Corporate Member Ltd v Oriental Assurance Corp* [2012] EWCA Civ 1341 where a stay was rejected in a reinsurance dispute despite a 'follow the settlements' clause and contentions of back to back cover.

it is not appropriate to embark upon a comparison of the procedures, or methods, or reputation of the standing of the courts of one country as compared with those of another.[76] Rather, in *Trade Indemnity plc v Forsaringsaktibolaget Njord*[77] Rix J emphasized the weight to be attached to the evidential location of the issues of fact and law likely to arise as between reinsurers and reinsureds. He set out that in a case involving an allegation of the misrepresentation of facts by the reinsured on the placing of the reinsurance, where the real issue was what the true facts were (rather than what was represented or materiality), great, and in most cases determinative, weight should be attached to the fact that the centre of gravity of the dispute is the place of the primary business of the reinsured, as distinct from that of the reinsurers where the reinsurance risk was placed. However, the position may change if the legal issues are complex, or the legal systems are very different, because in those circumstances the general principle that a court applies its own law more reliably than a foreign court will point to the more appropriate forum, whether English or foreign.[78] This may very often be the case in reinsurance disputes and is evident from the approach adopted by the English courts in a number of cases. In *Assicurazioni Generali SpA v Ege Sigorta AS*,[79] a case involving Turkish insurers and English reinsurers, Colman J stated:[80]

> I have no doubt at all that in a case where the meaning of a complex English law contract is in issue, particularly in a technical field such as reinsurance in the London market, it is appropriate to place weight on this factor in determining whether the English Courts are clearly the appropriate forum. Indeed, I would go so far as to say that, in determining whether the fair trial component of the overriding objective and of the interests of justice component of the *Spiliada* test is most likely to be satisfied, it would be completely unrealistic to leave out of account the fact that a trial before a Turkish Court will involve the slips and wordings being translated into Turkish and then construed in translation by the Court with the assistance of expert opinions also translated into Turkish as to what the meaning and effect of the English words should be.

Similarly in *Gan Insurance Co Ltd v Tai Ping Insurance Co Ltd*[81] the Court of Appeal **7.56** upheld the decision of the judge at first instance,[82] that England was the most appropriate forum for the resolution of the dispute between the claimant reinsurers who were based in London and the Taiwanese reinsured. The court took into account the fact that: the claims co-operation clauses that were at the centre of the dispute fell to be determined according to English law; they were standard London reinsurance

---

[76] *Amin Rasheed Shipping Corp v Kuwait Insurance Co* [1984] AC 50; *Trade Indemnity plc v Forsaringsaktibolaget Njord* [1995] LRLR 367.
[77] [1995] LRLR 367.
[78] See *Spiliada Maritime Corp v Cansulex* [1987] AC 460, 486.
[79] [2002] Lloyd's Rep IR 480.
[80] [2002] Lloyd's Rep IR 480, 486–487.
[81] [1999] Lloyd's Rep IR 472.
[82] [1999] Lloyd's Rep IR 229.

market clauses designed to protect London market reinsurers; and they were expressed in English and utilized the English concept of a condition precedent.

7.57 In *Brotherton v Asegurado Colseguros SA*,[83] the claimants were leaders on a facultative line slip under which they reinsured the original insurer's liabilities to the original insured, a Colombian bank called CAJA. The claimants sought to avoid the reinsurance contracts for the non-disclosure of allegations of corruption against the President of CAJA and commenced proceedings for negative declaratory relief (ie a declaration of non-liability). David Steel J held that England was the most appropriate forum because: the contract was governed by English law; the primary issues of fact revolved around misrepresentations and nondisclosures by London brokers to London underwriters in London; most of the relevant factual and expert witnesses were in England; and the proceedings on the direct policy in Colombia were of no concern as the claimants' case was not based on the truth of the allegations against the President of the bank, but on the content of those allegations.

7.58 In *Excess Insurance Co Ltd v Astra SA Insurance and Reinsurance Co*,[84] Potter J held that the *forum conveniens* of the dispute was England because the overall 'centre of gravity' of the case, as a reinsurance dispute under treaties brokered in London and governed by English law with English arbitration clauses, was England. In contrast where there is a likelihood of multiple proceedings involving the insured which centre around another jurisdiction, this may prevent England being the *forum conveniens*.[85]

7.59 In very many cases, therefore, reinsurers who have had business placed with them on the London reinsurance market will have good grounds for asserting that the appropriate forum for the dispute is England. Another factor may be the availability of a comprehensive determination of issues between many different reinsurance parties in one place. In *The Golden Mariner*[86] a reinsurance contract was concluded in England between 46 reinsurers, most of whom were from other jurisdictions but who were following Lloyd's underwriters. An application to stay English proceedings was rejected on the ground that England was a convenient forum for individual insurers around the globe to have the validity of a claim determined in a single hearing binding on all concerned.

7.60 A recent case in which an implied choice of law assisted in determining the proper jurisdiction for the dispute is *Stonebridge Underwriting Ltd v Ontario Municipal*

---

[83] [2002] Lloyd's Rep IR 848.
[84] [1995] LRLR 464, upheld on appeal [1996] LRLR 380.
[85] In *Limit (No 3) v PDV Insurance* [2005] Lloyd's Rep IR 552 retrocessionaires claimed a declaration of non-liability in England in respect of original claims by a Venezuelan national oil company, in respect of environmental impairment liability. This was before the original insured or its insurers had commenced any proceedings in Venezuela, and the Court noted that there was an air of unreality and considerable uncertainty about the English proceedings. As it was desirable that the issues between all parties be determined in one place, and as the centre of gravity of the dispute was in Venezuela, jurisdiction was declined.
[86] [1989] 2 Lloyd's Rep 390.

Insurance Exchange.[87] In that case, it was held that English law was probably the applicable law of a reinsurance contract placed in London by London brokers with a London reinsurer and incorporating a number of standard London market clauses. That implied choice of law helped to determine that England was the proper jurisdiction for the dispute as to whether sums were due under an excess of loss reinsurance contract contained in a London market slip policy. The reinsurer argued that nothing was payable because of the annual aggregate deductible provisions and a breach of the notification requirements in the claims co-operation clause which was a condition precedent to liability under the reinsurance contract. The fact that the reinsured was a Canadian mutual did not mean that Canadian jurisdiction was required.

The underlying insurance contract and reinsurance may contain terms which must **7.61** be construed in order to ascertain jurisdiction. In *Dornoch Ltd v Mauritius Union Assurance Co Ltd*[88] there was an argument over which legal system should be applied to construe the jurisdiction clause in a reinsurance contract.[89] The reinsurance slip simply stated 'Jurisdiction clause' whereas the underlying insurance had an express Mauritius jurisdiction clause. It was argued that whether the underlying exclusive jurisdiction clause was incorporated was a matter of Mauritius law as that would be the law which would apply if it was indeed incorporated. The Court of Appeal affirmed the decision of the judge who applied the law of the forum, which was English law. The case did not concern whether the agreement existed at all, but the meaning of one of its terms. Where there is more than one possible putative law it made no sense to decide which one to choose by applying one of those putative laws. The court simply had to apply the law of the forum where the dispute is being decided.

The presence in a reinsurance contract of an English exclusive jurisdiction clause is **7.62** a factor to take into account when considering whether to stay proceedings pending determination by a foreign court. In *Amlin Corporate Member Ltd v Oriental Assurance Corp*[90] reinsurers claimed declarations that they were not liable to indemnify the reinsured because a typhoon warranty had been breached. The reinsured applied to stay the claims pending the outcome of claims in the Philippines where it was arguing the same point. The Court of Appeal upheld the judge's refusal to grant a stay. The fact that reinsurers were bound to follow the settlements of the reinsured was not a general exception to the normal rule that a stay of proceedings could only be granted in rare and compelling circumstances.

---

[87] [2011] Lloyd's Rep. IR 171. See also *Tryg Baltica International (UK) Ltd v Boston Compania de Seguros SA* [2005] Lloyd's Rep IR 40.

[88] [2006] 2 Lloyd's Rep 475.

[89] The competing forum, Mauritius, took a different approach to the question of deciding the proper law of the reinsurance contract (not applying the Rome Convention). If the law of Mauritius was applied, the principles concerning the central issue of the construction of fidelity cover would be significantly different.

[90] [2012] EWCA Civ 1341 (unreported, 17 October 2012).

GLOSSARY

Adjustment Premium   An additional premium which can be payable to an excess of loss reinsurer, after deduction of deposit premium.

Aggregation (see 4.52)   A clause which protects a reinsurer's exposure by adding together losses which are related to one and the same cause or event (depending on the wording used) for the purpose of a limit of indemnity (or deductible).

Aggregate Limit   A limit on the total amount payable during a specified period (usually the period of the policy but if the policy is a multi-year one, annual periods could be specified) under the reinsurance (or by way of deductible) for all losses, whether or not related.

Avoidance (see 6.47)   The reinsurer's option where the reinsured has made a misrepresentation or material non-disclosure which induced the reinsurer to enter into the contract, so that the contract is treated as never having existed.

Binder (see 2.35)   An authority given by a reinsurer to a third party to accept business on its behalf.

Bordereau (see 6.84)   A summary of information on risks provided by the reinsured to the reinsurer under a proportional treaty, showing the premiums and losses ceded.

Brokerage (see 2.52)   A broker's remuneration paid to brokers for their services (often a percentage of premium).

Capacity (see 1.02)   The financial ability of a reinsurer to take on additional risk.

Captive (see 1.16)   An insurance company that is wholly owned by a non-insurance company in order to insure the risks of the parent company and its subsidiaries or associated companies.

Cede (see 1.52)   To transfer to a reinsurer all or part of a risk undertaken by an insurer under a reinsurance contract (usually a treaty).

Cession   The portion of the sum insured ceded to a reinsurer.

Claims-Made Basis (see 4.73)   Cover for claims made during a designated period, normally a year, whatever the actual date of loss.

Commutation (see 4.37)   A global settlement of paid and outstanding losses and future potential losses (IBNR) under a reinsurance contract by payment of an amount estimated to cover all liabilities (or a proportion of all liabilities if the commutation is to settle a dispute between the parties), which then releases the parties from the contract.

Cut-Through Clause   A clause making a reinsurer directly liable to the underlying insured and entitling that underlying insured to bring a claim directly against its insurer's reinsurer if the insurer is insolvent.

Deductible (see 1.61)   The amount of loss the reinsured retains for its own account.

Equitas (see 2.48)   A company formed by Lloyd's of London to administer the run-off of open obligations of underwriting syndicates.

Facultative Obligatory Reinsurance (Fac Oblig) (see 1.71)   A reinsurance contract where the reinsurer is obliged to accept the risks chosen to be ceded by the reinsured so long as they fall within the risks identified in the agreement.

Facultative Reinsurance (see 1.41)   Optional reinsurance normally of a single risk negotiated individually where the reinsurer may decline to take the risk.

Fronting (see 1.15)   The cession of all or most of the risk to a reinsurer so that the reinsured retains little, if any, of the risk in the underlying policy.

Gross Line   The amount of liability taken on by a reinsured company before the proportion ceded under a reinsurance agreement is taken into account.

Gross Loss   The total amount of loss (the ground-up loss) sustained by a reinsured company before recovery under a reinsurance agreement.

Honourable Engagement Clause (see 3.09)   An arbitration clause affording the right to determine a dispute in accordance with market principles and good faith and to construe the reinsurance contract purposively.

Inception Date   The date on which a reinsurer comes on risk.

Incurred But Not Reported (IBNR) (see 4.37)   A reinsurer's future liability for losses that have already occurred, but have not yet been reported to the reinsured. The reinsurer will normally maintain loss reserves for these potential losses.

Inwards Treaty   For a company both writing reinsurance and seeking its own reinsurance, an inwards treaty is a reinsurance treaty which offers reinsurance to another party.

Leading Reinsurer (see 2.38)   The reinsurer which sets the terms and generally has the largest participation, whereas the other reinsurers often agree to be bound by the terms set by the leader (although a leader is not usually an agent of the following market—but see 'Line Slip' below).

Line   Where a number of reinsurers cover the risk, the amount of risk agreed by each reinsurer, normally expressed in an amount or percentage.

Line Slip (see 2.35)   An agreement by reinsurers that they will be bound by the agreement between the lead reinsurer and the reinsured or broker as to what individual risks are accepted.

Net Line   The amount of the underlying insurance retained by the reinsured (after deduction of the reinsured proportion of the risk).

Net Retention   The amount of risk which a reinsured keeps for its own account and which is not reinsured.

Non-Proportional Reinsurance (see 1.35)   Excess of loss reinsurance, where the reinsurer does not share proportionately in every risk, but comes effectively on risk when the reinsured's loss exceeds the agreed excess point.

Obligatory Reinsurance (see 1.51)   Treaty reinsurance under which a reinsurer must automatically accept any risk which falls within the category it agreed to reinsure.

Outwards Treaty   For a company both writing reinsurance and seeking its own reinsurance, an outwards treaty is a reinsurance treaty which provides protection to the company's own account.

Outstandings (see 2.48)   Claims where the loss has occurred and been reported, but the liability of the reinsured has yet to be ascertained. The word can also be used to describe a loss where the reinsured's loss has been ascertained but payment has not yet been made by the reinsurer to the reinsured in accordance with the periodic payment arrangements found in the treaty reinsurance.

Over Subscribed Where the slip is passed around the market by a broker and the lines written by reinsurers add up to more than 100%, there is over placement and the slip will need to be signed down.

Primary Layer In excess of loss reinsurance, the primary layer is the bottom portion of the risk (except for the retention or deductible) and each layer above that can be identified as a separate layer of reinsurance (often with different reinsurers).

Proportional Reinsurance (see 1.37) Quota share and surplus reinsurance (also called participating reinsurance) where the reinsurer shares in a proportion of the losses and the premiums of the reinsured.

Provisional Notice of Cancellation (see 6.11) Where a reinsurance contract is written on a continuous basis cancellable each year by written notice, a party may send a provisional cancellation notice that is then rescinded if the parties agree to continue the reinsurance for another year.

Quota Share (see 1.54) Proportional reinsurance where the reinsured must cede to the reinsurer an agreed share or percentage of each and every risk within a specified class of business.

Reinstatement After payment of a loss under an excess of loss contract with an aggregate limit, the cover can be reinstated by payment of a reinstatement premium. The contract terms will specify whether there are a limited number of reinstatements permitted.

Reinsured (see 1.12) An insurer which enters into a reinsurance contract with a reinsurer.

Reinsurer (see 1.12) A company that agrees to reinsure an insurer under a reinsurance contract.

Retrocession (see 1.18) Reinsurance taken out by a reinsurer to cover a risk or risks for which it provides reinsurance to an underlying reinsured.

Retrocessionaire (see 1.18) A reinsurer who agrees to offer retrocession cover to another reinsurer (sometimes known as the retrocedant) in respect of a portfolio of reinsurance.

Risks Attaching (see 1.65) A reinsurance contract may reinsure risks under new or renewed policies which incept during the period of the reinsurance contract.

Run-off The remaining liability of a reinsurer which is not writing new business, but administering and paying claims under contracts written in the past or the liability under a reinsurance treaty that has been terminated. Run-off liability continues until the underlying insurance contracts have all expired or been settled.

Signed Line (see 2.29) The extent of a reinsurer's liability for the underlying sum insured expressed as a percentage on a slip.

Signing Down (see 1.44 and 2.31) Where a slip is over-subscribed, each of the signed lines on a placing slip are reduced proportionately so that the reinsurers collectively provided 100% (rather than more) of the sum insured (also called writing down). The line of a reinsurer who has subscribed on the basis that its line is 'to stand' cannot be signed down without that reinsurer's consent and in such circumstances the lines of the other reinsurers will be proportionately reduced.

Slip (see 2.13)   The summary document containing the outline details of the risk and the terms and conditions of the proposed reinsurance. It is shown to reinsurers by a broker who may agree to the reinsurance by signing and stamping the slip.

Surplus Treaty (see 1.56)   A proportional treaty where the reinsured must cede and the reinsurer must accept surplus amounts of insurance business subject to express limits and retention.

Syndicate (see 1.02)   A group of members at Lloyd's underwriting insurance or reinsurance business through the agency of a manager or underwriter.

Time Bar (see 6.85)   The limitation period applying to a reinsurance contract—either express or imposed by the Limitation Act 1980.

Treaty Reinsurance (see 1.50)   Reinsurance covering a portfolio of the reinsured's business which must be identified in the contract.

Ultimate Net Loss (see 3.10)   The sum paid by the reinsured to settle the underlying insurance claim and associated costs, less any reinsurance recoveries or salvages. It is the amount for which a reinsurer is liable to a reinsured under a non-proportional reinsurance contract. Contracts usually provide for payment by a reinsurer as the loss develops, without the reinsured having to await the final ascertainment of the loss.

Written Line (see 2.18)   The documentary evidence of a reinsurer's liability for the underlying sum insured expressed as a percentage on a placing slip (subject to reduction by signing down).

Writing Down (see 1.44 and 2.31)   See Signing Down.

INDEX